<small>ACCLAIM FOR</small>

"Raw and real, yet also heartwarming and at turns hilarious, Cate Montana writes like the sister you wish you had. She is the wise voice of experience and insight that will push you to examine and explore while wrapping you in the warmth of the divine feminine."

Kathleen McGowan, *New York Times* bestselling author of
The Expected One

"Original and captivating! *Unearthing Venus* is both visionary and an everywoman story that painfully, brilliantly and eloquently captures what it is to be a woman today and every day."

Peggy Holman, author of *The Change Handbook*

"I loved this book! I laughed out loud so many times. Cate Montana's unabashed self-honesty makes you realize you're not alone on this path of seeking answers, even while still having all the usual womanly doubts and fears."

Kathy Campbell, marketing consultant

"A rare and naked exploration into the illusive power of the feminine. If you enjoyed *Eat, Pray, Love*, you will absolutely consume this book. A major new voice of our time!"

Pavel Mikoloski, publicist

"A glorious and compelling view of a woman coming into her power, *Unearthing Venus* not only has me rethinking my relationships with the women in my life, it's inspired compassion for women and given me a clearer view of how easy I've had it as a man in a man's world."

Bruce Smith, editor at *The Mountain News*

"It's a rare experience to read a book about a woman's experience without victimization, philosophizing or fairytale coatings. This is a real woman's journey to find herself in a man's world, falling into the same obsessive pitfalls all honest women face. Cate Montana has lived hard and deep, giving us a powerful, insightful book that raises important and necessary questions we need to ask for humanity to evolve."

Dian Parker, author of *Violets and Ice*

"I ate it up! I related so personally to the character's struggle! At age 29 I feel at a complete loss as to what the feminine even means and how, as a female, I am supposed to fit into this man's world.
This book made me excited and hopeful."

Katherine Elliot, artist

"Fascinating and entertaining!"
Deb Brandt, former News Director at KUOW FM, Seattle

"I could not put this book down. A journey of courage, determination and honesty, it grips the soul and induces one to rethink feminine attitudes and mind. Bravo!"

Patricia Donnelly, artist

"An amazing and inspiring book that empowers you while invoking deep insight into the age-old issues surrounding the masculine and the feminine."

Francesca White, owner of Lemuria Book & Boutique

"This book has the feminine honesty needed to push women into a deeper understanding of themselves, their histories and patterns and, ultimately, their real connection to this world."

Annette Graville, dance instructor

unearthing venus

My Search for the Woman Within

A MEMOIR

Cate Montana

WATKINS PUBLISHING
LONDON

This edition first published in the UK and USA 2013 by
Watkins Publishing Limited, Sixth Floor,
75 Wells Street, London W1T 3QH

A member of Osprey Group

1 3 5 7 9 10 8 6 4 2

Designed by Luana Gobbo

Printed and bound in China by Imago

ISBN: 978-1-78028-597-9

www.watkinspublishing.co.uk

Distributed in the USA and Canada by Sterling Publishing Co., Inc.
387 Park Avenue South, New York, NY 10016-8810

For information about custom editions, special sales, premium and
corporate purchases, please contact Sterling Special Sales
Department at 800-805-5489 or specialsales@sterlingpub.com

This book is dedicated to Margo Ernst, my mother.
You always said I would write a book someday. It's probably not what you expected. Certainly it's not what you would have liked. But then I could be wrong about that. I think it's what you knew in your heart of hearts—what we all know in our heart of hearts. Thank you for the gift of life and the chance to evoke a deeper truth and express it for both of us.

Acknowledgments

I send thanks and appreciation heavenward to my dearest friend Amantha for being such an outrageous example of the Divine Feminine, providing so much support and encouragement for digging into what was, for me, wildly unfamiliar territory. Shine on, dearest sister, wherever you are! To Marcia who read each unedited chapter as it fell out on the page—your enthusiasm for the material kept me going to the end. Thank you! To Sadhguru, aside from everything else (and there's so much), bless you for kicking me in the right direction despite my contrary inclinations.

Deepest thanks to my editor at Watkins, Michael Mann, who "saw" this book and chose to guide its heart song into the marketplace. To John Tintera—you've become such a comfort and friend along the publishing path. Thank you! To Deborah Hercun, Jade and Rebecca and all the rest of the production staff at Watkins, many thanks for the hard work making this book a pleasure to look at, read and hold. Hats off to my agent, Susan Mears, for taking the manuscript on a long overdue vacation to Bali and actually reading it and falling in love with it. Last, but not least, a big hug to my friend Pavel Mikoloski who insisted Susan read it!

A brief note to the reader . . .

All the events in this book actually occurred, precisely as written, with a very few minor exceptions which are as follows: Conversations were recapitulated as best I could remember them, and, if not exactly precise, their essence remains true to what was said. Due to the profoundly intimate and often controversial nature of discussions and actions that take place, I have changed the names of friends, ex-husbands and lovers to ensure that no embarrassment is incurred by anyone. For a couple of people I have changed minor details about their life situations to further ensure anonymity.

CONTENTS

PART I

***

THE ODYSSEY BEGINS
(April 2010)

CHAPTER 1

The question

"What do you know about woman?" he asked, brown eyes flat, boring into me, through me. It was as if the universe itself was asking me the question.

I shriveled into my overstuffed chair, wishing I was just about anywhere but pinned under that gaze. *What do I know about woman?* Repeating it in my head didn't help. *What a damnable question.* I stalled with a weak attempt at humor.

"Aside from what I know being one?"

His gaze didn't flicker. No trace of a smile, he waited.

I had come to the interview prepared with questions, not answers. Seventy-five questions, to be exact. And now, within minutes of sitting down on the sofa next to me in the hotel lounge, I was the one under the grill. *Damn gurus. They don't play fair.*

I had to admit his question was justified. After all, if I was going to interview him for a book about the feminine element of creation, he needed to know what I knew just as much as I wanted to know what he knew. I just wasn't ready to go first.

Covering my dismay, I trotted out an embarrassed lie based on what I thought he thought would constitute appropriate preparedness. "Well," I said slowly. "I've read some feminist literature." *Not!*

"And I've spent a lot of time meditating on the nature of the feminine and masculine as primal creative forces."

That much was true. But it wasn't the answer he was looking for. It wasn't the answer I was looking for either. His hands slowly smoothed a section of his linen robe. He glanced away, giving me breathing room, his long salt-and-pepper beard flowing across his chest as he turned his head to look towards the wide windows overlooking the marina. *He's wearing socks with his sandals*, I noticed idiotically. *With a copper ring and thread tied around one ankle.*

Was there any meaningful reply I could give that wasn't based on my life's experience? Probably not. But how could I make sense of what I knew? How could I express the tentative, quivering insights I was gathering into my own sex in a way that could be easily condensed and understood? *If I had answers about what woman is I wouldn't be doing this stupid interview!* I wanted to shout.

His gaze turned back my way. In moments I would have to speak. The reporter in me desperately wanted to make sense—to at least *seem* intelligent. This interview was part of a job, after all. But my pounding heart told me the moment ran deeper than good impressions. Sadhguru Jaggi Vasudev—mystic, guru, UN delegate and international humanitarian—wanted something greater from me. Something real and visceral . . . if not coherent.

It's this guy's job to make people uncomfortable. It's what gurus do. My soul lifted in response to the thought even as my mind quaked. *Good job he's making of it so far.*

❈ ❈ ❈

My interest—actually it was more like an obsession—with the feminine started when I was 48 years old. I was living in the Pacific

Northwest, working as the Northwest editor of the national newspaper, *Indian Country Today*. As a clueless white journalist whose total knowledge of Native American history had been derived from grade-school sociology texts and the 1953 movie, *Captain John Smith and Pocahontas*, working for the paper gave me a shocking initiation into the Native viewpoint and a knowledge base few Americans are privileged to acquire.

It's hard to get a handle on your own culture while you're living in it. It's like being a fish swimming in the ocean. You're oblivious to the water until something comes along and hurls you, gasping, into a boat or onto the shore. Then all hell breaks loose while you're flopping around getting used to the new perspective. But eventually you catch your breath and look back at the water with shocked eyes and shaking innards and go, *Wow. I swam in that? I used to do so and so and think such and such and didn't even know it? Holy crap!*

Culturally, working at *Indian Country Today* was like that on a daily basis. But there was one interview I conducted for the paper back in the summer of 1999 that had a particularly powerful impact, awakening my fascination with the feminine and changing my life forever.

John Perkins was a white guy and founder of a non-profit organization called The Dream Change Coalition. The group took Westerners to live with tribes in the Amazon regions of South America in an attempt to foster in ordinary people just the kind of enlarged, organic worldview I was developing whilst working in Indian Country (as Native Americans often refer to their culture). Author of several books, including *Confessions of an Economic Hit Man* and *Hoodwinked,* John was an economist and graduate from the Boston School of Management. His story—which I had no idea was about to knock me on my ass—started when he entered the Peace Corps back in the 1960s.

Sent into the heart of the jungles of Ecuador to set up financial systems for the Shuar tribes, John swiftly realized they had little use for his services. Most tribal members had never seen a bicycle, let alone a bank. He spent several fruitless months traveling with his guides deep in the jungles. On one foray, several days' walk from the nearest road, he was struck by a deadly fever. Unable to travel, John was close to death when a Shuar tribal shaman appeared out of the jungle.

"The Anaconda told me to find you and heal you," the man said. "Will you let me?"

Barely conscious, facing certain death, John agreed. The shaman took him to his camp and, within days, had him out of danger. Awed and grateful, John spent several weeks recuperating with the tribe. Days before he was due to leave, the shaman came and asked if he wanted to stay longer with the tribe to learn their ways.

"No white man has ever trusted us enough to let us use our medicine," the shaman said. "I would like to teach you so you can take our knowledge back to your world and build a bridge between our peoples."

John stayed for almost a year, then returned to the States, going to work as an economic consultant for the World Bank, the United Nations and several Fortune 500 companies. For years, he lived a tortuous double life helping corporations and international banking agencies deplete third-world countries' resource bases under the guise of Western aid and development. Yet the shamans knew his heart. Like something out of the movie *The Emerald Forest*, no matter where he went, after the business confabs were over, a native guide always waited at his hotel door to invite him to retreat to the interiors to learn their tribal ways. Shucking his pinstripes, he spent weeks in the jungles every year.

Straddling two opposing worldviews eventually became unbearable, and John had to choose which master to serve. He left his consultancy and subsequently made a lot of money building and selling an alternative energy company in New England. Then he went back to the Shuar tribe.

"Look," he told them. "I'm retired. I've got the time, and I've made all this money. I want to help you save your rain forests."

"That's nice," said the elders. "But it's not us killing the rain forests. It's your people in the north with all your dreams of fancy buildings, cars and hamburgers that are killing the rain forests. You say you want to help? Then go back to your people and help them change their dream of greed into a dream that honors life—a dream that nurtures the earth instead of destroying it."

Humbled, John came back to the States and founded the Dream Change Coalition. Several years later, he decided to reverse the intercultural education process and bring a shaman to America.

Ipupiara was a native of the Uru-e-wau-wau tribe and had never been out of Brazil before. When John picked him up at La Guardia Airport in New York, he didn't know what to expect. However, Ipupiara was calm and smiling in response to the clogged streets, huge crowds and massive buildings. Driving along in the midst of Manhattan, Ipupiara suddenly shouted, "Stop!"

Startled, John had the cabbie pull over. Ipupiara leapt out of the car, dashed across the crowded sidewalk and, to the amazement of onlookers, knelt at the corner of a massive skyscraper. Placing his forehead against the stone, he reached his arms as wide as he could to embrace the building and went into a trance. Minutes later he stood up, grinning from ear to ear, and got back in the cab.

"What a great consciousness that building has!"

"But our people don't think that buildings are alive," John responded.

"You're kidding, right?"

John shook his head. Ipupiara's brows furrowed with worry. "John, your people are in much worse trouble than I thought if they don't know they breathe life into their creations."

Ipupiara gradually settled into his new environment, rapidly soaking up Western ways as he went about the work of cultural bridge building. He moved into a tiny apartment in Washington, DC, and started conducting workshops. Six months had passed when John got an urgent call from him one day.

"John," said Ipupiara. "Where are your women?"

"What do you mean, 'Where are your women?'" John replied, puzzled. "They're right here, working as bankers and teachers and doctors, raising their children and living their lives. Why do you ask?"

Ipupiara sighed. "You know that in our tribe men and women have different jobs, yes? The men hunt. They fish. They cut wood for fires and cut down trees to build huts and canoes. The women cook, make clothes, gather wild edibles and care for the children. As elders, men and women have equal say and guide the people. But there is one job the women perform that is the most important job in the tribe. In fact, the survival of the tribe depends upon this one task."

Intrigued, John asked what that task was. "My friend, you must know that, left to their own devices, men will hunt until there are no more animals in the forest. They will fish until there are no more fish in the rivers, and cut down trees until there are no more trees. It is their nature. It is the job of the women of the tribe to tell the men when to STOP. John, where are your women? Why are they not telling the men to stop?"

The story hit me like a boat anchor.

I knew in my gut Ipupiara was right. Man-kind clearly had a different agenda and operating system running to woman-kind. And, in the West, that system was clearly out of control. My society had no clue what the word 'stop' meant. But, as a woman, what the hell was I supposed to do about it?

Unlike women in the Shuar tribe and females in other, 'less civilized' cultures, I held no authority *as a woman*. In fact, I had less authority as a woman than any other social position available to me in my tribe. In the West, women only had authority when they became something other than a woman—like a teacher, the CEO of a company, a senator or a judge. And women most often held the authority of those positions *despite the fact* that they were female—an automatic strike against them that still had to be compensated for even at the beginning of the 21st century.

Hearing Ipupiara's story forced me into an immediate reassessment of my status in the world as a Western woman and the beliefs I held about that status. I'd always considered myself to be fully liberated. I'd gone to college, developed careers, traveled alone, taken lovers, got married, got divorced, bought homes and racked up credit card debt. I was so liberated I'd scorned the entire feminist movement, writing it off as the whining of a bunch of angry women with axes to grind.

I'd never been overtly discriminated against . . . well, okay, maybe a couple of times. And . . . well sure, women were definitely still exploited as sex objects—to such a degree that I didn't even notice it anymore. And yeah, the United States was the only modern nation in the world that refused to mandate sexual equality. And Roe v. Wade was under attack again, but . . .

The 'ands' kept adding up.

And then I remembered an evening back in 1984 when I was working at the CBS-TV affiliate in Atlanta as a videotape operator. I had just finished the evening news. One of the stories I'd helped edit that day was about the gang rape of a young black girl at her downtown school. As I was walking through the tape room, a network programming feed from New York was recording. It was the CBS Sunday Night Movie, and on the monitor a woman was running, screaming, being chased by some guy with a knife.

At the same time, overhead on the on-air monitor, a woman was being beaten by her boyfriend in some TV show. Everywhere in the tape room, on ten different monitors, I saw women being brutalized, heard them sobbing and screaming for help. And I remembered thinking at the time, *what the hell kind of world am I living in?*

Had anything really improved since then?

I contemplated the deep respect the Shuar women obviously commanded. I compared their feminine values and the life-honoring role they played in their society to my own participation in the world. Slowly and painfully I became aware of things I'd never allowed myself to see—like the fact that in many regards I was still a second-class citizen and a victim in my culture. Even more pernicious was the fact that I was also a victim *of* my culture. I'd been programmed to accept its masculine values to a degree that I'd lost all track of sustainability and sanity and joined the men in their 'let's cut down all the trees' approach to living.

I was one of the five percent happily consuming 40 percent of the world's resources, busily looking out for number one. I'd accepted the belief that caring and concern for others had no place in the 'real world'—especially if I wanted to get ahead. I'd unconsciously accepted that money and technology answered most ills and that equality with men meant acting the 'same as' men.

I'd accepted that if people were poor and suffering, they just weren't working hard enough; that opportunities were unlimited if I was willing to compete. I believed if I treated my house as an investment instead of a home and worked my ass off, eventually things would work out okay. But things weren't working out okay.

Over 26 percent of my fellow Americans suffered from a diagnosable mental health disorder. Drug addiction and suicide were epidemic. One out of every three kids was obese and a diabetic. World resources were being polluted and depleted at an alarming rate. Vast cesspools of political and corporate corruption were being uncovered. The economy was teetering, and the ridiculous gap between the top 0.5 percent of the world's wealthy and the rest of humanity was revealing a picture of such shocking greed and exploitation it was almost ungraspable.

Something was radically wrong with my society. And for the first time in my life I began to get why. The US was sick, not because of some 'ism' or failed economic plan, but because something enormous was missing. And the 'enormous something' that was missing was *woman*—not women like me who had been raised in a man's world to think and act like men. But rather *woman* and feminine values in general.

The world lacked nurturing and compassion, heart and intuitive council, connection and empathy, response-ability and caring, and the simple common sense that comes with aligning oneself with *life* . . . not the arbitrary goal of personal profit at all costs.

But what could I do about it? What would give women the power to say, "Stop?" How could we create effective change as *women* in my culture? How could I help implement that? Or was shifting society by wielding power like a man on man's playground the only answer?

For 11 years I stewed over these questions as the world continued its troubled journey, making little headway towards answers. Eventually, my wandering footsteps led me to India and Sadhguru. His outspoken advocacy for a re-establishment of the Goddess and a re-awakening of feminine values in the West got my immediate attention. Maybe I could present Sadhguru's thoughts and knowledge on the subject? Excited, I approached the Isha Foundation with a book proposal about understanding the feminine from his perspective. After many months the Foundation and Sadhguru agreed to the project. In April 2010, I flew to LA for my first interview.

Which brought me back to the Santa Monica hotel lobby, sweating it out under my interviewee's unrelenting gaze.

More agonizing silence crawled past as I sat there, shaking and undone. Over a decade of passionate inquiry and 58 years spent wearing this woman's body and I couldn't genuinely answer his first, most basic, question? *What do you know about woman?*

Argh!

How could I be so lost? So confused? How could I be so utterly ignorant of my own essence? Perhaps it was the impossibility of a short answer that muted my tongue? If only I could take the long way around and tell him the story of my life, it would all make so much better sense.

Maybe even to me.

PART II

* * *

THE MAIDEN
(1957–1969)

CHAPTER 2

Life in 1950s' suburbia

My mother really wanted to be a boy. She confessed she wished to be a boy so desperately that she believed her older brother when he told her that if she wished *really, really hard*, on her tenth birthday she would magically become one. It was unclear whether her desperation was a commentary on the general life of women in the 1930s or on her own life specifically, growing up under the stern hand of a well-to-do German physician and his coolly distant, socialite WASP wife.

Even as a self-centered only child I could tell my mother wasn't particularly happy. But then I'm not sure happiness was really an important issue for women in the 1950s. As long as the domestic picture looked right, happiness was assumed to be there. Actually talking about being *un*happy was considered self-indulgent and thus vaguely improper—at least in my family. At our little Tudor-style house on the outskirts of Washington, DC, all was right with the world as long as the cocktail shaker hit the counter at precisely 6pm and the family sat down to dinner together at eight.

Just as the food wasn't too spicy, neither was anybody's life. It didn't matter if the dog had just barfed on the oriental rug or the neighbor's kid was caught peeing on the dogwood tree in the backyard, whether dinner had burnt or I had brought home another dismal report card, everything was automatically 'fine' whether it really was or not.

"How was your day, dear?" my mother asked every evening as my stepfather walked through the door at precisely 5.45pm.

"Fine," he replied, handing her his gray felt hat and heavy black overcoat to put away in the hall closet. "How was *your* day?"

"Fine," she said as she hung up his coat. A dutiful kiss on her cheek, and they moved as one towards the bar on the mahogany side table in the dining room.

It was a dance they never misstepped, five evenings a week. On weekends, the silver shaker came out at five instead of six—a daring move away from propriety. But then my mother was a divorcé. Leaving my father when I was three and marrying my stepfather, Jack, when I was seven, automatically put us far beyond the proper pale. The neighbors didn't know she was a divorcé, of course. And never would. Divorce was a sordid condition only whispered about. In nice households it didn't exist.

Perhaps her fallen state was one of the reasons my mother drank a little earlier in the day on weekends.

My mother's parents lived close by in Arlington, and I spent almost as much time at their house as I did at my own. My grandmother, who was gradually becoming immobilized with Parkinson's disease, rarely said anything. Elegantly dressed, diamond rings drooping on flaccid fingers, she sat, rigid, in a large gold wing chair in front of the big television set all day watching soaps and *Queen for a Day* in black and white.

"My husband has leukemia," sobbed the heavy-faced blonde TV contestant. "I lost my job at the factory after I lost my left foot because of the diabetes." The audience started clapping. The response meter started to rise. "We don't have insurance, and our daughter and her baby have been living with us ever since her husband was killed in Korea. And then . . ." she broke down, weeping. "And then our dog died." The meter went wild. I clapped my five-year-old hands in glee and watched as the distraught woman was crowned in misery's glory, clutching her fake sceptre, beaming gratitude for her new GE washer and dryer set.

But no matter how awful the tale, my grandmother's face never altered.

Grandpa made up for her lack of emotion. Breaking all the social rules about keeping one's burdens to oneself, he actually complained about his cancer and angina and having to care for my grandmother. Trapped in a house with his dying wife, his physical and emotional pain was a live presence that was uncomfortable for everyone to be around. But we never talked about it. We just went, supported and smiled.

For a divorcé with sick parents, a kid, a new husband who mixed anger with alcohol, and no social outlets aside from grocery shopping, everything couldn't have been 'fine' in my mother's life. Certainly, she had time to think up other ways to describe it. I left her home alone in the morning at 7.30, slamming the heavy front door shut before running to catch the school bus just up the street. Coming back from my elementary school classes at 3.30, she was still home, alone.

Just as it was impossible to imagine June Cleaver with her feet up on the coffee table, cigarettes mounded in an ashtray, telling Wally and Beaver to "fix your own damn sandwiches," so it was impossible to imagine my mother doing anything but waiting patiently to serve. Nicely dressed in a cashmere sweater and skirt, lipstick applied, dark shoulder length hair freshly released from pin curls, she was always there—like perfect background music.

True, she smoked Viceroys like a fiend, and lipstick-stained, caramel-colored butts filled all the crystal ashtrays in the house until they were whisked away in the silver 'silent butler' before my stepfather came home. Not because she wasn't supposed to smoke—everyone smoked—but because decks were always cleared for The Husband's Return. Table set, drinks ready, house clean, homework put away, dinner in the oven, Chet Huntley and David Brinkley reassuringly talking on the television in the den, my stepfather always entered a perfect world at the end of his day.

Both Jack and I took my mother's presence, her unceasing work, her interest in us and her love, completely for granted . . . gifts we didn't even know we possessed. What she thought about life and her role in it, whether she was happy or not, no one even thought to ask.

We lived in the fiefdom of fine in a cleanly sea of white. We had a house, bought and paid for, two cars, a TV, a charcoal grill in the backyard to cook steaks on in the summertime, and the latest modern conveniences—which meant a refrigerator and a washing machine. A maid came twice a week to clean. My stepfather brought home the weekly paycheck, paid into his government pension fund and invested in stocks.

It was just like on TV—clean, neat and prosperous, the ultimate manifestation of the American Dream.

Never mind that in 1958 the only people who could afford tidy suburban nests were white men. Single women were not legally allowed bank loans until 1973—a discriminatory policy that extended well into the 1980s. And in pre-Civil Rights days in the South it was impossible for people of color to enter the suburban arena. Our maid and World War II movies were about the only reasons I knew African Americans and people of the Jewish faith existed—and my stepfather's vicious tirades. "Those sons of bitching niggers and goddamn Jews," he'd rage as he took another slug of bourbon. "They're screwing up the whole goddamn country."

His words of hate sliced the air, carving away at invisible faces, drawing blood. I could feel it and shrank back in my chair, dinner forgotten.

"Jack, please. Not in front of . . ." I didn't have to look up to know the silent pause and head nod were directed at me. "Would you like more potatoes? Good, aren't they? Let me get you some more." Before he could answer, she rose and hurried into the kitchen, leaving me nervously alone within an all-too-easy arm-grab reach.

Sometimes she could placate and distract him. Sometimes not. It was a dangerous thing to do, stepping in front of Jack's anger. You never knew what would trigger him or where it would redirect next. And although he never vented physically beyond arm-grabbing, shaking and high-decibel threats to "knock your goddamn head off and shove it up your goddamn ass," the truth of the matter was we were both relieved when Jack's anger found targets other than us.

Tidy and prosperous we might have been, but my family was a far cry from the TV ideal fostered by shows like *Leave it to Beaver* and *Lassie*. And mine wasn't the only troubled home. My friend Janet's father drank and beat the kids with his belt, sometimes leaving his little son to sleep naked in the driveway at night. My friend Alice's mother had a compulsive disorder of some kind. She constantly washed everything, including Alice, in harsh detergents. The furniture was swathed in clear plastic slipcovers and swabbed daily with ammonia. Even the carpets had plastic runners all through the house, and woe to the unwary child who stepped off the runways during play.

My friend Mary's mother got pregnant every year like clockwork, even though her traveling salesman husband was mostly gone. The crazy widow near my grandparent's house chased kids out of her yard with a broom, screaming, red hair flying—an entertainment none of us could resist initiating. And there was something so bad about the couple next door to our house on 37th Street that my parents wouldn't even let me in their yard.

I found it perplexing that my TV peers didn't have parents who fought and drank, didn't have disabling migraine headaches, didn't bring home consistently bad report cards or have to struggle with issues like whether or not to tell their parents they'd been molested by the paperboy and his gang of friends like I had been. Was there something particularly wrong with me that, at age seven, I had to deal with such things?

Actually he wasn't *our* paperboy. I would have recognized him at the time if he had been. But months later when Mom and I were at a local gas station, I recognized him. A scrawny, pimply youth, he was riding a bike with newspapers in the back panniers. I got all excited and pointed him out to my mother. "He's the one! Mom, he's the one who grabbed me in the woods!"

My mother got a good look at him, fired up the engine and put the car in gear.

"What are you doing? Mother, he's the one!"

I don't exactly know what I expected her to do. The image of her sweeping out of the car, grabbing him by the shirt collar and whaling the tar out of him crossed my mind as proper justice. Instead, she stepped on the gas and drove away.

Didn't she trust me to recognize him? Was she leaving because nothing really bad had happened? The guys, who must have been about 13 years old, had separated me from my friends, pulled my pants down and tried to touch me 'down there.' Not waiting to see what would come next, I hit the bent-over paperboy as hard as I could, pulled my pants up, kicked another assailant and ran back home. I never asked any of my other little girlfriends what happened to them. And they were horrified I'd told my parents about it. They never said a word to theirs.

Emptiness filled the car and my stomach that day as my mother fled confrontation. That she took no action was a shattering event in my young life. The unconscious faith that I was protected and safe, that wrongs were always righted when the truth was told, evaporated. My mother was my whole world. If she wouldn't defend me, who would? Jack? I had no bond or trust in him. My grandfather was old and sick. I went to bed that night feeling very alone. It didn't occur to me that my mother, at just under 5' 1" and a 100 pounds soaking wet, could have been physically afraid of accosting a strange male—even a youth. I just figured my friends had been right not telling their parents. After all, this wasn't TV. What could real parents do?

By the time I was eight I had made up my mind that family life sucked. The attitude showed in many ways. Playing 'grown-ups' with my friends, Janet always wanted to play Daddy, Mary always wanted to be 12 (a big number at seven!), and Alice always wanted to be '18 and a mommy.' Me? I wanted to be 18 and away at college.

I had also decided the last person I wanted to be like when I grew up was my mom. Being a wife and mother apparently required endless patience and self-sacrifice, the ability to shut up when you wanted to scream, the capacity to do endless menial tasks that nobody else wanted to do, plus the ability to be yelled at and abused without talking back or getting angry or mean in return.

I was constitutionally unable to do any of this. Young as I was, my mother was already having to run interference between me and the man I called Dad—a man I had learned to both despise and fear and yet love over the years. After all, he'd been in my life since I was four. And what else can children do but love their parents? He was The Father and The Husband. He supported my mother and me. He put a roof over our heads and food in our stomachs. He paid for the riding lesson on Thursdays, the piano lesson on Mondays and the ballet lesson on Saturdays. Paying for these things, I was told, meant he loved me. My job was to appreciate the bounty and do as I was told.

When adults asked me what I wanted to be when I grew up, I always answered, "a neurosurgeon." It was a profession I'd learned about from my grandfather who had been a surgeon before a massive coronary removed him from medical practice. Just knowing the word was impressive enough to garner a startled "Oh" from just about everybody. Pleased, I worked it to good effect. It wasn't that I was really interested in medicine. I just knew that an answer that triggered amazement and admiration from both men and women alike seemed like a good ticket to a future that would sail me far from the shores of a life like my mother's.

Certainly it wasn't the times themselves providing a desire for radical independence. It was abundantly clear that if I grew up pretty, subservient to men and domestically inclined, the rest of my life was handled. On television, women ran through houses in yellow chiffon dresses using Lemon Pledge, hung adoringly on Mr Clean's bulging biceps and swooned over washing machines. Men made money, drove big cars, used big guns, made the world turn and were catered to in every way. Children were to be seen and not heard as they learned the few simple roles that would take them through life.

If you were a boy, you emulated the hard ridin', tough talkin', flint-faced John Wayne. If you were a girl, you could be the charming blonde, blue-eyed Doris Day; the exotic, cleavage-showing Elizabeth Taylor; sex-goddess Marilyn Monroe or, for the more domestically inclined, June Cleaver—not the actress who played her, the role itself. Did anybody know or care who played Beaver's ever-patient, soft-spoken, cookie-baking mother?

If you wanted boys to like you, the rule was to stand around looking adorable while deferring to them in everything. I was taught to never say anything smart in class, never to win at jacks and certainly never show I could catch a baseball better than a guy. "Boys don't like that, Cate," my mother cautioned. "How many times do I have to tell you not to act like a hooligan around them?"

"But I *can* catch better than Bobby Barrett," I wailed to my mother. "And they *want* me on the team!"

"They may want you on the team now. But later they won't want you or like you at all. Trust me."

I didn't believe her. Why would boys be stupid enough to care if a girl beat them at something? What difference did it make? Plus, I could tell she was giving me 'do as I say, not as I do' advice.

For despite her seeming conformity, there was an unfettered gene in my mother that thumbed its nose at feminine propriety. She liked wearing pants when she could get away with it. She loved to drive fast, leaving guys behind at stoplights, zooming ahead like Our Lady of Pasadena from the Beach Boys song that hadn't been created yet. A strong swimmer, my mother would stroke far out into the ocean at night when we went to Virginia Beach every summer on vacation. Once beyond the breakers, she would float for ages, watching the stars, refusing to swim back no matter how loudly Jack bellowed, pacing the edges of the waves.

Even he feared to follow her out there. Which was, perhaps, why she did it every vacation. The restless gray ocean inspired both passion and peace in her like nothing else could. And despite steady lip service to the contrary, she wasn't eager to see my wings clipped. She supported me in my horse-riding passion as long as I did the obligatory girl thing of taking ballet. She tolerated the long camping trips Jack insisted on. She also agreed to the gift of a pellet rifle for my eighth Christmas.

I was as excited by this stunningly unexpected present as I was bored with the big-breasted, plastic Barbie and huge dollhouse that came along with the rifle that year. The doll's gorgeous looks, which I'm sure my mother hoped would provide an encouraging message, were ridiculous. I didn't have to look in the mirror to know the chances of looking like that when I grew up were remote. Early on, I told myself I didn't care.

The rifle, however, was another story. A gun that could penetrate three inches into the DC phone book was no kid's toy. It even had sights that needed to be adjusted, or 'sighted-in' in gun parlance, to shoot accurately. Never mind that within 24 hours of unwrapping it, I found myself at the center of a local neighborhood shit-storm. The gun was the gift of the season for me.

My little girlfriends, however, were uniformly shocked when I proudly showed it to them and couldn't wait to race home to tell their parents. Janet's mom and dad were elected as neighborhood arbiters to 'discuss the matter' with my parents. When mom and Jack refused to take the gun away from me, I lost two girlfriends whose parents would no longer let them play with me. All the boys, of course, were uniformly green with envy. Later in life I would discover that most men seem to find the thought of women and guns erotic. Of course, men find women and just about any object erotic, so I'm not too sure there's much to be read into the fact.

But the gift of a gun to a city girl and my peacekeeping Mother's defense of it against blatant social pressure were astounding to me. Jack was an avid hunter and outdoorsman. His support wasn't surprising, and the gun had been his idea in the first place. But my mother? It was many years before she gave me an account of the following story that explained her actions. Back then, all I knew was that a couple of weeks before Christmas I was sent to bed earlier and earlier so that my parents could head to the basement after dinner. What they were doing down there I was absolutely forbidden to know.

If only I had been privy to the following scene!

"Damn." Jack leaned in for a better look. "Try another one." He reached up and pulled the paper target off the thickly padded wall.

Forty feet away at the other end of the basement a cigarette glowed, orange-red in the semi-dark.

"I can make that shot all night long with my eyes closed."

"Yeah? Okay, big mouth, try this."

Walking over to one side of the basement, he got down the stepladder and carried it to the backdoor. Opening it, he put down the ladder several yards away. Then he got another target and stapled it to one of the rungs. The paper wafted gently to and fro in the freezing night air, barely illuminated by the ceiling light in the basement. Moments after stepping aside, the first *pfft* sang out. A reload. Another *pfft*. A reload. Another *pfft*.

"Hold it!"

Stepping up to the ladder, he jerked down the paper and walked back into the light. Whistling, Jack looked at my mother in amazement. Three neat holes punctured the black bull's eye in a perfect triangle. He closed the door, reached over to pick up his cigarette and took a deep, contemplative drag. At the back of the basement my mother's glass tinkled as she sipped bourbon. "Hell, I could pick off your cigarette tip from here."

"Excuse me?"

"I said I could shoot the cigarette out of your mouth from here."

"You wouldn't dare."

"Really? You got the balls, I got the gun."

"Shit." Defiant, Jack took another drag from his cigarette, stuck it in his mouth and stood in front of the padded section of wall, lips and chin stuck out.

"Want to smoke it down some more?"

Jack took the cigarette out of his mouth. "If you don't have the guts, just tell me, hotshot." He stuck it back in his mouth and jutted his lips and chin out once more. *Pfft!* Jerking back, shocked, the cigarette dropped from his lips. On the cement floor the severed tip still glowed. Six inches to the right lay the cigarette, tobacco frayed, the paper torn an inch away from the filter.

Turns out my mom was captain of the sharpshooting team in college. Who knew? Amazing the things daughters don't learn about their mothers until it's too late.

An image of easy self-contentment and peace comes to most people's minds when they think about 1950s' America. But actually it was a time of deep military unrest and outright civilian terror. Over 50,000 American soldiers died in the Korean War between 1950 and 1953. The Vietnam War started in 1955. The Cold War and nuclear-arms race exploded onto the scene, with Russia and the United States growling at each other like feral dogs. Pictures of mushroom clouds blossomed on the front covers of *The Washington Star* and *Post* and *Time Magazine*. Nuclear oblivion was the icy thought we all took to bed at night.

Living near ground zero of the most important political target in the Western world, I was no stranger to the thought of atom bombs dropping on my head. Our house was about ten miles from the Pentagon, and the bi-monthly emergency drills at school were not about taking cover from hurricanes and tornados—and all the kids cowering under their wooden desks knew it. At least once a month I woke up screaming, dreaming we were under attack, envisioning incoming missiles overhead. When my mother heard me answer her question "And what do you want to be when you grow up, little girl?" with a darkly gloomy, "You mean *if* I grow up?" preceding my neurosurgeon answer, her protective instincts finally kicked in.

"We should build a shelter in the backyard," she said one night in a conversation I was privy to only because I had learned that the heating duct grill between the living room and the upstairs hallway was a direct line into Adult Matters.

"I'm not sure it would do any good even if we had one," Jack answered. "We're too close in." The ice in their glasses tinkled loudly in the sudden silence. "They'll drop more than one here, you know. Just to make sure they wipe out the government."

'They', of course, were the Russians. The Reds—other people on the other side of the world with kids. But they were the bad guys. Commies. The ones who deserved to die, not us.

"We could move back to Michigan."

"What would I do there? Jesus, Margo, I'm a diplomat, not a car salesman."

"I was just thinking."

"Well, try thinking something else."

CHAPTER 3

The farm

My mother's fears played directly into Jack's overall life plan. He had been raised on a farm in Maryland and, despite the fact that he shot peaceful herbivores and mounted their heads on the walls of his den, was quite the nature lover. He longed for the privacy of rural existence and was quite opinionated about the fact that a farm was the only place to raise a kid.

For the first time Jack and I agreed on something. I was a natural loner who much preferred sitting under the huge elm tree next to the fern-clotted spring in our backyard and looking out for fairies to running around the neighborhood with a pack of screaming kids. And the word 'farm' instantly translated in my eight-year-old brain into the word 'horses.'

When my grandparents agreed to bankroll the move, the search for the ideal country haven locked in Jack's mind got rolling. For months, we spent every weekend scouring northern Virginia properties with a real estate agent. Finally, two months shy of my ninth birthday, my family bought Fieldmont, a 360-acre farm of rolling Virginia hills, forests and fertile bottomland. An hour commute to DC, Fieldmont was close enough for my stepfather to keep his job, yet far away enough to put a damper on Cold War fears. Over half a mile from the nearest neighbor, the house was also far away enough from other people to keep Jack's frequent and loud blow-ups out of the public domain.

It was only 65 miles. But in social terms we may as well have migrated to the moon. Overnight, my mother went from the isolation of the suburbs filled with other isolated women to the extreme loneliness only a farm wife knows. Aside from supplying a better chance of surviving nuclear war, I think farming was about as far removed from her ideal lifestyle as possible. Certainly she never expressed a personal desire for such an experience—at least not that I ever heard, even glued as I was to the heating grate.

But Jack had decided to move and that was that. In much the same way that women followed their men's lead over the frozen Bering Straits, the Alps and the Atlantic Ocean as local climate and social pressures dictated, so my mother followed her husband into the country at his desire and for my sake. The upside was that she could wear blue jeans whenever she wanted.

I was sick with German measles the day they drove me up the long, dusty drive to the rambling stone and frame antebellum house on the hill. The house gleamed achingly bright in the sun, surrounded by walnut trees, ancient boxwoods and pines, with its white pillars supporting a long front porch and balcony. Underneath the porch the ceilings were painted a soothing blue to confuse the wasps into thinking it was the sky so they wouldn't try to build their nests there.

Awakening from my fever and lying dwarfed in a bed big enough to fit Abraham Lincoln, I looked around my new room in amazement. A large, floral, hand-painted pitcher and washing bowl topped the walnut and marble dresser across a room so big I could have rollerskated in it. A lone light bulb hung from the 12-foot ceiling, its white painted wires twisted with an old fly strip.

Two huge windows overlooked the front field with its meandering creek and small pond. Beyond were more pastures and then the gentle rise of the Bull Run Mountains. Flowers ran riot in the yard in long-neglected beds that had been planted before the Civil War. Somewhere a cow bellowed. Across the field a horse nickered.

I think that first June day out of bed awoke the explorer in me, never to sleep again. Certainly the farm supplied the foundation for everything important that would follow in my life . . . the questions in my mind about God and life's meaning, and the yearning for substantive answers that would eventually take me on the inward journey towards spirit and set me on the path of the Goddess.

Long before I consciously knew She existed, I would experience Her many faces on the farm: beauty, terror, love, birth, death, decay, fertility, destruction and creation, hope and despair—all delivered through her disguise as Nature. As a child I knew nothing of these esoteric things. All I knew in those days was that, on the farm, I flew free.

I rode the horses my parents bought me across unending solitary miles of countryside in the withering summer heat, swatting the deerflies on Jeb's arched neck, carmine blood staining his sleek chestnut coat. I rode through scented fall rains and the deep winter snows, fingers stiff and numb on the reins. I rode bareback in the moonlight—my familiar world washed to black and silver—the dying squeal of a rabbit as an owl made its kill on silent wings or the harsh yowl of a bobcat raising the hairs on my neck, chilling me to the bone.

My roan mare, Comet, carried me tirelessly down sodden muddy trails and through fields warmly scented with sunshine and wildflowers. We splashed through creeks and rivers, leaped over stonewalls and fences, and threaded through forests where wild turkeys exploded from cover under our noses and leaves sifted down forming gold and amber puddles that crackled underfoot as we passed.

I hunted for kittens in the hay barns, waded for tadpoles in the creek and swam naked in the huge pond behind the barns. I lay in the tall wheat-colored grasses and absorbed the sky. I watched spring crops of corn and oats get planted, sweated alongside the farmhands pulling in hay bales on the long, scalding summer days, ploughed through thigh-deep winter snows to rescue newborn calves, dug gates clear of ten-foot drifts, and cleaned saddles and tack, watching yard-long icicles hanging from the barn eves melt in the sun.

Rendered both ecstatic and miserable in my own skin, life blistered me whilst weeding the garden and taught me true terror when running around open pastures during electrical storms, trying to catch equally frenzied colts. It dragged tears from my soul watching a cow's hard labor end in stillbirth. It dazzled me with a lake of fireflies in the nighttime mists of the creek bottom. It placed the miracle of a long-legged foal still wet from its mother's body under my wondering hands. It drenched me in the scent of new-mown hay and honeysuckle and filled me with peace.

Life was a feast—a banquet only previously hinted at—and not until I sat down to eat did I realize how starved I'd been. In suburbia, the life force was sleepy, domesticated and distant. In the country, the Goddess roared into view, plunging me deep into Her mysteries, wrenching open my mind and heart, insisting that I pay attention to Her and Her only, indiscriminately feeding me life and death in equally abundant share.

"One is no better or worse than the other," She whispered. "Life . . . death, they are the same to me."

But my ignorant and sensitive humanity told me differently, and I suffered terribly as pets and a favorite foal died—and both my grandparents. Then pets and foals were born, and I thrilled accordingly. It wasn't hard to see that the spark so recently extinguished, causing such sadness and tears, was the same spark being lit anew.

But what about people? Where would I go when my body was a silent shell, empty of its tenant? Had I lived before? Would I return? Would my grandparents? Our priest at the Episcopal Church where my mother dragged me once a month said, "No." The steadily repeating seasons, however, whispered a different, more reassuring, message. I lay awake pondering these things as the wind sang through the metal eaves and the single-pane windows with their ancient blown glass rattled eerily through the long winter dark.

Middleburg, Virginia, was a place out of time. A village of stone houses and 18th-century taverns-turned-modern restaurants, tack shops and hunt country-chic clothing stores, it was not unheard of in 1960 for some of the old-timers to ride their horses into town to the Red Fox Tavern for a quick afternoon snort. Sometimes, to the delight of tourists from Washington, DC, who flocked to the countryside on weekends every fall, the Middleburg Hunt was seen galloping straight down Route 50 through town in hot pursuit of a fox.

Known as the Old Dominion, the whole area was the transplanted creation of the English country aristocracy into the New World. Vast estates, many with antebellum homes that survived the Civil War, covered hundreds of square miles. Fieldmont was in Orange County, which was named after Orange County, Ireland, famous for its thoroughbred horses and foxhunting. I rode with foxhounds in the Orange County Hunt that had kin back in the Old Country.

Fieldmont itself had had only three owners since George Washington surveyed and signed the King George grant, wresting the lands from the Indians and giving it to the Mercer family back in the 1760s. Buying the farm from the third owner, the widow Mrs

Field, we inherited an antiquated English social legacy and a bygone Southern tradition—for among other things Fieldmont came with a family of 'tenants.' Agreeing to take care of and employ those tenants was part of the purchase price of the farm.

Mr Reynolds, now bent and spry in his omnipresent knee-high rubber boots, not a day under 70, with one blue eye gone from a dose of lye and the other eye shrewdly assessing, had been born on the farm. So had his hefty, redheaded daughter, Betty, who worked in the house.

Mr Reynolds and Betty lived across the 30-acre field in a small house with no indoor plumbing. Their property, which my parents eventually deeded to Betty, contained an outhouse, chicken coop, pigsty and an enormous garden down the hill next to a creek that poured into Little River. They had a Jersey cow, Sally, that grazed the 30-acre field and got milked twice a day in a milking barn that hadn't seen any other cow but Sally for a long, long time.

"After Mr Fiel' passed, Miz Fiel' said we was to raise sheep." Mr Reynold's weather-beaten face hardened perceptibly and he spat a maroon stream of tobacco juice on the ground in a gesture that spoke volumes about that particular decision.

"When was that?" asked my mother, eyeing his juice-stained beard stubble nervously. Mr Reynolds scratched one sweaty armpit of his long-sleeved, gray farm shirt, considering. "Reckon 1935 or so." He shifted his weight in his rubber boots.

"Used to stan' down by the crick. When it rained and the crick raised, well, ba Gawd, them sheep jus' stood thar and drown." His blue eye glittered happily at the thought. Another stream of juice bit the dust. "Sheep's stupid." He stared hard at my mother. "We's gonna raise sheep?" he asked suspiciously.

We didn't raise sheep. My parents decided to raise Black Angus beef cows and, inevitably given my obsession, horses. By age 11, I had eight horses to look after. Mr Reynolds helped out. But the burden of duties—riding, cleaning stalls, overseeing the animals' welfare, grooming, cleaning tack, planning for horse shows, foxhunting, pony club and other equine events, as well as helping rebuild the stalls, laying out a riding ring, building the fences, designing and building the jumps—was on my shoulders.

Rarely did I drag back to the house from the horse barn after school until well after dark. After a year or so, my parents hired a part-time trainer to help me. Bobby took on the task of breaking in all the colts to ride and showed me how to train them properly, reluctantly teaching me everything he knew.

I say reluctantly because what self-respecting 19-year-old male wants to be saddled with a scrawny girl child to teach? But I dogged his every move, pressing my pony hard on his heels as he rode the bigger thoroughbreds in our stable over the enormous stone walls and field fences that connected farms and estates. Eventually, my tenacity and guts earned his grudging respect. A few years later, my blossoming body earned his interest. But that's another story.

President and Jackie Kennedy rented an estate a mile cross-country from our house, and I often rode with Carolyn in the back of the hunt field where the children were supposed to ride. A picture of Jackie riding an elegant horse in the front field of our farm, with Carolyn tagging along on a scruffy pony, hung on our living room wall.

My mother tried hard to fit into Middleburg society—and failed. A kind, reserved soul with no pretensions and airs, it was impossible for her to gain entry into a social scene based on airs, pretension and who knew whom. We knew nobody and sported an Irish last name. And though we were well off, my family was poor compared to the neighbors. For here the lords of US business and politics dwelled: the DuPonts, the Mellons, the Curriers, the heirs to the Pillsbury, Mars and Sears fortunes and many others.

There were basically two ways to enter the dream of the landed gentry: to be born into it or to have enough money to buy your way in, and the 'Who's Who' of the Old Dominion had both avenues covered. There was another way, however, and by accident my parents found it. They sent me to the expensive local private elementary school where all the rich kids went.

It didn't gain them entry, but it worked for me.

Soon the houses where I played and had sleepovers were mansions with *Gone With the Wind* porticos and sweeping staircases, black butlers, cooks and upstairs and downstairs maids. I dined on fine china, drank from crystal in dining rooms the size of some people's houses and played bridge in salons straight out of *Pride and Prejudice*.

I rode to the hounds with my friends and sipped brandied coffee from silver stirrup cups served from silver platters held by nervous servants dancing around the horses that restlessly stamped and shifted, bridles jingling, breath steaming in the cold morning air from flared nostrils. Afterwards I attended stately hunt breakfasts in my mud-spattered black boots and black Melton coat, forking down delicacies with hands still reeking of horse sweat and adrenaline. At Christmas there was a grand hunt ball.

I adored any event centered on horses. But regular parties were different. At 15, I was painfully shy and would have gladly refused every invitation if my parents had let me. But they didn't. The first major invite found me an hour before party-time, decked out in a gorgeous white beaded dress Jack had bought at Neiman-Marcus, sitting at our kitchen table with ears the size and shape of scarlet cauliflowers, covered in a rash of itchy nervous hives.

"I can't go like this!"

"Of course you can't," my mother said calmly as she stirred some concoction together in a glass over the sink. "Here, drink this."

I glared at it suspiciously. "What is it?"

"Baking soda and water. It'll reduce the hives."

"I don't want to reduce the hives. I don't want to go!"

"You're going. Drink. You can thank me later."

I gagged down the disgusting brew, the hives went away, and all too quickly I was in the car, chauffeured by Jack, party-bound.

It was a futile scene of itchy rebellion that would be repeated over and over until one particular summer party when I was 17. I was standing on the sweeping back portico of a friend's house near the refreshment tables. The manicured lawns were dotted with elegantly dressed, brightly chatting young people. Beyond the lawns, horses grazed and contentedly switched at flies in their pasture. A light mist was rolling in out of the creek bottom. Maybe I could slip away down to the broodmare barns? Surely I wouldn't be missed.

"Would you like something to drink?"

Startled out of my horsey reverie, I glanced up into the blue eyes of a young man I didn't know. Blond, crew cut and handsome, he stood there in a lightweight Italian wool jacket and red tie looking absolutely terrifying. I swallowed hard and nodded. But with the arrival of my champagne punch something else arrived. As I took the offered glass, carefully avoiding the young man's fingers, something palpably clicked—literally it felt like a switch being thrown on a breaker panel somewhere in my brain. I relaxed, glanced up through my lashes, thanked him and began talking. And laughing. And, wonder of wonders, flirting.

One of his friends joined us. We talked. I laughed, touching Blue Eyes lightly on his jacket sleeve when he made a joke, warmly making contact. When dinner was served, he escorted me to a table and didn't go away. When it was time for me to leave, he kissed me goodnight. My first kiss! Floating on air I glided to the car where my friend Jennifer's mom waited to drive both of us home. I got in and talked and talked and talked.

The miracle had occurred. Social glibness and female mating skills, long quiescent in my DNA, had been awakened. The agony of shy awkwardness behind me, life would never be the same.

I made up for lost time and, by age 18, had entered high society. I gave elegant sit-down dinners for my rapidly expanding circle of friends, planning everything from seating arrangements to what wines to serve with which course and which liqueurs should be offered afterwards. I entered the diplomatic party scene at some of the Washington, DC, embassies and giggled with my girlfriends over our coming-out parties (as in debutante), discussing the white dresses, elbow-length gloves and full string orchestras our parents would shell out for with admirable nonchalance.

Beneath all the aristocratic trappings, the problems my new friends and their families faced were no different from the problems in my old Arlington neighborhood—alcoholism, drugs, battery, adultery and dysfunction. The only difference was that, in this crowd, vice wasn't hidden. It was cultivated. Of course, even in this world of excess there were excesses. Despite visits to expensive sanatoriums, my friend Marilyn's mother drank herself comatose everyday until she finally shot herself through the head. In response, her mostly absent lawyer father handed Marilyn over to the cook to raise until she was finally sent away to boarding school. But in the realm of The Beautiful People this was standard operating procedure.

In truth, I still much preferred the company of the dogs under the exquisitely laid tables or the cat cruising the butler's pantry to most of my well-heeled peers affecting the sophisticated boredom of their parents. In their silence, it seemed animals had much more profound things to say.

Deep down I knew I wasn't really one of the beautiful people. I was a pretender, speaking boarding-school French even though I was really a day student. Decked out in expensive evening dresses that my mother scrimped and saved to buy me, I wasn't truly comfortable in that world. Yet it was so beautiful!

Who cared that the beauty was superficial? I *hungered* after more of what the top one percent elite was giving me a taste of.

I already had a better education, more material advantages and more opportunities than 98 percent of the world's population. But it wasn't enough. I lived on a farm in a lovely antebellum house, but my friends lived on estates in mansions. I rode $3,000 horses and, not having a horse trailer, had to hack cross-country for miles to get to the hunt meets and horse shows whenever I could. My friends deigned to get on their $30,000 mounts delivered to events in huge private horse vans, bored with the grubby but necessary effort of appearing at least a few times a year in equestrian garb.

I didn't just love this life: I adored it. And I was jealous of my truly wealthy friends. Yet when it came down to 'setting my cap' for a rich boyfriend (and eventual husband), I just couldn't do it. I know that's what my parents hoped for. Even my grandmother had once told me, "Honey, you can love a rich man as well as a poor one. So why not go after the rich one?" But I was a romantic. If I was going to have a boyfriend, it would be because of love, not money. Besides, did having a wealthy husband make any difference in the long run? With the exception of one older couple I knew, most adults didn't seem very happy whether they had money or not.

Even so, I watched some of my poorer friends' mothers— handsome women who were husbandless for one reason or another—marry rich, fat old men they couldn't possibly have been attracted to. Next thing I knew their moms were away in Cannes at the film festival or in Monte Carlo, leaving the kids to be waited on by servants, free to enjoy the cars, boats, great stereo systems and lavishly stocked liquor cabinets. Poor people said, "Money can't buy love." But in my world nobody seemed to care.

Was money the only thing keeping my mother married to Jack? Was the need for security the only glue binding her to his side? How many times had I helped pack her bags after hair-raising, drunken shouting matches? How many times had I encouraged her, indeed begged her, to leave? But she never got any further than the bottom of the long front hall before she changed her mind and turned around to silently drag her tan leather suitcases back up the stairs. "The devil you know is better than the devil you don't, Cate. Remember that," she would softly say, closing her bedroom door in my protesting face.

My mother was far from the only woman I knew clinging to her gilded cage for safety and for her child's sake. And what about Betty, our maid and tenant at Fieldmont? What choices did she have? Although her circumstances seemed different on the outside, wasn't it all the same dynamic? Like my mother and all these other fashionable women, she lived to serve. She lived *because* she served.

It was just a fact of life.

CHAPTER 4

Contemplating flight

Bend, grab, lift, toss. Bend, grab, lift, toss. The sun was merciless even at ten in the morning. I stopped and wiped a grimy hand across my forehead. Runnels of sweat formed grooves in the particles of hay glued to my breasts under my long-sleeved shirt. I itched. And there was hay down my pants again.

Horses sweat, Cate. Men perspire. Women merely glow. "Yeah right," I muttered, lifting another 50-pound bale and tossing it onto the fourth tier of bales on the wagon—a straight lift upwards of about six feet. Tommy, our summer help, smiled down at me in thanks before he placed it. I continued walking.

It was a good crop of alfalfa. The windrows stretched across the field, curving with the contours of the land. Likely we'd pull in over a thousand bales this year. I took another swipe at my forehead. Stacking the fifth tier, eight feet up, hay and dust sifted down in my face with each toss. Sometimes I could make it, sometimes not. I tossed the last few bales onto a lower tier and sprinted up to the passenger side of the Ford truck hitched to the wagon, grinding slowly along. I slapped the side.

"That's it."

Mom glanced my way. "Want to ride back in the cab?" I shook

my head and waited for the wagon to come up to me, then swung aboard to help Tommy stabilize the load on the way back to the barn.

By noon, the thermometer was hovering at 96°. We stopped for lunch, hauling coolers out of the truck, setting them in the shade along the fence line. Across the fence the seed heads at the tops of the long golden stalks drooped listlessly—the next field to cut and bale. I sat down under a tree next to my mother and handed out the thick ham sandwiches, potato chips and RC colas she had packed on ice that morning.

We ate contentedly. A welcome puff of breeze brushed my face and I looked around. A few thunderheads were forming in the south, a reminder that we'd better get back to work soon.

Mom fetched her cigarettes from the truck, and Tommy started the long walk towards the barns on some errand. Idly, I watched his retreating back. At 17, he was headed into his last year in high school and then college, or perhaps a job. I rolled onto my back and stared up at the sky. What the hell was I going to do?

Given my family, it seemed college was inevitable. Even my grandmother had had a degree—in ancient Greek, no less. But for me, school was an endurance contest. Oh, I was smart enough. Over the years my mother had accrued enough notes from my teachers saying so—along with statements like "If only Cate would apply herself"—to wallpaper the downstairs bathroom.

Thing was, school was utterly, devastatingly, soul-killingly meaningless to me. Who cared about the indicative mood of the imperfect tense of the Latin word *nolle*? I was unwilling enough in the present tense. And, for God's sake, unless I was going to be an engineer and build bridges, why did I have to know geometry and calculus? Why couldn't I study music? Or dance? Or theater or art? Or better yet just hang outdoors and ride all day?

I was a right-brain student in a left-brain society that didn't know, or care to know, about any educational alternatives for people like me. My teachers paid the price in frustration. I paid a price in humiliation. My parents paid a price in expensive private schools and tutoring until finally, in my sophomore year after being admitted into a Catholic high school and handed over to the nuns, I capitulated. It was simply too painful being the class dunce anymore. I buckled down and studied as if the subjects mattered— and became a straight 'A' student.

I had finally bought into the mindset that it didn't matter that I hated what I did—that it was the end-goal of other people's definitions of success that mattered. The nuns were happy. My parents were relieved. Maybe I might get somewhere in life after all.

But four more years of college? It seemed like a prison sentence. Horses were my whole life and qualifying for the US Olympic Equestrian Team was my dream. Unfortunately, this was not a goal my parents supported. They didn't want me becoming a professional rider and trainer because it wasn't a thing "girls like you do." The other problem with my plan was the kind of horse I needed to get to the Olympics didn't live in my barn.

The only possible route to get where I wanted to go was to train the super horses of the super-rich and get into high-level competition that way. For a while my parents indulged me and let me work at a fancy jumper stable nearby. For a brief three months I was in heaven riding show horses under the trainer's close supervision. But show jumping is a dangerous sport. When my mother arrived one day unannounced and discovered me on a snorting, plunging horse, leaping fences she could walk under without brushing the top of her head on the rails, fear and worry— ever her constant companions—got the better of her.

"If you want to pursue this after you're 18, I can't stop you," she said. "But you'll be on your own and not living under my roof, that's for damn sure."

Her decision spelled the end of my dream. For while the

thought of being on my own was intoxicating, at 17 it was also unfathomable. The ins and outs of finance, negotiating apartments, paying insurance—it was all a mystery to me. Sure, I had a bank account into which my parents paid a steady allowance of $25. But that was the limit of my financial education. I didn't even know how to balance a checkbook.

Everything in my life was taken care of: my teeth, my hair, my clothes, my education, my car, insurance, food. As much as I wanted to pursue my dream, the idea of taking responsibility for all that was terrifying. Plus, leaving home to pursue that dream would eliminate the trips to Europe and the parties with all my fancy dresses—and my own horses, and my piano, and . . .

I sighed and reached over to pull a strand of hay from its stalk, stuck it in my mouth and chewed ruminatively.

Was Tommy scared, facing the future? Or was there some unknown male gene that made guys unafraid to venture forth? Did something more practical than male bonding happen on father/son camping trips? Did they get advice on how to operate in the world? Rules to steer by? Secret trust funds to ensure they always had a net and would never have to worry? Or was testosterone that powerful?

My gaze slid speculatively towards my mother, sitting in the open door of the truck cab, smoking, feet up on the running board. She expected me to follow in the family tradition and graduate from college—preferably with my MRS degree. Then I would be safely out of her hair and the happy responsibility of a husband. *Shit.* I sat up and spat out the hay stalk. *Look what happened to her. Some happy.*

"How old were you when you married Cliff?" I asked.

If she was surprised by my question, she didn't let on. She took a puff on her cigarette. "Twenty-five."

"Why did you get married?"

"All my friends were married, and I was bored," she replied.

"Cliff and I had known each other forever. Our parents were friends. When he asked for the hundredth time after he got back from the war, I finally said, 'Yes.'"

I was stunned. She got married because she was bored? "Why didn't you keep teaching instead?"

She took one more drag, then turned on the seat to stub out the butt in the truck's ashtray. No sense catching the hay field on fire. "Teach kindergarten for a couple years, then ask me that again."

Hmmm. "Did he know?"

"What?"

"That you . . . weren't in love with him?"

She shrugged. "I'm not sure." She brushed invisible flecks of hay off the door handle. "I don't think it would have made any difference."

Staring across the field, I plucked another piece of grass and twirled it between my baling twine-chapped fingers. Finally I ventured the question I'd never quite dared to ask. "Why did you divorce him?"

I held my breath. Despite Jack's violence, my mother hadn't left *him*. His rages, which fortunately never went beyond pushing, grabbing, shaking, screaming and verbal abuse, made it easy to imagine worse. Leaving my father in 1955, when women never divorced no matter how bad it got, must have been a desperate flight from a relationship too terrible to imagine.

She barked an ugly laugh, reached towards her cigarettes, stopped and looked at me for a long moment. Honesty or evasion? For some reason she chose honesty. "Because he loved me too much. Drove me crazy. Made me feel guilty as hell." She shook her head.

"When we were dating, he wanted me to leave my parents' house and get out on my own. When we were married, he wanted me to have my own life: to go back to work if I wanted. Or even school. He was always at me to be more independent." Her eyes went opaque with memory, and a sudden blush suffused her sunburned cheeks. "And he constantly wanted . . ." She stopped abruptly and I watched the momentarily open door to her inner life slam shut.

She glanced at the distant clouds gathering and stood up. "Better get back to work."

I didn't try to know my real father until I was 35. He hadn't reached out to me over the long years since I was little, so why should I bother? But then a friend was reunited with a daughter he hadn't seen since she was an infant, and I saw the joy in his face as he told me about his invitation to her college graduation.

"Why all the excitement?" I asked. "You haven't seen this kid since she was a year old."

He looked at me as if I were crazy. "Are you kidding? She's my little girl. I've never stopped loving her even though I've never seen or even talked to her."

It was a revelation to think my own father might feel the same way about me. It probably shouldn't have been. I mean, by that time I was an adult who had been through my own first divorce. I knew it took two people to make a hash of a marriage, not just one. And I no longer styled myself as my mother's automatic defender. But love? It seemed a stretch to imagine my father felt much of anything for me. Nonetheless, after a few days, I nervously put the word out through the family grapevine that I wanted to connect. Two days later Cliff called.

The moment I heard his voice I knew who it was. But with the words, "Do you know who this is?" all the resentment and loss I didn't know were in me smashed home. I pretended ignorance. How could I admit, after all those years, that the *instant* I heard his voice a connection was there? That I was awash with feelings of warmth, comfort and safety? That the joyous cry "*Daddy!*" was bursting from my heart?

Although I wanted nothing more than to hurl myself through the telephone line into his arms, I couldn't let the word escape my lips. I withheld myself that first conversation and made him work for it. It made me ashamed to be so cold, but I couldn't help it. There was damage and distance to deal with. But somehow, as we talked, it all just melted away. He was real and present in the conversation, and I couldn't help but respond in kind. After a couple of increasingly intimate talks, he invited me to visit him and his family in Philadelphia.

The week tilted my world upside down.

Cliff was the father I had always yearned for—kind, contemplative and even-tempered. An affectionate man, intelligent, quick to laugh and slow to judge, he listened to my life stories and asked questions about my philosophies with genuine interest, something neither my mother nor Jack had ever done. He let me set the pace on intimacy, said nothing but wonderful things about my mother and never pried. My three adult half-brothers, his wife, his friends and his dogs adored him. Never once did I hear him raise his voice. And, like me, he was a music aficionado and played the piano.

Why, oh why, had this father been taken from me? How different my life would have been had my mother stayed with him! I lay awake in his comfortably middle-class home and stared at the ceiling, imagining a different life course.

I would have been loved and respected by this man. I would have been raised to believe family life was a good and nurturing thing and lived the truth of it. I rolled over, staring out the window at suburban lights and late-night traffic. I would never have lived on the farm—an impossible thought! Would probably never have had even one horse, let alone a dozen. That too was impossible to imagine. And the glitzy social scene? *Humpf.* I would have gladly traded that experience for something as substantive as a benevolent father's hand on the reins of my life.

A benevolent father, what a concept.

What would it have been like to be honored and cherished as a young girl? Protected, yet allowed to flower? Raised to understand that true strength lies within the mindful heart, not a raised fist? Taught by example to be thoughtful and emotionally mature? What would it have been like to watch my mother be treated with affection and tender estimation, even admiration? To have witnessed a virile man standing by her side in support, not looming over her in suffocation? My mind extended the imagery. What would it have been like to go to church and hear words of kindness and love, not judgment and law? *To have a benevolent father in both home and Heaven . . . wow.*

The late September night was stifling. Restlessly, I turned over on my back and listened to the steady tick-tick of the bedside clock. I had suffered rage instead of reason, control but not protection, manipulation rather than encouragement—a home life that mirrored the dominant patterns of my society. Until I visited my father's house, I had rarely contemplated that there might have been a different way. But if Cliff was the epitome of everything that was right about the male and fatherhood, Jack was the epitome of all that was wrong. The contrast between what had been and what might have been made my heart ache.

And yet . . .

If my benevolent father had raised me, I wouldn't be the same person. Who knew how I would have been, what I would have chosen, what I would have become? Sure, I would have been comfortable and happy . . . perhaps even complacent. *It would not have been a life conducive to growth.*

The hairs stood up on my arms and prickled on the back of my damp neck. There had to be some reason I had experienced the wrong side of the male of my species. Perhaps Jack had been the right and inevitable path for my soul's journey? Looking back, I can see for certain now what I only could guess at then. The Goddess had had plans for me. She made sure I had less pleasant soil to grow in than Philadelphia; made sure I was unprotected, un-honored and isolated, with only Nature to turn to; made sure I was battered just enough by all that was wrong so I would question what was right; made sure I was abused just enough to weep, but not enough to shut me down into quiet despair like my mother.

It was inevitable that we talked about her. Which was, perhaps, one of the reasons my mother had never encouraged me to know my father. Contrary to my firm belief that all the blame for her unhappiness belonged to Jack, Cliff carefully explained that there was a back-story I didn't know about. He didn't say a whole lot. But some of the stories he related from their youth, courtship days and the four years of their marriage definitely connected the dots—like the fact that Grandma had beaten her to the bathroom floor with a silver hairbrush as she got ready for school one morning.

"She was an abusive cold bitch of a woman," Cliff said morosely over cocktails one night. "Your grandfather always made excuses for her, not that he was all that warm and fuzzy either. But compared to your grandmother he was a saint." He was silent for a long moment, toying with his glass. Then he glanced up at me. "It almost killed me to have to leave you with them. I was afraid . . . I was afraid Ruth would get hold of you and that you'd turn out like your mother."

He didn't mean it as criticism, and I didn't have to ask him what he meant. That Cliff still loved my mom was clear, and the faithfulness of his heart over all the long years touched me deeply. But we both knew my mother was unaffectionate and somehow out of touch with anything that really mattered—like emotions, dreams and questions that bubble up from the soul. Now I knew a tiny bit better why.

Having an abusive, highly controlled childhood finally answered why she had been attracted to a man who sought to control her every movement, squeezing the life out of her. Jack gave her all the excuses she needed to remain hidden and unresponsive. He supplied her with the pain she associated with love: the pain she must have thought she deserved, meted out as it had been by her own mother's hand.

Were there even darker reasons, I wondered? Ancient places in her woman's soul so damaged they demanded punishment from many fronts? And my grandmother! No wonder she had been turned to stone, paralyzed by a disease as implacable as her own heart. What fate had twisted her so? Had she been abused as a child as well? I knew she had been raised in a stern Roman Catholic household. Had she believed the priest's talk about original sin? Was that why she shrank from self-love and life? Was that what she was trying to beat out of her little girl? And my mother, being a sensitive soul, had absorbed it all. Was Jack her unconscious payback for the sins of Eve? Was this the inheritance she thought she deserved?

It was a frightening thought, and I couldn't help but wonder if I too carried this withering burden of feminine self-hatred and pain. My body was a carbon copy of my mother's—broad-shouldered and athletic—just eight inches taller. Did we share a crippling soul inheritance as well?

I never got an answer from my mother's lips, only answers from my own life. As the years passed, she drifted ever further away, spending every free moment not involved in farm and domestic duties absorbed in the historical novels piled deep beside her single bed in the sunny master bedroom upstairs. Her only notable evolution was drinking and smoking, which she did in ever-increasing amounts.

She had her first heart attack at 45.

PART III

* * *

THE SIREN
(1969–1973)

CHAPTER 5

Speaking of sex

Coming to puberty in the 1960s, sex was everywhere in my world—and it wasn't just the exploding attitudes of permissiveness and 'free love.' Male-dominated corporate advertising ensured that scantily clad women were draped across everything: billboards, magazine covers, calendars, ads for cars, washing machines and deodorant. By the late 1960s, the only way to make advertising non-pornographic was to ensure the models were so anorexic they had no breasts.

Entire magazines were devoted to coaching women on how to catch and keep a man by looking great, satisfying him sexually and cooking fabulous meals. No one seemed to notice just *who* would benefit from these all-pervasive messages. Certainly no one cared that the slick covers featuring impossibly slender models and recipes for award-winning fudge cheesecake sent a mixed message guaranteed to drive the most balanced of women into a schizophrenic state about themselves.

Sex and relationships became so linked in people's minds they developed into a single publishing category. Almost every radio song twanged on about love and sex, the agonies of yearning for it and the heartbreak of losing it, completely confusing the two.

Even the term 'rock 'n' roll' was an early 20th-century African-American euphemism for having sex.

From age 12 onwards, bra size and the topic of boys, how to attract boys, how 'far to go' with boys, speculations about how not to get pregnant, who had done what with whom, and who was going to do what with whom, had formed the excited basis of most of my girlfriends' conversations. Despite my glitzy society upbringing, the topics didn't interest me much, even in high school. Between taking care of my horses, schoolwork, being editor of the school newspaper and president of the athletic club, I had no time to really think about boys. How did my friends come to know so much? And where did they find the time and opportunity to do all the things they whispered about?

Sex, apparently, was taking place everywhere but in my own home.

My mother was modest in the extreme. No more than one top button was ever undone on a blouse or dress. If I happened upon her in a state of undress, even if she were wearing bra and panties, she'd jump in the closet and hide. My mother and Jack didn't kiss, never held hands and never touched each other as far as I could see. Between that and the fact that they slept in separate beds, I held out the faint hope that sex, whatever it really was, never occurred between them. It wasn't just the normal squeamishness kids have about their parents and body functions. I just plain didn't like the way Jack smelled.

My mother never glanced at the sex-advice-filled magazines lining the grocery store checkout lines. We didn't use the 'S' word in the house. Even the colorful anatomy plates in the *Encyclopedia Britannica* failed to shed much light on the subject. As a result, I entered puberty knowing very little about this human mystery aside from what my girlfriends giggled about and what I gleaned watching the passionate kisses that sealed the end of every romantic movie on TV.

It was rather like hanging out with an 800-pound gorilla in the room—a vast, looming presence I knew was there, but couldn't refer to. Not surprisingly, my first emotions concerning sex were curiosity and shame. When a little first-grader whispered, "I know a bad word" into my seventh-grade ear at school one day, I knew that 'fuck' wasn't something I should ask my mother about. The syllable packed the punch of the act itself. I could sense it. And it filled me with excitement and dread.

Sexually enlightened cultures (as opposed to sexually permissive ones) do exist. Unfortunately, growing up I wasn't privy to information about them because none of those cultures were considered 'civilized' or modern. They still aren't. Looking back, it's pretty amazing to realize how much more healthy my own sexual coming of age would have been had I been raised as a native in some place like Burkina Faso, the 'Land of the Proud Ancestors', in West Africa. But I wasn't, and I undoubtedly drag around sexual scars to this day because of it . . . along with almost everybody else in the US.

It wasn't until I was in my 40s that I ran across the writings of Malidoma and Subonfu Somé outlining the sex education of children in the Dagara tribe of Burkina Faso, and read anthropological texts about other cultures' sexual ethos. Better late than never, I suppose. But what an eye opener!

For example, in the Dagara tribe there isn't even a word for 'sex.' It's not that coitus doesn't exist (else the Dagara tribe wouldn't exist either). It's just that within this group of people, like many indigenous tribes around the world, sex is not considered an 'act.' Thus, there isn't a noun for it in their language. But if not an act, what do they think it is?

For the Dagara, sex is a sacred journey of discovery two people take that moves them through multidimensional layers of consciousness and psychic connection. A powerful moment where the conception of life takes place, sex is a doorway through which the Dagara unite with the spirits of their ancestors going back thousands of years. As such, it is regarded as a most sacred process that requires much spiritual preparation and awareness to engage.

When I was 12, peering at brassiere ads in newspapers, wondering what it would be like to have boobs, girls my age in the Dagara tribe were being taught to view their wombs as sacred spaces. While my mother was hiding in closets, the elder women of the Dagara were training their daughters to psychically walk through the energetic doorway of their own bodies into alternate dimensions, taking their sexual partners with them in spirit.

While American boys masturbated over stolen *Playboy* magazines in the bathroom, boys in the Dagara tribe were being taught to honor the feminine and the psychic power of woman that would soon aid them in entering the spirit dimensions. At an early age they understood that 'sex' was not only a pleasurable way to provide the tribe with the next generation, but they fully grasped its inter-dimensional spiritual potential for 'journeying' into larger spheres of knowledge. For them, friction and genitalia were merely the packaging. Great fun, no doubt about it. But it was what lay on the inside—what two people might explore together during the experience—that mattered.

Talk about a different mindset!

When I reached menarche and 'got the curse' in the spring of my 13th year, my mother shyly bought me a box of Kotex, explained that a woman's eggs are fertilized by a man's sperm, then asked me what I wanted for dinner. When I ventured to ask her how this fertilization actually took place, she got all flustered and said, "Jesus Christ, Cate, go out and watch the cows."

I did, and gained a liberally egalitarian view of sex. The steers humped other steers and the heifers. The heifers humped the heifers and the steers. Once a year the bull singled out the cows that were in estrus and devoted himself to them for a couple of days. That was it. The rest of the time he was completely indifferent. And, of course, everything happened 'dog-style.' For me, the missionary position came as a complete surprise.

My introduction to sexuality would have shocked tribal elders the world over. But, except for the cow instructions, for my generation in America it was pretty standard. For us, the only sacred rule of sex was that a girl was supposed to be a virgin when she got married—a hypocritical social holdover from times when young maidens were bartered by their family for land, titles and power. By the mid 1960s, I just couldn't see—aside from avoiding pregnancy—what possible relevance virginity had in anyone's life.

But my mother did. She had such a thing about me being a virgin that she wouldn't even let me use Tampax. I spent many dreadful afternoons stuck on the sidelines at pool parties with a bulky Kotex pad between my sweating legs, pretending to ignore the knowing sniggers and glances of my juvenile friends, hating my body and hating my mother and her old-fashioned attitudes. In those moments, I wanted to crawl into a hole and die.

And if my mother's paranoia over the state of my hymen weren't enough to keep me on the straight and narrow, there were always the Sisters of Notre Dame Academy. The nuns didn't outright lecture us about it (they didn't mention the 'S' word either). But aside from a high school diploma, ensuring our virginal purity until graduation was their main responsibility. The priest made it a point during weekly confession to always ask, "Are you *sure* there isn't something else you want to tell me, my child?" As if any of us had unsupervised time on campus away from the nun's hawk-eyed gazes to get away with anything. Which just went to show how naïve I was. Many of my girlfriends managed to get away with quite a bit!

Despite the fact that my best friend got pregnant two months before graduation and had to leave the convent in disgrace, as far as I was concerned, the worry and lectures were a waste of everyone's time and breath. Like most young people of my generation, I had little respect for a heavy-handed rules and regulations approach to virtue. Not that it made much difference. I was far too busy with other concerns and, aside from my social scene, I had little association with the opposite sex. Dating was something girls in public school did.

And so the years crawled innocently past until, suddenly, I found myself approaching my sophomore year at Mary Washington College (the women's college of the University of Virginia) as a sweet 19-year-old who had only been kissed twice. The first time sweetly by Blue Eyes at that summer party long ago, the second time disgustingly by my long-time mixed-doubles partner from whom I'd extorted an invitation to my senior prom at the convent by threatening not to play any tennis tournaments with him that summer at the country club.

The obligatory poker-like tongue in my mouth as the sun rose at the end of our night-long date of celebratory parties was disturbing and far from pleasant. But then he exonerated himself by briefly nibbling my neck and breathing in my ear. Shivers ran all over my body in ecstasy! I briefly surrendered to his ministrations, simultaneously realizing *Oh my, this is trouble!* and not caring one whit. Then he went back to kissing and I escaped his grasp, breathed a hasty "Thanks for the evening" and exited with as much dignity as I could muster.

We never had another date, and my continuing virginal state was a matter of no concern until one late afternoon during the summer of 1970. I was speeding back from the grocery store as another car whipped past on the other side of the twisting country road at an equally crazy speed. In that moment, it suddenly occurred to me that one wrong flick of the wrist could send me hurtling into the afterlife at a combined speed of over 140 miles per hour—and that, if such a thing happened, I would die a virgin.

Being a teenager, there seemed something dreadful and stupid about that particular fate. So, right then and there, I determined to do something about it.

Despite the lack of interesting boys around me, I didn't have far to look for a potential defloration partner. Bobby, my horse trainer, had been in my life and in my barn ever since I was 11. The secret I had told no one—not even written in my diary—was that I had had a terrible crush on him from the first day we met at a friend's stable. As an employee and man eight years my senior, I never experienced any of the shyness with him that I experienced early on with boys my own age. Our passion for horses gave us a common bond. And, despite the age difference, there was an intense sexual chemistry between us almost from the beginning.

We'd carried on a mutual flirtation in the barn and across fields and forests ever since I was 12. A flirtation that, by the time I was 19, was just waiting to explode into action. "Sugar, let's tie up the horses," he would suggest, flashing me his irresistible grin as we rode far from Fieldmont and prying eyes.

Mock outrage at his suggestions had become less and less convincing. Kicking my horse into a gallop to get away from his welcome impertinence only made him laugh. He'd let me ride off some steam (and fear), then range up his horse next to mine and reach out a calloused hand. Linked, we'd race side by side, soaring over stonewalls and rail fences, filled with the joy of being together doing what we loved most. Giving my virginity to the man who'd been my closest human companion for eight years, whose lean jockey's body I had admired for so long and whose desire for me was undeniable, was inevitable. I never gave a thought to the fact that he was married.

And so it was, on a hot sunny day in the latter half of August in 1970, that we finally tied up the horses. Between the wait of years and the barrier of my virginity, it was a brief, sharply painful experience that left a great deal to be desired in the romance department. But it got the job done. Afterwards, I washed the blood off in a nearby creek under his admiring and protective gaze, put my boots back on and got on my horse. We rode home holding hands, making plans for a real tryst.

That night I lay in bed, absolutely thrilled.

I'd 'done it'. I was a woman now. I was so proud of myself you'd have thought I'd made some major discovery like penicillin.

CHAPTER 6

Becoming an adult

We tend to think of childhood as a time of unfettered innocence and irresponsibility that lasts until puberty. In truth, childhood is a state of mind—a state of mind in which feelings of wonder and joyous aliveness predominate, borne out of an unthinking awareness of our connection to the world and all its creatures. A state of awareness in which the self experiences no separation from the world and others and everything is vibrantly alive. There is no future. There is no past. Everything is Now. And everything Now, including the self, is amazing and beautiful just because it exists.

This ecstatic state of perception is called spiritual enlightenment by mystics, the frame of mind Jesus was talking about when he said, "Verily I say unto you, except ye be converted and become as little children, ye shall not enter into the kingdom of Heaven." It's the consciousness we yearn for, the 'childhood' we feel nostalgic about as we watch our own kids at play. They have something we once had but lost, and we cannot seem to recapture it.

Growing up happily immersed in Nature extended my childhood state of mind considerably past puberty. It also gave me subtlety of mind and a deep sense of internal quietness that made self-awareness possible. I even remember the exact moment I realized my childhood was ending. I was 17, curled up in a big leather chair in my bedroom, writing in my diary about the strange, intangible film that seemed to be descending over everything, distancing me from . . . me. It wasn't anything I could put my finger on. But it was real and disturbing enough to write about. I wondered, at the time, if this distancing was what adulthood was all about.

For now when I saw a flower, I was no longer like a little child, simply seeing the flower. Increasingly there was something intangible between me and the flower. A 'veil' comprised of all the things I recalled and associated with 'flowers'—my knowledge of pollination and hay fever ads on TV for nasal congestion, and the time I grabbed flowers off the church altar and got yelled at by my mother, and the time I wanted a corsage, but my escort forgot to buy me one. Seeing a flower was no longer a simple act of direct perception and involvement. It was a subconscious rehashing of my past experiences.

This subconscious reservoir of information was building up, creating the distancing I was sensing, pushing me from being the 'direct experiencer' of reality into more of a 'narrative observer' position in life. Which meant I couldn't just flop on the ground and dive into the glory of an evening's sunset anymore. Now there always seemed to be mental considerations. Was the grass wet? Would I stain my new pants? What time was it? Did I close the grain-bin doors? What was that annoying tree doing blocking that part of my view?

When I listened to music, lying prone on the floor beside the stereo, I was no longer able to crawl inside the sound and be swept away. Now I was kept *outside* of the music by thoughts of how loud it was, or too soft, or the fact that there were scratches on the record, or that I didn't like the next passage coming up.

What the hell was going on?

I didn't know anything about consciousness. I didn't have a clue that the way the brain functions, organizing, associating and retaining every impression and experience from pre-birth onwards, was building a neurological network of knowledge that was decreasing my ability to simply 'be' in the world: that by age 18 I had finally lived long enough for all the gazillion bits of sensory input to create a lens of perception through which to operate.

But I got it intuitively. My diary musings were right on target. This veil, this neurological network, was indeed my adult ego; an identity that thought certain ways and liked and disliked certain things; an identity with certain concerns that constantly assessed its environment, judging whether things were acceptable or not, deciding what to do about it if they were or weren't.

I was beginning to 'see through a glass darkly.' Full adulthood would arrive when I no longer remembered any other way to be.

Losing my virginity hastened the process towards adult amnesia. Any elder in the Dagara tribe could have explained why, and probably most of the children. Unlike Westerners, they were accustomed to thinking in terms of non-physical realities and were well aware of the subtle energetic dynamics of sexual congress. Had any of these people been available as advisors, they would have told me that when I joined my body with Bobby's, I joined with him not only physically but psychically as well. Looked at from a more scientific perspective, this invisible information sharing process during sex was actually a quantum event. When Bobby and I merged our bodies, we quite literally merged at the quantum level as well, subconsciously exchanging energy information.

In the yogic tradition of India there is even a word for this sexually transmitted information absorption: Runanabandha.

Traditional mystics and yogis warn people against having multiple sexual partners, not because of any moral or ethical concerns, but rather because they understand that absorbing too many people's energetic information can confuse the body, sometimes leading to mental degradation and what Western medicine has diagnosed as hypersexuality, or sex addiction.

So, what did my body pick up during my defloration? It's hard to say exactly. It was probably whatever resonated most with me: Bobby's subconscious tendencies, guilt, fears and other emotions, plus all the random information similar to what was already clouding my once child-like perceptions. His energetic information was added to the energetic pot of what constituted the growing personal identity of the adult 'Cate' and vice versa. And because energy can neither be created nor destroyed, the energy of his information and the energy information of every subsequent lover would have stayed with me for a long time. According to some Native American traditions, it would be seven years before the energetic imprint of Bobby's touch and sperm left my body!

But back then, safe in my ignorance, no hint of this touched me. I got back on my horse and rode away that day thinking I had at long last experienced the ultimate human experience! And if somebody had explained the situation in greater detail, I probably wouldn't have believed it. Oh, maybe the scientifically documented cases of people with organ transplants suddenly experiencing strange thoughts, habits and food preferences that turned out to belong to their organ's former owners (now dead) might have gotten my attention. But I wouldn't have applied it to my life or my sexual experiences. I was 19 and invulnerable. Psychic quantum information sharing was light years from my consciousness. Secure in my technological world of ICBMs, transistor radios and indoor plumbing, I did The Twist, ate at McDonalds and thought I knew it all.

I waited in the chill dark listening for Bobby's footsteps. The field down by the pond was filled with weeds and Scotch thistle. Only the immediate area around the camper was mowed, and I was certain I would hear him coming.

"Cate?" My name whispered in the night. How stealthily he'd approached!

"Here," I hissed and got up to open the door. Instantly his arms were around me. We kissed for a few breathless moments, night-cooled lips exploring, then separated to sit down on the bed.

If my hurried, uncomfortable first time had been an afternoon snack, my second sexual encounter was a leisurely four-course meal. We talked and kissed and slowly, slowly he seduced me into the sheets, sliding my flannel nightie over my head, lowering his body over mine. It . . . wasn't painful. It was delicious, sweet, slow and gentle. We laughed softly afterwards, still embraced. I felt warm, cherished and deeply satisfied. It was the moment of intimacy I had waited years for.

Bodies stirring again, the afterglow kisses deepened. Coming up for air, I noticed something odd. Over Bobby's shoulder a bright shaft of light was slicing the night, hitting water, then pasture, then the trees lining the rutted lane coming down from the barns. Mind elsewhere, I stared for a long moment, puzzling it out.

"Shit!" I levitated onto one elbow. "It's Jack! Oh my God, get out! Get out!!!" Bobby bounded up, fumbling for his clothes, his socks, his shoes. "Where's my undershirt?" he gasped. The lights were getting closer. I could hear the engine's roar, the auditory rage of my stepfather spilling before him, coming at us down the hill.

"Forget it!!! Go!!!" I cried. I could see the headlights now as Jack's jeep tore down the lane. Bobby slammed out the door just as the vehicle swept around the last section of fence before the water, lights raking the camper. I heard his footsteps this time as he ran. The jeep careered up to the camper and screeched to a halt.

KA-BLAM!! KA-BLAM!! KA-BLAM!! Rifle fire tore the night.

Naked, I dove back under the covers, fishing wildly for my nightgown. Wadded at the foot of the bed, I snatched it out and shoved it over my head with shaking hands. The door to the camper ripped open and Jack stormed in, flashlight blazing, eyes deadly, rifle in his hands.

My mind whirled as I rocked violently in my seat. How long would it take Bobby to get around the pond, across the dam, up the hill and through two more fields? Barefoot and naked, running through briars and thistles? Would he lose his car keys? Had Jack locked the pasture gate where Bobby had hidden his car, preventing escape? The jeep slewed to a stop, spewing gravel. My mother was standing in her bathrobe at the backyard gate, clutching the front of her robe.

"Get out of the goddamn car!!" Jack roared.

"Jack, what is it?" My mother's voice trembled. "What's going on?"

I fumbled with the door handle, stalling for time. Cursing, he reached across, opened it and shoved me out into the driveway. I minced around the back of the jeep, barefoot in the gravel in my shortie nightgown. Ignoring my mother, Jack pulled the rifle out of the backseat, shoved it down beside him and raced off down the drive. *Oh God, don't let him kill him! Oh God, oh God . . . please!*

"Cate, what's happening?"

Shame mixed with the terror coursing through my body as I saw my mother's frightened eyes. What the hell could I say? My mind split in two, one half spinning a story of self-protection, the other half chanting one pounding word—*run!*

Jack found only an open gate, tire tracks in the grass and no target for his rifle. Storming angrily back into the house, he banished me to my room, then spent the rest of the night hashing the situation over with my mother.

Although it was 1970 and I was 19 and well past the age of consent, my parents had strictly conservative moral and religious ethics. I was still living under their roof, subject to their rules, and those rules were clear: virginity and parental obedience were not optional, they were mandatory. Getting caught, almost literally with my pants down, breaking both those rules was no light topic of discussion.

I sat in front of the mirror on my dressing table, blank-faced, listening to the shouts and crying going on downstairs, looking for evidence of the tenderness and terror that had marked the night. My face showed nothing. In fact, I felt nothing. To drum up some emotion, I silently chanted a litany of my wrongdoings and their repercussions. *You betrayed your family's trust. You committed a sin and had sex out of wedlock. You committed adultery! You almost drove Jack to murder. You've hurt your mother. Your reputation is destroyed. No man will ever want you again.*

Still nothing.

The numbness and shock didn't go away. Days later when Bobby managed to get a concerned call through to me at home, I was indifferent. Desultorily I agreed to a meeting. Sitting on my horse that afternoon, watching his car come up the back dirt road far from Fieldmont, for the first time since I was 11, my heart didn't give its customary flip-flop of excitement. When he pulled me close to comfort me, I felt like a stick figure carved of wood. When he tried to kiss me, my lips were unresponsive. When he asked to see me again, I brushed him off.

Something had died that night after all. The brief flame of tenderness and exuberant sensual responsiveness in me had been snuffed out. I never saw Bobby again.

CHAPTER 7

Missing the mark

It all should have been different somehow. But how?

I shared my generation's rejection of the moral codes of my parents and wanted freedom on my generation's terms. But after the rebellion, then what? I had nothing inside to lean on, no authentic truths or spiritual lodestone gained from personal experience to guide me. Just the system of religious rules I had been caught rejecting.

Three weeks after my disastrous night in the camper I was on a plane bound for the University of Arizona and my sophomore year in college. The decision to expand my cultural and educational horizons, which only weeks before had worried my parents, was embraced with relief in the end. Anything to get me out of harm's way and Bobby's bad influence.

Arriving at a huge university campus at the peak of the Vietnam War with the whole student protest movement in full swing was more confusing than galvanizing. Girls in tie-dye halter-tops and bellbottoms wandered around barefoot with flowers in their hair. Peace signs decorated people's clothes, store windows, cars and vans. Marijuana smoke hung like a pall in the dorms. Head shops dotted the downtown business landscape like pimples on a teenager's chin. Protest rallies mobilized thousands of students, and the Arizona National Guard was brought in to manage the situation.

The whole atmosphere was charged with a sense of change and larger purpose. Consciousness-raising groups were forming. Transcendental meditation was attracting students in droves. Women's studies were becoming a viable subject. Feminist groups held meetings. But none of it touched me. The little I knew of the world from personal experience had taught me not to rock the boat. Jack, my grandfather, my mother, the priests and nuns were right. It was best not to question anything. I was just there to finish out my school/prison sentence and check out the desert.

I watched the social upheaval swirl around me as if from behind a glass wall.

Can I possibly describe how shallow I was? How my shallowness was the very fullness of what I thought I knew? I'd absorbed my parent's beliefs and my teacher's knowledge. I'd soaked up Jack's violence, my mother's submissiveness, my culture's paradigms, my family's political party's ideologies and my priest's platitudes. They were 'me,' constituting the truth of how the world was.

The 'veil' I had noticed two years before was now a suffocating blanket, muffling everything. I drew my second-hand philosophies tightly about me, wearing them proudly, safely assured of who I was—a shrouded young ego clinging to her only truth.

Within a week of my arrival I smoked pot for the first time with the girls across the hall. Within a month I met Gregg out on the campus tennis courts. A junior majoring in business administration, Gregg had his own apartment off-campus with a roommate. I wasn't physically attracted to him, so he wasn't anyone I was interested in dating. But he was a great tennis player, and he was from Washington, DC. With this as a superficial bond, we started hanging out together.

Back in those days, men and women's dorms were segregated. At Arizona, the women's dorms were locked at midnight on weeknights and at 2am on Saturdays and Sundays. To have a key to your dorm, sophomore girls had to have written parental permission. Sophomore boys did not. My parents, figuring I had no business being out later than dorm curfew on any given night of the week anyway, refused to give that permission. Which meant that at 12.10am one Thursday night in early October I couldn't get back in my dorm. No amount of door pounding or waiting around in the cold desert night outside the building produced another student arriving with a key. Gregg, who hung around to see me safely inside, got tired of waiting and offered to let me sleep on his sofa.

I felt awkward accepting his offer. But it was windy and cold, and I was tired. Brian, his roommate, would be there after all. And it wasn't like they were strangers or anything. They were both nice guys. So I accepted Gregg's offer.

Within moments of the door locking behind me it became clear that Gregg had no intention of letting me sleep on the sofa. The moment my coat came off, he grabbed me, kissing me roughly, hands on my breasts. I pulled away, protesting. He persisted. I used all my strength and shoved him away.

"Stop it, Gregg! Leave me alone!"

He grabbed me again, pulling me close. "Why else are you here? You know you want it as much as I do." He bent to kiss me again. I wrested my mouth away.

"I'll call Brian!"

"He's not here. It's just you and me."

He shoved me towards his bedroom. I fought, but he was a large man and too strong for me. *This isn't happening!* I thought wildly. In desperation I let my body go limp and let my weight carry me to the floor. My arms got free, and I slapped and kicked at him, but he got me by the hair and dragged me by it across the room. I cried out and scratched and grabbed at his hands, trying to relieve the searing pain.

"No!" It should have been a scream, but wasn't. *This can't be happening. I should scream.* I simply couldn't scream. Something blocked my throat, and the words wouldn't come out, not even a primal shriek. *Why can't I scream? I should scream . . .* Panting, feet scrabbling for purchase against the rug, he almost had me through the hallway door.

Gregg's elbow banged sharply against the doorpost. Cursing, he lost his grip. Unsupported, I fell flat and lay there for a moment. In the gloom of the hall his strong athlete's body towered over mine, a huge dark shadow dressed in white Lacoste. "Please, don't do this!" I begged. And suddenly the image of my mother backed against the kitchen counter as Jack advanced flashed in my brain. The very same words had come from her mouth, too.

He grabbed my hair again, and my mind splintered. Was it Jack leaning over me? Was it Gregg? Somebody's teeth were in my face, bared in an animal effort. "Come on," he snarled. Ah . . . it was Gregg. But why was I on the floor? Had I tripped on the hem of my long skirt backing away as Jack came down the hallway screaming "Whore!" Or . . . no, it was Gregg. Wasn't it? My mind chittered insanely *I'm sorry I'm late I'm sorry I couldn't get in the dorm please don't do this I'm so sorry . . .*

"Cunt!"

Something gave way inside. Something broke. Sobbing like a little girl I went limp, and Gregg dragged me into his bedroom. *I can't I can't don't . . .* Before I knew it, he'd torn off my jeans, pried my legs apart and was on top of me and inside me. I lay still, unresponsive, mind numb, body in shock.

It was too late to scream.

❖❖❖❖

The ordinary tick-tick of the clock as the second hand moved around the luminescent dial was the only sound in the room. Somewhere, outside in the real world, someone laughed.

I moved, inch by slow inch, out from under Gregg's inert, sweaty body. As gravity took him the rest of the way to the mattress, he snorted, rolled over and started snoring. My face was smeared with tears and sweat. The sticky wetness between my legs felt like blood. The thought of his semen filling me was revolting. With a shudder I got his leg off mine and rolled as far away from him as I could get. My mind touched on the sweetness of Bobby under my sleeping bag in the camper and skittered away. I stared at the wall in the dark. What was wrong with me? What had kept me silent? *Oh God, why did I let him do it?*

Guilt flooded through me, adding to the pain. It was my fault. My fault I went out on a school night. My fault I didn't wait at the dorm. My fault I didn't scream. My fault I slept with Bobby. *My fault my fault my fault . . .* It was too much to bear. My chest felt like it would burst. Tears ran hot onto the pillow. I hadn't fought hard enough. *Why why why?*

The answer was deep down inside, unreachable.

How many times had I been told to be 'seen and not heard?' How many times had my mother told me to let men do what they wanted in order to keep the peace? How many times had I watched her let herself be abused? Passive silence was a program burned deep into me. But in that moment of exhausted despair I couldn't see the truth. The rape had not been my fault. A woman's 'No!' means no. It was not about how hard I could fight a man off to prove it. But all logic escaped me. Self-loathing and contempt were all I could feel.

I only got what I deserved.

Horrifying as it was, the savage thought was a comfort. It set things right. Made sense of the situation. *I'm not a virgin, after all. I came back to his apartment. What did I expect? Candlelight and roses?* Following this ugly track, the looming pit of despair and guilt receded a little further. *Jack was right. I'm nothing but a whore.*

Somehow the ghastly harshness of my thoughts protected me, shielded me from facing the depths of the assault I'd just experienced. They insulated me from the shattering violation, sequestered me from feeling the ancient feminine soul wound it had ripped open. Clutching bitter self-judgment like a teddy bear, I finally fell asleep.

Many people, my parents and the nuns included, would have no trouble labeling me a sinful person for my actions. And, like me, they might also have believed I'd only gotten my just desserts and been righteously punished for those sins. And yet the Aramaic word 'sin' originally was an archery term that meant 'missing the mark.' It had nothing to do with wrongdoing and being a bad person. It just referred to an inaccurate shot at something.

If the ultimate target of sexual union is indeed union—a pleasurable, overwhelmingly intimate 'knowing' and bonding with another person, mind, body and soul—then my dreadful initiations to sexuality had way missed the mark. But how could it have been otherwise? Raised by parents from a generation and culture that knew next to nothing about intimacy, my sexual understanding was ridiculously shallow, based on nervous teenage gossip and whatever magazine articles I could sneak into my possession. Rebellion was my main reason for losing my virginity, that and a vague sense that it was 'time' to do so and that I was missing out on something if I didn't. And, of course, there had been attraction and opportunity.

Yes, I was responsible for my choices. But ignorance plus the natural arrogance of youth combined with hormones and social permissiveness were a disaster waiting to happen. I walked right into the mess, joining the untold millions of sexually uninformed women who had gone before me down the same unhappy path. Screwed up by everything from childhood sexual abuse to misused quotes from the Bible, Puritanism and Victorian prudery to bathtub gin and 'free love', generation after generation we fell into bed for pretty much all the wrong reasons, then wondered why we reaped a harvest of guilt, confused values and lowered self-esteem afterwards.

Yes, I had missed the mark. But if there was any 'sin' involved in the modern moral sense of the word, it was the sin of my society that tacitly approved of and economically supported sexual exploitation of women, infantile fantasies, moral confusion, sexual ignorance and lack of mature wisdom.

Would the rape have happened if Gregg had been taught a deep respect for women? Could he have possibly done what he did if feminine values had been instilled in him through education and example? If he had had wise, sexually wholesome mentors instead of *Hustler Magazine* as his guide, could he have possibly justified his actions? Would he have used force if brute physical strength wasn't the accepted mode of getting what you want in our world?

Probably not.

So why wasn't he provided this? Why weren't all men?

As it turned out, for all her preaching to the contrary, my mother had trod a similar path of sexual injudiciousness in her youth. Which was, perhaps, why she had been so vocal and adamant about *my* virginal purity. But, intimacy not being her forte, I was 30 before I found out during a confession that occurred late one night on a trip to Paris.

At the time, I was fresh from my first divorce. Emotionally eviscerated by my failed marriage, depressed and confused about my future, I took a leave of absence from work to backpack around England by myself for a month in September 1981. I met Mom in France afterwards as a well-deserved reward for weeks of hiking and sleeping in cheap pub rooms unlikely to make it to the pages of any decent tour guide. We were well into our second (or possibly third) round of after-dinner brandies in our elegant hotel room one night when I discovered *she* hadn't been a virgin when she got married either.

"You're kidding!"

"Not kidding." Mom lolled against the carved headboard of her bed, feet on the satin duvet, brandy glass in one hand, cigarette in the other. Beaming triumphantly at my surprise, she sipped her drink. Below the tall open French doors, summer foot traffic was at its peak at 2am as Parisians sauntered through the warm fall night from bars to bistros and back again.

"You slept with Cliff beforehand?"

Her eyebrows slanted in sardonic amusement. "Now, what makes you so sure it was your father I slept with?"

My double take sent her into gales of laughter. Paris and the brandy were definitely having their effect. "You must think me awfully dull, Cate."

Not anymore! I positively stuttered over my next question. "So who then?"

"Bob Heidermann."

"Who?"

My mother sighed and swirled her glass ruminatively. The viscous liquid tracked down the insides of the snifter like melted amber. "The love of my life," she said, softly. An inner light glowed, hesitant yet warm, and for a brief moment I could see the young girl in love once more. Debating the wisdom of her confession, she tipped the brandy to her lips. Perhaps that taste was the deciding factor, for she launched into her tale.

Like my Bobby, her Bob (same name!) was a guy from the 'wrong side of the tracks.' They met during her senior year in college at a Christmas party while she was home for the holidays. When he asked my mother to marry him the summer she graduated, she was thrilled. But her socially conscious parents refused the match. Heartbroken, she broke up with him and never saw him again.

There is a saying in the Bible that the sins of the fathers are visited upon their sons, and the same must hold true for mothers and daughters. Like me, Mom had been guilty, yet smugly pleased she had 'done the deed' with him. Like me, she was the one who broke off the relationship due to parental disapproval. Eventually she settled for a man she didn't love, got married to Cliff and had me. Finally, divorcing kindness because she felt unworthy of it, she remarried and endured Jack.

Following in my mother's footsteps, I also settled for a man I didn't love. It seems impossible to believe now, but for the rest of the semester after the rape Gregg and I dated—if hanging out with someone you actively dislike, but continue to sleep with, can be called dating. My friends at school were astonished at my decision. A few of the more feminist-inclined sophomores wondered why I hadn't ripped Gregg's balls off that night, or at the very least called the campus police afterwards. My three freshman roommates were more cavalier and forgiving. Two of them had been date-raped so far during the course of their young lives, Sandra twice. To hear them talk about it was no big deal.

Post-trauma I was inclined to agree with my roommates. It didn't seem like such a big deal to me either. My mother always said, "You make your bed, you lie in it." Wasn't that what I was doing? Gregg and I were intimate now. Why not continue? I mean, what did it matter? What did anything matter?

Suddenly seeming to have no attention span at all, I sleep-walked through my classes, falling further and further behind in my studies. School, uninteresting to begin with, just didn't seem important anymore. I assuaged my guilt over my flagging grades and continued relationship with Gregg by smoking more pot. Not surprisingly, the weekly phone conversations with my mother became more and more stilted. What could I tell her about my life now? "Hi, Mom, I'm having a great time getting stoned so I can handle being raped. But don't worry. I'm okay?"

As the weeks passed, her mom-radar went into high gear, and concern over my apathy grew into alarm. But I just couldn't muster the energy to do anything about it. Post-Traumatic Stress Disorder wasn't a term or condition that existed back then. Bad things happened, you dealt with them or not as the case may be. If I thought about my situation at all, which I pretty much didn't, I figured I was managing fine.

Fresh campus protests exploded, and troops cordoned off the streets as students rioted and helicopters buzzed overhead. Tear gas hung in the air like a stinging fog, and I stayed in my high-rise dorm room, windows closed, mind shuttered. Looking down on it all was like watching a movie. The world had nothing to do with me or me with it.

Continuing to sleep with Gregg was the most painful thing I could find to do. A highly effective method of punishing myself for my actions, it helped me avoid my guilt. It also served to make me an accomplice rather than a victim. Unconsciously I put myself in control. Instead of this man, or any man, continuing to inflict pain and outrage on me, I was inflicting it on *myself*. By choosing it, I had the power, not them.

Emotional pain, as my mother had discovered, was a great distancing device. It kept her, and now me, from thinking too deeply about the condition of our lives. It prevented both of us from addressing the unfathomable and terrifying question of what it was in us *as women* that made us subconsciously believe we deserved violation and disrespect. For unless at some level we felt we deserved it, why, oh God why, would we seek it out?

"Sweetie, Jack and I want to fly you home for Thanksgiving. Would you like that?"

Would I like it? Thanksgiving was my favorite holiday. There was something so right about holding an annual feast after the fall harvest to give thanks for life's bounty. I loved helping prepare the turkey, especially the stuffing, shoveling as much of the uncooked bread-mess into my mouth as I could while Mom wasn't looking. And the Thanksgiving foxhunt on Saturday was an annual treat, with a gala hunt breakfast afterwards that I looked forward to all year long.

A flicker of interest registered. *Thanksgiving. Home.* Emotion rose, unbidden. Tears welled in my eyes. Sitting in the stuffy, graffiti-marked dorm phone booth, I imagined standing in my favorite horse's stall, Jeb's satin-and-steel neck warm against my cheek, his dusty horse scent filling my nostrils. I mentally twined my fingers through his copper mane, inhaled the smell of straw, sweet feed and manure, pungent and comforting. *That* was real. *That* was life, not this strange disembodied state and place of exile. A wave of homesickness hit me with shocking force.

"Um." I cleared my throat. "Gee. It's only four days and so close to Christmas. Are you sure?"

"If you want to come, we're sure. We'd love to see you." *We're worried* hung unspoken on the line.

Yes yes yes yes yes!

I cleared my throat again, harder this time. "I'd l-love to come home, M-Mom." I barely got through the flight details, hanging up hastily before the dam burst. Back in my room I threw myself on my narrow bunk bed and cried. It was the first time since the night of my rape, and the wracking sobs came harsh and uneven. But there was light at the end of my dark tunnel at last. The farm was calling, and I was headed home.

I transferred back to Mary Washington College in Virginia the following spring semester. Goodbye, Gregg, goodbye, Arizona. My parents were thrilled to have me back, and I was glad for many reasons, not the least of which was being able to drive home on weekends to ride. Telling Gregg my decision just before the Christmas break upset him. But I couldn't have cared less. I was leaving the trap I had set for myself and couldn't wait to get away.

When he showed up at my Virginia dorm just after spring break three months later and asked me to marry him, it couldn't have come as a bigger or more unpleasant surprise. As nicely as dismay and indifference could make the words come out, I said, "No."

"But, Cate, I love you." His face was a mask of almost desperate sincerity.

Was it love that had driven his 'persistence past my initial resistance,' as he liked to call it? I shook my head, trying to clear it of all the bullshit. *Whatever*. I might be into self-punishment, but continuing to accept that kind of love was beyond even me.

I didn't marry him.

Instead, through the rest of college and afterwards, I went on to create and then endure other unsatisfying relationships with other inappropriate men I didn't love or even like all that much. Attracting guys was no problem, even though I wasn't beautiful or pretty in the traditional sense. *Thank God*. I'd watched the turmoil that the curse of beauty caused. One of my friends was a teen model for *Cosmopolitan* magazine, and she was never sure why a man was with her, for her prize looks or for herself, whatever that might be. Every woman I knew ached to be taken seriously and truly be 'seen.' And the most beautiful of them all were usually the least satisfied.

No, I wasn't beautiful. I was safely what people called attractive, with an athletic body that I wielded like a club, doing damage both ways. I was a Siren, calling men to me, then leaving them because there wasn't any other glue to the relationship. I didn't do it out of love, often not even out of desire. I did it because I didn't know what else to do with my body, which, between hormones and the general philosophy of the day, I was confused into believing *was* my self.

Besides, who didn't believe it was important for a woman to be attractive and have a man? It meant I was successful as a woman. Didn't it? Certainly a warm male body next to mine at night made me feel satisfied with myself—made me happy. If a man was in my bed, by golly, I was a viable human being.

So much for the Feminist Movement, the Equal Pay Act, Title IX, Career Day talks at my high school and the general atmosphere of Women's Lib. Sure, all these things gave me the example and assistance to seek my way in the world. But none of these influences could compete with generations of sexual programming. Needing to have a man to feel right about myself was such an ingrained social expectation, I wasn't even aware of it.

And the act of lovemaking itself?

For something that was so wonderful, sex certainly came with a lot of baggage. Not only did I have to worry about my looks, morality, pregnancy and STDs, I also had to worry about performance. As far as I could tell from the magazines, the whole point of sex was orgasms, not connecting and bonding and making babies but 'getting off.' The essential ingredient of successful sex was to make sure you stimulated your partner properly for them to have The Big O. Then, in order for them to feel good about themselves as sexual partners, *you* had to have one, too.

Turns out it wasn't so hard ensuring my partner's pleasure. Just being horizontal and breathing was sufficient for most men. Providing them proof they were fabulous lovers by getting *me* off—well, that was an entirely different matter. It's not that I didn't enjoy sex. Despite my rocky beginnings, I loved it. Only problem was The Big O escaped me utterly unless I fantasized about being abused and raped. And this totally freaked me out. Not only did it make me feel twisted and dirty inside, it confused me. Having experienced rape, I knew the reality of it did not turn me on. So why did the fantasy? What was going on? What was the matter with me?

I was confident I was neither masochistic nor sadistic. Pain, physical or emotional, was not something I enjoyed receiving or giving. In fact, seeing any animal or human in pain put me in an absolute panic. Even torture scenes in movies had me running from the living room, hands clapped over my ears so I couldn't hear the screams. "Cate, come back! It's only a movie, for Christ's sake!" Jack would call out in exasperation. But I had to run away. The terrifying cinematic sights and sounds were all too real to me.

Real?

It's hard to talk about, let alone explain, but starting around age five I had recurring nightmares of torture and abuse that happened almost on a nightly basis. I never told my mother the content of the nightmares that had her rushing into my room to wake me up several times a week. They embarrassed as much as frightened me, and for some reason I felt I should keep quiet about them. One dream that recurred frequently was particularly horrifying.

In the dream, *a crowd mills below me, a blur of gray robes and muted voices in a twilight scene. I don't understand the language they are speaking. A beefy, sweating man grabs my jaw with a filthy hand and pries my mouth open, thrusting his fingers inside my mouth, poking at my teeth. I snap at his hand, connecting with acrid flesh, drawing blood. He jerks his hand back and slaps me.*

Stars burst in my vision. Unthinkingly, I place my hand under my pregnant belly, supporting my unborn babe. The shake of his head 'no' goes unseen as I am shoved towards the front of the wooden platform. The men seethe forward, all hot eyes and ugly smiles. I watch, uncomprehending, as a soldier steps through the crowd, drawing his short sword. His mouth gapes open, pink with anticipation against his dark beard. With a swift lunge he slits my belly open, top to bottom. I drop to my knees in a mess of intestines, blood and water. A little arm with a perfect hand and tiny fingers lies in the filth before me.

It was the worst of the nightmares that populated my young mind. The others were mostly just fleeting impressions of fire, the agony of burning, cold dark rooms, implements and brutal men's faces, despair and wild confusion, pleas unheard and a throat raw from screams.

Where would a child get such terrible visions? At such a tender age when no television show, movie or book was available to me that contained such images and ideas, where did these dreams come from? And were they even dreams? I had no idea.

Long before puberty they faded away. But their mark on me remained, carrying over into my adult sex life as fantasies. Despite the fact that I had not summoned them, I was deeply ashamed of them. They were a sickness in my soul, and for many years I kept them secret, desperately wondering how to get rid of them.

But as much as I wanted them to go away, I also wanted to understand their origin. Stepping back and studying the act itself, it was easy to get the impression that sex was something the male 'did' to the female. In fact, if you didn't know what was really going on, the scene could appear pretty grim. How many little children have sleepily happened upon their parents and mistakenly thought that Daddy was 'hurting' Mommy?

Passion can wander the gamut from tender playfulness to bondage and back again without ever entering the realm of inappropriate force. But it's a fine line. For the woman, sexual surrender and submission are close companions. It's thrilling riding the edge between the deliciousness of being 'taken' and the distress of being taken advantage of. On the masculine side there's an art to supplying enough drive versus too much: between much-desired mutual ravishment and entering the realms of rape.

How easy to justify and apply brute force in a world where violence creates kings! How easy to tip the scales in the wrong direction. And in my world, the scales had been tipped for a long time. Since the fall of the Goddess religions and the rise of the patriarchal Gods of Islam and Judaea, women had been regarded as soulless chattel. For thousands of years, we lived or died at the whim of the men who owned us, mandated by God Himself to have power over us and treat us harshly to ensure obedience.

How many generations of abuse did it take to imprint soullessness on a woman's genetic line? How many generations of brutality to instill submissiveness into her being? How many generations did it take to embody the impact of male contempt and embrace worthlessness? How many generations of torture and rape did it take for a little girl to wake up with nightmares? To be born into psychic confusion, mixing pain with what should be the ultimate physical pleasure? Fifty years of relative liberation in a few Western countries was hardly enough time to wipe the psychic slate clean of thousands of years of horror.

I never asked my mother if she shared similar visions and fantasies. That would have been way too personal a conversation for her. Besides, I was too embarrassed to ask. But as I grew older and less self-conscious, I did open the conversation with other women. To my vast relief several friends spoke painfully of similar thoughts. I wasn't alone! It was difficult sharing brutal fantasies and we all had deep reluctance exposing ourselves because of the embarrassment and disgust they triggered. But it helped getting them out into the open.

We also speculated over the causes. Where did these fantasies come from? Nobody in their right mind wanted such things in their head, and most of us had had these visions since childhood. Figuring out their roots seemed important and we came up with everything from soul memory and past life recollections to genetic inheritance, to the psychic retrieval of archetypal images that belonged to the collective consciousness of humanity existing in the noosphere. You name it, we considered it.

But for all our fancy ideas surrounding the abuse we fantasized about and the shame we felt because of it, never once do I recall any of us expressing outrage or anger at the perpetrators in and of our dreams. None of us directed any blame towards men. Even the knowledge that the degradation and abuse of women was *still an ongoing reality* in our modern world didn't trigger any feelings of anger towards the opposite sex.

In 1975 two million American women were battered by their husbands and we remained silent and unmoved. In 1992 we said nothing about the 1.3 women in the United States age 18 and over who were being forcibly raped *each minute*—a statistic that left out the 22 percent of rape victims who were *younger than age 12* and the 32 percent of girls who were between ages 12 and 17.

My friends and I said nothing as female babies in China were being abandoned on garbage heaps for wild dogs to eat. In 2012 the United Nations declared an estimated 200 million women were missing worldwide, killed by bride burnings, widow burnings, dowry-related suicides and infant exposure and abandonment.

Two hundred million women had perished in my lifetime for the crime of being female, and I didn't even know the word 'femicide' existed?!

Islamic nations frequently denied women medical attention. If they were admitted to hospitals they were routinely denied anesthesia during surgery. Globally, military troops used mass rape as a method of psychological warfare against citizens. Female political prisoners were raped to death in prisons and pregnant women shot through their wombs and left to bleed to death.

My dream/memory of a sword through the womb of a woman on an ancient slave block in Rome . . . what was the difference between that and a pistol shot through the womb in prison in Abu Ghurayb? In three thousand years only the means of the execution had changed, not the method or the soul-shattering contempt behind it.

How could I not care about the fate of my sisters around the world? How could I remain unmoved when their agony lived in my own mind? How could I know what was happening and just let it slide by on the nightly news? Even now, writing about these horrifying hate crimes against women, there's an astonishing lack of outrage in me. Instead of anger and distress I feel a cool sense of separation that could almost qualify as indifference. How is this possible? It's like I don't believe these things are really real. Because if I did wouldn't I be on fire about it, marching in the streets, shouting from the rooftops?

What the hell's made me so numb and unfeeling? Is it gender specific PTSD? Have I been brainwashed by comfort? Too absorbed by busy-ness? Do I make no huge outcry because somehow deep inside I fear I'll be punished if I demand justice? That I'll lose my hard-won grasp on liberation by making a fuss? Or do I subconsciously believe women are to blame for their own abuse?

Damn Eve and her stupid apple!

Is it possible we've swallowed this story of guilt rammed down our throats for thousands of years and now we subconsciously believe we're to blame for the fallen state of the world and deserve whatever we get? Do we really believe the rapes and beatings are our fault? That the mere presence of our bodies leaves men no choice but to rape us if we're not willing? To beat us if we're not obedient?

"Shame" is a small answer for such a staggering situation. And yet what else could it be?

Looking back I can't believe I once took pride in not being a feminist. And yet how could I possibly have been a feminist? My mother raised me to keep the peace. I was educated in schools created by and for men. I was taught to define success in masculine terms, to define justice through men's history and ideals. I was indoctrinated through male-dominated media to accept men's ideals of femininity. I believed that bosom-baring babes on the cover pages of all my favorite magazines was the only way women could be seen and heard.

I accepted myself as a sex object and lashed out against feminists, because taking the masculine stance made me man's equal. Like Patty Hearst, I—along with hundreds of millions of other women in my generation and generations following—had been kidnapped and brainwashed into adopting the philosophy of our former captors, identifying completely with the patriarchal status quo as the only way of escaping the inescapable reality of still being its victim.

PART IV

***

THE WARRIOR
(1974–1986)

CHAPTER 8

Life in television

In 1973 I graduated from college with a BA in English that made me marketable for exactly nothing. Since I'd failed to garner an MRS degree at the same time, January 1974 found me packing my car and a small U-Haul trailer, headed to the University of South Carolina in Columbia to work on my Master's degree in journalism.

Soon after my arrival I started dating Brad, a really nice, good-looking radio disc jockey who lived in my apartment complex. He was so nice we didn't date for long, and soon I was on to someone much less appropriate. But during our brief affair I spent a lot of time hanging out at the radio station during his evening shift. I found the control rooms fascinating and would sit for hours in the news booth practicing mock broadcasts, making faces at Brad through the glass panels, trying to get him to crack up on air. After he dropped one of my demo reels on the program manager's desk, it seemed a DJ career was well on its way to happening. And then I met Frank.

Tap tap tap. I didn't hear the knocking through my headset. *TAP TAP TAP.* I jerked around to see a dark-haired man standing patiently outside the sound booth. I slid my headset off and opened the door. "Yes?"

"I need to pull one of the cart machines to work on it."

"Sure thing." I took the headset off and slid out of my chair.

"Frank," he extended a hand. A neat row of colorful little screwdrivers was clipped to a white plastic pocket protector on his shirt. "I'm one of the transmitter engineers."

"Cate Malone. Nice to meet you."

We yakked as he disgorged the cartridge player from its rack. Then I followed him back to engineering.

"Actually I work at the TV station," he said. "I'm just out here tonight helping out."

WIS-TV was the local NBC affiliate station in the state capital of Columbia and partner to WIS radio. Frank tinkered with the equipment for a moment more, then glanced up. "If you like, I can take you on the ten-cent tour of the studios sometime."

Visit the TV station? Would I like to? I leapt at the chance. Pleased with my enthusiasm, he agreed to meet me at the station a few days later.

We walked up the narrow stairs, past the announcer's booth and back into the control room where all the daily programs and commercials were placed on the air by the switcher—a guy sitting at a complex console filled with colorful buttons, glowing lights and fader bars, surrounded by cartridge players, reel-to-reel tape machines and audio meters. Next to the switcher was a bank of consoles that controlled the images from the enormous cameras down in the studios. To my right, behind the sliding glass doors to the tape room, two huge Ampex quad tape machines whined. The switcher went into a commercial break, hitting a few buttons. A projector on the film chain rolled.

"So, what do you think?" Frank asked, pulling up a tall metal stool. I sat down next to him, checking out the contents of the counter that ran the length of engineering. A jumble of stripped-out equipment, circuit boards and soldering tools, its top was marred with driblets of silver solder and burn marks. Around me the transmitter racks glittered with randomly colored lights. With no windows in the production and engineering areas, there was no telling whether it was night or day.

"I love it!"

"Lights, camera, action, huh?" he joked kindly.

"Yeah," I responded sheepishly. In the background a disembodied voice from the director's control room could be heard asking for the studio cameras to be turned on. Out of the corner of my eye I watched the switcher scoot his chair across the small space between his console and the camera controls to hit some switches. Frank looked pensive.

"So," he said after a moment. "How'd you like to work here?"

"What?" Startled, I jerked my attention back to his face.

"We've got a videotape job opening up. If you're interested, I'll recommend you."

"I . . . I don't have any broadcast experience."

He shrugged. "It's on-the-job training. To be honest with you, the Equal Opportunity Employment Commission is breathing down our necks. We've only got one woman in production. You'd be doing us a favor."

I looked around the room with its ambient electronic glow. It didn't occur to me to be affronted that I was only being offered the job to fill a government-mandated quota; that it wasn't really me he was interested in as a human being with viable potential, just my gender and what it could legally offer.

"Think about it," he said.

There was nothing to think about. I was 22, between semesters, still bored with school and eager to start my own life independent of my parents. "I don't need to," I replied as calmly as I could. "What do I need to do to get the ball rolling?"

"Standby one," said the director. "Take one." On the overhead on-air monitor, the picture flipped from the local news story that was running on the film projector behind me to the face of our local news anchor, Ed Carter, who immediately started reading copy introducing a network story I had recorded earlier on a satellite feed from New York.

"Ready tape one." Phil, the director, sounded tense. I stopped fiddling with the long cord connecting my headset to the intercom system overhead. Tape one. That was me! Nervously I stood by my tape machine, finger poised over the big round play button. "Roll tape one!" I punched the button and snapped on my headset. "Rolling!"

Television is all about timing. In those days, it took one of the massive half-ton tape machines using a two-inch-wide black electronic tape, seven seconds to get up to playback 'speed' and lock the signal. Switchers and directors needed to be able to time the pre-rolls, counting down the seconds to the exact moment they needed the tape to roll to get out of one story and into the next seamlessly.

"Take tape one." The story from my machine punched up on air. I watched proudly.

My first solo newscast! Granted, it was the noon news and not the primetime evening newscast. But that was probably a good thing. I focused back on my machine, watching the tape counter click off the seconds. The story was almost done, and I had a scarily short amount of time to get the next story cued up—19 seconds to be exact—seven of which would be eaten up by the pre-roll. Twelve seconds. Twelve seconds. My heart thudded in my chest.

The story came to its end, and, not watching the on-air monitor to see if Phil was off the tape or not, I punched fast forward.

"Goddammit, what the *FUCK's* going on tape one? Goddammit!"

Phil's voice screeched in my left ear over the headset that linked all the news production people, cameramen, video engineers, audio guy, technical director, studio director, news director, graphics . . . about 15 people in all. Instantly I realized my mistake. I'd put the machine into fast-forward while the picture was still on air, spinning the image into a blur of video hash before he could cut back to the studio.

"Get me the next goddamned tape. *Fuck!* " Phil was spitting tacks. Fingers trembling, heart pounding, my mind a fog, I watched the tape counter spin like an out-of-control altimeter in a death dive. Before I knew it, the tape had raced past my next story. Panicked, I punched rewind and the machine gradually, incrementally slowed. Finally it reversed.

"Do you have it?" Pause. "Goddammit tape one DO YOU HAVE IT?"

I was nowhere near.

"I need it NOW! Goddammit WHERE'S MY TAPE??? Talk to me goddammit. Give Ed a stretch. Tape one WHAT THE FUCK'S GOING ON!!!???" I couldn't take the time to fumble with my headset switch. I focused on finding the place to cue up the tape. Phil continued to rant and rage. Finally! I snapped on my headset. "Cued!" I cried.

"Intro Ed!" The anchor re-pitched the story. "ROLL TAPE ONE!" I hit play. Seven, six, five, four, three, two, one, the story came up on air. Instead of a network reporter talking about national oil shortages, a story about water quality in Lake Superior surfaced. It was the wrong cut.

"FUCK!!!" I could hear Phil without the headset, his scream echoing up the stairs from the director's booth. "Go back to Ed. Take camera two. *GODDAMMIT TAPE ONE I'M GONNA COME UP THERE AND CUT YOUR FUCKING TITS OFF AND THROW THEM IN YOUR GODDAMNED FUCKING TAPE MACHINE!!! DO YOU HEAR ME?* "

The whole world could hear him. "GET ME THE NEXT TAPE AND GET THE RIGHT FUCKING ONE THIS TIME OR BY GOD YOU'LL FUCKING WELL BE SORRY! CUE ED TO COMMERICIAL. FUCK!"

Phil's curses streamed throughout the two-minute break. Mortified and shaking, I found the next story and cued it up. The rest of the newscast passed in a blur. I stayed on headset through the end credit roll until we went back to network programming. The news was finished. Was I? Sappy music from *Days of our Lives* poured from the monitors. I walked back behind the projectors where no one could see me, slid to the floor and burst into quiet tears of humiliation.

You could either take it or you couldn't. The pressure of live shows, the incessant watching of the clock segmenting life into 60-, 30-, 20- and 10-second commercial increments, plus the obligatory three-second station IDs: *WIS-TV, Columbia.* The 10- to 12-hour shifts, the language, racing to go to the bathroom on a two-minute commercial break, eating on the job, hours standing on headset in front of the machines editing commercials and shows in cold, windowless rooms, the constant need for perfection . . . all for $95 a week.

Every little slip—the wrong tape airing in a show, the wrong commercial, a clipped word, three seconds or more of blank air time not filled with precisely the content printed out in the daily Program Log, all of which had to run on the precise second, was written up at the end of every shift by the tape operator and switcher on duty on the dreaded 'Discrepancy Sheet.' Directors also had to do this after a newscast or other live show. I shuddered to think how long it had taken Phil after my first newscast to describe exactly what had gone down that day at high noon.

If you had too many discrepancies credited to your name over a certain period of time, your job was at risk, plain and simple. We used to joke, "Hey, it ain't brain surgery." But you'd never know it by how seriously we all took the job of accurately pumping out endless minutes and hours, days and weeks, months and years of news and entertainment onto the airwaves.

After I settled into the job, it turned out the same coordination and sense of timing that made me a good horsewoman made me a good tape operator and editor. The tape room was like a dance. Sometimes the movement was slow and lazy. Sometimes—when equipment broke down and you had to get backup tape machines and projectors loaded in impossibly short amounts of time; or the newsroom timed the space between stories so tight it was a matter of split-second responses to get things on air—it was crazy. But I loved it. Exciting and challenging, TV had glamour like no other industry except Hollywood.

Within months I was assigned the primetime tape shift. Within a year I was in training for the next on-air switcher position, a job even more demanding than tape operator that was in direct line to a director's job. When an opening was announced, production guys all over the station were congratulating me on my shoo-in promotion, including Andrew, my co-worker and boyfriend at the time. And then George, the production manager, called me into his office.

"I'm giving the next switching position to Andrew."

Fully expecting confirmation of my promotion, I couldn't quite grasp what he'd just said. "Excuse me?" I said.

"I know you've been in training, but I've decided to give the job to him instead."

My stomach did a sideways lurch. This wasn't happening. "But I have seniority! I'm the one who got him the tape job in the first place!"

George had the grace to look uncomfortable. "Look, you know

and I know—hell, the whole station knows—you deserve this promotion. But you and Andrew live together, and I'm trying to figure out a way to make this work for both of you."

"How does this work for both of us?" I strangled.

"Guys just don't like girls getting ahead of them . . . you know, in work and things like that."

My mind flashed to my mother's advice about not playing ball better than the boys. "Let them win, Cate," was her sage advice. *What complete crap.*

"Women take disappointment better than men," he said, plowing on.

I stood there, trying to wrap my mind around his logic. Mistaking my silence for agreement, George brightened. A placating smile emerged.

"Look, nobody else knows this and don't say anything, but there's another switching position coming open next month. It's yours. You do great work. I'm just trying to make sure this whole thing doesn't upset your relationship, that's all."

Unfortunately, responses like "Since when are you a shrink?" or better yet, "My lawyer will be talking to your lawyers," didn't occur to me.

I left his office, hurt and seething. Sticking all the personal stuff in with what should have been a straightforward employment decision muddied the waters. It took the situation into emotional territory. Yet even though George had started it, I feared getting emotional. My mainstay approach at work—"Be one of the guys and don't rock the boat"—had worked well so far. I really didn't want to be seen as a feminist asshole mouthing off about sex discrimination. But now, when it counted, it seemed I wasn't one of the guys after all.

I accepted George's decision, acknowledged everyone's sympathy and watched Andrew slog through his training as the butt of everyone's jokes. It was a humiliating month for both of us that did nothing to improve a shallow relationship based on casual friendship, a bed and the economic fact that two people could get along money wise better than one.

Thirty days later, true to George's words, a second switching position came open, and soon I was a primetime switcher with Andrew relegated to the morning shift. Shortly thereafter I met someone else, and Andrew and I broke up. A year later, after working in television two and a half years, an ABC affiliate station, WCBD-TV in Charleston, South Carolina, hired me as their daytime director. My career in fast forward, I packed up my furniture and moved to the coast and one of America's most beautiful cities.

Television gifted me the hide of a rhinoceros, a sailor's vocabulary and nerves of steel. Within six months of moving to Charleston I realized that I didn't really like directing. It was okay. But my abilities lay more in technical editing than in creating visual effects and clever ads. I actually missed running tape. Unsure what to do about my career, I had been working at WCBD for a year when I got a phone call from some guy in Los Angeles that I'd never heard of and whose name I can't remember. To this day I haven't got a clue how he got my name, but the mid-October phone call changed my life.

"Cate Malone?"

"Yes."

"This is (fill in the blank) in LA. Your name came up on a list of tape operators who might be interested in freelance work."

"Okay," I said hesitantly, not sure what this might entail.

"As you know, NABET (the National Association of Broadcast Employees and Technicians) is about to lead ABC network production engineers on strike. Which means there won't be any network technicians available for Monday Night Football on the 31st in St. Louis."

"Uh huh."

"Would you be interested in working the game? Running tape?"

"Um . . ." my mind whirled. *What the . . ?*

"We'll pay you $100 a day, plus $25 per diem, plus all travel expenses, hotel, etcetera. You'd be there four days. What do you say?"

I was flabbergasted. One twenty-five a day for the network? I made $165 a week working at one of ABC's affiliate stations. And in 1977 that was decent money. Holy shit. This was the big time! "Cate?"

I could picture this fast-talking guy in a slick LA office overlooking smog and the Hollywood hills, list in hand, pencil poised over my name. To strike or not to strike? That was the question. *Just do it already.*

"Sure. Yes. I'd love to."

"Great! I'll have someone contact you tomorrow to go over the details. You leave next Friday. Welcome aboard."

Eight days later I was officially a strikebreaker—better known as a scab by the guy whose job I was taking over—and the first female production technician ever hired to work on a remote crew for ABC Sports. Filled with nausea and nervousness, I was rethinking my decision long before the rental car got to the crowd of angry, sign-waving, middle-aged men gathered around the Busch Stadium gates. As we pushed slowly through the crowd, a few guys banged on the windows and yelled at me. What on Earth had possessed me to agree to this?

At last we cleared the crowd and parked near four large tractor-trailer rigs arranged in the parking area beside the stadium. Forty guys milled around pulling thick black camera cable, better known as 'horse-cock,' out of the truck bays, opening metal equipment boxes, looking efficient and knowledgeable. I got out of the car, and several men stopped and stared. One guy whistled softly, whether a sound of appreciation or dismay I couldn't tell. Gathering my remaining shreds of courage, I found out where the tape truck was and mounted the metal stairs.

There are times when life seems to stand still, to pause. And the grace of that moment, whether it lasts seconds or minutes, is that it allows time for meaning and larger connections to come into focus. The picture of your life expands, giving you context and sometimes even a hint of what's to come.

I had such a moment in my junior year at Mary Washington College. Mom had had her first heart attack, and I was trying to provide as much support as possible, commuting back and forth on a daily basis from school to the farm.

One beautiful spring morning I went for a ride before heading to classes. As I was riding up the road past the rambling old house I'd been raised in, the sun rose over the hills behind me, casting an elongated shadow of horse and rider against the green spring grasses. Something inside said, "Stop." So I pulled up Tammy and just sat, absorbing the moment. In the pause, a larger knowing crept in: I would soon be leaving this place—both the farm itself and a state of mind I took for granted. The quiet way of being that comes from spending long years of hours in nature's company was almost over.

In that expanded moment, I could 'see' a future adrift in a wilderness of forgetfulness and disconnection. I sensed that it would be many years before I came full circle—back into harmony with life again. For a long moment the knowing filled me. Then I urged Tammy forward. There were classes to get to, and I didn't want to be late.

When the tape-truck door closed behind me in St. Louis, I was sucked into that future. The darkened magic of a normal tape room with its soft song of equipment and disembodied voices on the intercom was enhanced and compressed in the tiny space of the truck. Its acoustically carpeted walls, intimately close electronics racks and ergonomic layout made it seem like a space capsule. Here, I would be conducting an even tighter dance with timing, speed and accuracy, working with the best professionals money could buy for a live audience of approximately 15 million people nationwide.

I spent the four days with my nerves packed off on ice where they wouldn't get in the way, and turned in a flawless performance. The Old Guard engineers were reluctantly impressed. That one of ABC's directors actually told me "good job" on the headset didn't hurt my future either. The phone calls started within days of getting back to Charleston. Was I available for a few NCAA games? How about a freelance commercial shoot? Wrestling? Hockey?

Soon the networks were asking me to come live in New York and LA to work in the studios. So I quit WCBD and Charleston. But instead of the Big Apple or Tinsel Town, I choose to continue freelancing in sports and moved to Atlanta. Once there, Joe Wheeler, the head of Turner Broadcasting's sports remote division, called.

"Can you run an Ampex HS200?" he asked.

I wasn't sure what one was. "Sure," I replied.

"Good. I need you at the NCAA football game at the University of Georgia next month."

Turned out that an HS200 was the slow-motion magnetic disk machine that could record up to 60 seconds of video that could then be played back at variable speeds and even stopped in a 'freeze frame.' Arriving at the truck, a sympathetic operator quickly grasped that I was clueless and showed me how to run the thing. I got in a couple of hours' practice before game time, and the show was a blast. Doing replays was an art and much more a part of the game than running tape. I immediately added 'slo-mo operator' to my résumé.

For the next nine years, I was on at least one round-trip flight a week, sometimes two, headed for some freelance football, basketball, baseball, hockey, kickboxing, golf, tennis, swimming, motocross or NASCAR event. I worked the 1980 and 1984 Democratic and Republican National Conventions for CNN, and Election Night coverage for ABC. I edited speeches for Ronald Reagan, recorded shows for HBO, edited US political coverage for the BBC and was hired by NBC to run tape for the Olympics in Seoul, Korea.

The hours were brutal, with 5am crew calls, long set-ups and occasional all-night editing sessions. A core member of the East-coast ESPN crew, I sometimes left conference games late at night, flying on a private jet with the technical director and lead cameraman to get to the next play-off game in time. I hauled thousands of miles of camera and audio cable through the rain, snow and sludge of spilled beer, ketchup and French fries under stadium stands. And I schlepped the 60-pound cameras up the steps to the booths, just like all the guys.

I watched the occasional fill-in techs hired from a local TV station for a one-shot chance like I'd had in St Louis, fingers shaking over the play button, knowing that if they screwed up, their lucrative freelance career was over before it had started. I watched them tremble and screw up and blessed Phil, my first director at WIS, for making me tough enough to take anything a network director could dish out—and some of the ABC directors were notorious rage maniacs.

I watched the wannabees come and go—in those days all men—and saw what a bitter pill it was for them to swallow, watching a woman go where their nerves wouldn't permit them to pass. And I smiled, waving goodbye.

It wasn't all terror and tension. There were lighter moments and distractions—at least for the guys. During games it was traditional for the cameramen to find sexy babes in the audience and zoom in on them. The cheerleaders on the field were always fair game for the tight cleavage and ass shots, better known as T&A (tits and ass). Not only were directors fond of using these 'color' shots to segue to commercials, but all the guys got off on them. Thrilled at being the focal attention of a network camera, most women were only too happy to comply, bending over to show their breasts and derrieres—even lifting their shirts to show it all off.

It was humiliating, but I recorded T&A just like all the other slo-mo operators, marking the 'best' (translate revealing) shots and freeze-framing them for the guys to punch up my machine's output in their viewfinders to get a bit of a lift (so to speak) when they were bored and cold out on their camera positions. Some of my girlfriends stuck watching games at home with their boyfriends asked me about the T&A footage and whether it bothered me. And did I participate in getting these shots?

I told them it didn't bother me at all (not true) and that women with feminist attitudes didn't get very far in sports television (true). Quickly labeled 'dykes' if they objected to such things (but if they were dykes, surely they wouldn't object?), they were never re-hired and the lesson didn't pass unnoticed. There was far greater pleasantness and job security in acting like I didn't mind. But if I ever opened the door to the tape truck and found the space jammed with cameramen, audio guys, grips and video engineers, I knew to quickly close the door and walk away. Porn was too much.

It didn't happen often. There were strict FCC rules about what could be aired, and the tales of what happened to the unwitting techs who mixed up tapes or mistakenly punched up porn on air were legend. But guys were guys. Combine a little down-time on a late

Saturday night with too much booze, a key to empty studios, couches, cameras, videotape and a couple of babes excited to be in a TV station and presto! Instant movie.

During the few moments these 'art films' were viewed, I'd wait around the tape truck outside, trying to ignore the knowing looks and bulging crotches as men came and went through the door. Normally the only woman on the crew, when the guys came out of the truck, I could feel their eyes on me, hot and speculative. And I hated it.

However, there was one standard industry pastime in which I could participate and even excel—and that was drinking.

My mother had a hollow leg and I inherited it. With great pleasure I drank crews under the table in the airport bars in the morning, on the planes in transit and in the sports bars after games until the wee hours. I sat in hundreds of hotel and motel rooms drinking beer, eating pizza, critiquing other network's sports coverage, in general being loud and crazy like the guys. I drew the line on crew sports of trashing rental cars, mooning restaurant diners and one-night stands. Drunk or not, I always retired to my room alone to catch a couple of hours' sleep before the whole cycle started again at 5am.

I was, in TV production parlance, a road warrior.

I'd reached the top of the heap in a glamorous, high-pressure, almost exclusively male profession. I had the approbation of my peers, got paid what they did, had a warmly attentive lover in Atlanta, lived in a great condo, drove a new car and was enjoying the good life. In all ways that mattered that I knew of I was a successful woman. For me, that was the same thing as being a success *as* a woman.

Consumed with the overwhelming need to prove myself as good as any man, delighted with my macho persona, I didn't even know there was a difference.

PART V

***

THE WIFE
(1975–1986)

CHAPTER 9

Husband number one

Animus possession. It sounded like something out of *The Exorcist*. And from a very young age I had a bad case of it.

The drive to embody masculine ideals (or at least my interpretation of them) guided most of my choices in life, from my career goals to how I presented myself: a confident, fast-talking, hard-drinking, rather loud woman with no makeup and a potty mouth. I also liked riding around on my motorcycle, collecting stares from men and women alike as I whizzed by on my ruby-red, four-cylinder 350-litre Honda. Underneath all this, of course, lay a very insecure, easily bruised, emotional girl whom I would go great distances to hide and protect. In fact, I managed to guard this inner self from view so well I even hid her from myself.

Not surprisingly, the Artemis archetype had pretty much ruled my life.

Everybody subconsciously plays out archetypal roles— quintessential human patterns of behavior like the mother, the patriarch, the wise woman, the martyr, the hero or the villain— varying and adopting roles as need and circumstances dictate. The ancient Greek goddess of the hunt, Artemis was the protector of wild animals, childbirth, young girls, virginity and the reliever of disease in women. Subject to the will of no man, she fearlessly explored the world with her hounds and bow and arrows. A female Nature figure imbued with powerful masculine qualities, Artemis gave me the strength I desperately needed as a young girl to stand up to Jack. Later in life she gave me the independence to stride out into the world alone.

Like most people, however, I didn't know I was playing a role. I thought I *was* the solitary and daring chick who rode her own bike, while all the other girls were riding behind their man. I thought I *was* the adventurous explorer out camping in the wilderness by myself: the daredevil whitewater kayaker shooting class-four rapids with the guys.

The fact that I was shitting my brains out in the bushes, terror turning my bowels to water, while the guys from the canoe club were excitedly riding testosterone highs, roaming the riverbanks, scouting their routes through the water, should have been a dead giveaway that I was only role-playing. But I didn't get it. Struggling back into my dry suit, I manfully rejoined them every time, pretending I was as pumped as they were at what we were about to attempt.

Never once did I question why I put myself through this. Never once did I wonder why I had to be the only girl allowed on the boys' gym equipment on the playground in first grade; why I was the idiot in the hayfields in 100-degree heat insisting on being the one walking and tossing the 50-pound bales overhead instead of taking the easier job of riding and stacking the wagon; why I had to outshoot all the guys on the trap-shooting range, get into drinking contests with TV crews and be lead editor on sports shoots, half-killing myself trying to outshine them all.

I just knew I wanted to be strong and powerful. And in my mind strength and power resided only in men. So I lived my *idea* of what a man was: aggressive, competitive, bold and opinionated. I refused to see that the tough-guy act had utterly failed me at some critical junctures in life, like the night of Gregg's rape. Whoever the woman was beneath all the role-playing, I didn't care to know or express.

A personality built around unconscious animus possession and role-playing is hardly a stable structure. Which is why, when I met my first husband, it was so easy for me to flip out of the whole Artemis program into a full-blown Hera complex in about six months. The highly emotional Greek goddess of hearth and home, Hera and I had absolutely nothing in common until I looked into the green eyes of a handsome Chicago lawyer and heard the mellifluous tones of his well-trained barrister's voice.

I was on a flight coming back to Atlanta after a Bears game at Soldier Field one cold December afternoon, cruising on an upgrade in first class. Duncan was headed to his final interview with an Atlanta law firm. Within moments of looking into his gorgeous eyes I knew *this is the man I'm going to marry!* The attraction was instantaneous, powerful and mutual—a sure sign at that stage of my unexplored life that there were tremendous gaps and wounds in both of us that needed the 'instant fulfillment' of an 'other' to fill. But who cared?

We fell in love like Mack trucks in a head-on collision.

On the surface we had a lot in common. We came from the same upper-middle class background, had the same love of the outdoors and similar values. His mother loved and rode horses. That's where the similarities ended. Duncan was steady, determined and responsible. I was spontaneous, romantic and impressionable. Duncan had marital history, child support to pay and a mortgage—all of which he took very seriously. I had no responsibilities other than paying the rent and remembering which flight I was getting on for the next gig.

By the time he settled into his new Atlanta home and we'd been dating for a couple of months, I had altered my model of masculine strength and power to include the ideals of responsibility, solidarity and mature thoughtfulness, qualities I neither possessed nor had ever experienced in a man. My subconscious screamed *Here is safe harbor!* as I laughed and talked over a fine restaurant dinner, sipping Scotch, bathing in the deep green sea of his eyes. *Here lies security!* . . . Something I hadn't even known I wanted.

In return, Duncan rapidly projected all his ideals of the unfettered feminine—playful, affectionate, relational and passionate, all qualities he had sorely repressed—onto me. Needless to say, when we tied the knot two years later, our marriage was a disaster. Not only were we crutches for each other's character lacks, I was dealing with some very superficial ideas about marriage. I thought being a wife meant keeping the house clean, cooking great meals, staying sexy to keep my man satisfied and throwing fabulous dinner parties to help speed his career. Worse, I was loaded with subconscious feminine expectations gleaned from endless magazine articles and movies like *Cinderella* and *Sabrina* about what love and married life were supposed to be.

Between the movies, magazines, dolls and genetics, the moment the wedding band went on my finger and the priest declared us man and wife, they all combined to kick into gear a domestic program as old as time: "Time to nest!" I dove headlong into the Hera archetype just as unthinkingly as I had lived out the Artemis urge. Unfortunately, just as I entered the Hera Housewife zone, Duncan came back from our honeymoon consumed by the 'Climbing the Corporate Ladder' and 'Breadwinner' programs. Within a month of our wedding he was sexually disinterested, obsessed with work, aiming for a partnership at his new firm, sailing deep into competitive male survival-of-the-fittest territory.

"Come watch a movie with me," I cajoled, stroking his shoulders as I stood behind him at his home office desk. He shrugged my hands away, never lifting his head from his papers.

"Maybe later," he said, absently.

I wrapped my arms around him. "You can do that later. Come cuddle."

He slapped his pen down and whirled around, breaking my embrace. "I'm fighting for my life here," he snarled. "Our lives. Can't you see that? Jesus, a little support would be appreciated!"

Wrapped in a Snow White dream of how things were supposed to be, his harsh words and rejection were like a spear through my heart. Clueless about what he was going through, certain I had done something wrong, I did the typical female guilt thing and thought it was all about me. I ramped up the French cuisine and the housecleaning between TV gigs, lost a few extra pounds, bought sexy lingerie and started lighting candles in our bedroom at night, all for naught. As the weeks passed with no affection and then the months, I became deeply anxious and insecure.

"Is he unresponsive? Disinterested? Is the bedroom a place where he just goes to sleep? Learn ten tantalizing no-fail ways to turn on your man and enjoy the fireworks again!" I put down the magazine, doubly depressed. Somehow I didn't think appearing at the garage door wrapped in Saran Wrap with a can of ReddiWhip was something Duncan would like. But what *did* he want? All the magazine articles were clear: when a man lost sexual interest, the marriage was over.

Intellectually I knew that sex was not what marriage and love were about. My mother had told me time and again, "Sex is not important, Cate!" But I didn't believe her. How could I? Aside from money, sex was everything in my society. Being sexually desirable as a woman validated me *as* a woman. God knows there were precious few other ways I could prove myself in that arena.

By the time our marriage had ground through 18 sexless months, the small pyramid of personal self-confidence I'd created by successfully playing the competent huntress in network television collapsed. I cried myself to sleep in an isolated huddle on my side of the bed every night I was home, pillow clamped over my face. I numbed myself with more and more alcohol. I stopped dancing and playing tennis and ignored the swimming pool in our backyard. Between no exercise and increasing amounts of booze, I gained weight. As I gained weight, I became even more insecure and depressed. Looking in the mirror with disgust, it was clear why my husband didn't want me anymore.

Couples counseling didn't help. Sullen and resentful at being asked to go, Duncan just didn't see what my problem was. Wasn't he doing well in the firm? Wasn't he busting a gut trying to make us secure? Why couldn't I just know he loved me and forget about sex for a while?

I couldn't. In my mind, sex and love were as inextricably combined as sex and pain. Married to a man I was deeply in love with, I wanted to give and receive tenderness and connection: to 'make love' for the first time in the fullest sense of the term. I wanted to be held and touched and appreciated. I wanted to do things for him, like bake bread and decorate cookies and make the house beautiful, not haul TV cable through the murk of a midnight commercial shoot. I wanted tenderness and play far more than monetary security. Surely it was possible to have both?

The yearning to nurture and be nurtured became over-whelming. My feminine nature was peeking out of its shell! But never having lived in a nurturing environment or been taught to value this sort of expression, now, wholly un-received, I could only despise my new desires as being weak and needy.

But even as I hated myself for it, I persisted in trying to connect on a deeper level. It suddenly seemed so obvious! I didn't need an expensive foreign car, a stock portfolio and a swimming pool. I would gladly live in a shack with Duncan. He had a dream of running a little hardware store up in the North Carolina mountains after retirement. Why didn't we just go do it now? Sure, things would be tight. Who cared? We'd be happy. At our second wedding-anniversary dinner in a fancy restaurant I found myself tearfully quoting Elizabeth Barrett Browning, "Come live with me, and be my love; and we will all the pleasures prove."

It only embarrassed him and pissed him off.

As an escape, I threw myself into my freelance work, even working bowl games over the Christmas and New Year holidays. In an attempt at self-punishment for somehow not being woman enough for Duncan, I gathered destructive things and people to me. I started smoking cigarettes, adding that to the booze and the overwork, trying to fill the aching need. Depressed, with no inner security, love or tenderness for my own being, I moved in a slow, unconscious dance towards death.

Three months after our second anniversary, I left. Tearfully. Sorrowfully. But I left, immediately adding 'failed marriage' to my internal list of perceived shortcomings. Unfortunately, leaving Duncan only compounded the aching void in my heart and soul. So now I lived alone in a little apartment near downtown Atlanta and took a different interstate exit off the freeway coming back from the airport. Big deal.

Where was meaning? Where lay fulfillment? Happiness? Joy? Were these just words in the dictionary, put there to torment me? No longer an end in itself, work became grueling and stressful. TV paid the bills and gave me the money to buy more Scotch and cigarettes. That was it. Blearily, I staggered out of bed each morning, and every day a strange woman with red eyes and puffy face filled with fatigue and dullness met me in the mirror.

I had done everything my parents and society said would make me happy: got a college degree, developed my career, kept my body fit, made money, found Mr Right, bought the house with the swimming pool and parked the foreign cars in the garage. And the dream had been a lie—a big, fat, fucking lie.

For another few months I labored on, heart broken, making money to support a life with no dreams in it. Even buying a beautiful new luxury car, my mother's never-fail answer to happiness, didn't bring me any joy. I was smoking almost three packs a day, and the cigarettes made me cough and gave me constant headaches. Something in me knew if I didn't quit smoking by the time I was 30, they'd kill me for sure. But the night before my 30th birthday I bought another carton in the liquor store on my way to a friend's house for dinner. Standing at the cash register, I broke open a new pack, knowing that buying them had sealed my fate. I didn't want to live anymore and, to be honest, I didn't care.

Resolutely, I got drunk that night. Driving home at three in the morning, driving fast, seatbelt unfastened, eight stereo speakers blaring, sun roof open, I accidentally dropped my lit cigarette on the floor. Not wanting to burn a hole in the carpeting of a car that still smelt new, I leaned down, fishing around, trying to find it. Glancing up just in time to see a telephone pole hurtling straight towards me, I cut hard to the left before impact, clinging to the wheel as my car slammed straight into the pole.

I never lost my grip, and it saved my life. Within moments of impact, terrified of fire, I wrenched the door open and somehow got out, staggering onto someone's lawn before I fainted. A very black place filled with nothingness greeted me. No tunnels of light. No waiting relatives. No dreams. Nada. Finally, I came back from the nothingness riding a soul-shivering scream that filled the darkness. Sitting bolt upright, I opened my eyes. The scream had come from my own throat, and swift hands were pressing me gently but firmly back to the ground. Lights from a nearby ambulance scrolled the darkness, and two paramedics leaned over me, murmuring soothing words. I must have scared the crap out of them coming to with that banshee screech! But they calmly staunched the blood running into my eyes, asking me questions, assessing the damage.

I was instantly sober and, miraculously, almost unharmed. I had wrenched an ankle and my face would need stiches, but "It's not that bad," one medic assured me, bending down and lightly kissing me on the lips in response to my anxious queries. "Don't worry, honey, you'll look fine again soon."

"Frankly, miss, you're lucky to be alive," a third man chimed in as he rolled a gurney next to my prone body. And I knew it was true.

It was nearing dawn by the time they loaded me into the ambulance. Birds were twittering in the trees overhead and their sound was sweet. Somewhere a crow called. The doors closed and the siren whooped a brief whoop. Strapped down and rocking gently with the motion of the vehicle, I examined the interior. I'd never seen the insides of an ambulance before and looked around curiously.

On the way to the hospital a burgeoning sense of wonder and meaningfulness filled me. I had hit the pole at 45 miles an hour, the entire car had folded around my forehead, and it hadn't killed me! Obviously, God, or somebody, wanted me to live. And since that was the case, it seemed the least I could do was oblige and quit smoking. I smiled at the attendant riding with me and told him how happy I was to be alive. I thanked him for being there to help me and told him it was my birthday. He leaned forward, telling his two partners. The driver laughed and hit the siren, letting it howl for a satisfying celebratory minute. The rest of the way to the hospital I lay there, contemplating life's glory and amazing strangeness. I'd smoked my last cigarette before my 30th birthday after all! And since I'd now been granted life twice, perhaps the rest of my days would best be spent trying to figure out what it meant and what the gift was really for.

CHAPTER 10

Round two

I quit hard liquor as well as the cancer sticks and moved out of the city. Within two weeks of the accident I was living in a condo overlooking the Chattahoochee River next to a state park where I could hike, kayak and get out into nature. And then, a couple of months later, I broke my rule about not sleeping with somebody I worked with.

It was at an LPGA golf tournament down in Florida. All the rest of the crew had checked in and headed out to dinner by the time Nick, a cameraman, and I arrived off the same flight. Dropping our bags in our rooms, we ate in the hotel. We'd worked together for years, but this was the first time we'd spent any time alone. Discovering a mutual love of kayaking and science fiction, we talked non-stop right back up to my room where one thing lead to another and he made his interest clear.

I was shocked. A man wanted me? I burst into tears after the first kiss—not the reaction he was expecting. As the floodgates opened, the whole wretched story of my marriage came out, from Duncan's coldness to my fears that I was unattractive, sexually inadequate, frigid, you name it. To his credit, Nick just lay there listening, stroking my hair, telling me it was all going to be okay.

It was. We slept together that night—just slept. His gentle understanding made me want him all the more. But he knew I'd taken a hit and took his sweet time reacquainting me with what a bedroom could be for, romancing me over the space of the next week even though I was a quivering bowl of willingness by the second night.

We lived almost a continent apart, but it was a love affair that was to last for many satisfying years. Nick was older, patient, a thorough lover and, wonder of wonders, genuinely more interested in my pleasure than his own. Eventually, he earned my trust enough for me to tell him the shameful secret of my fantasies. Completely undismayed, he made it his business to teach me how to make love with love and receive pleasure. Under his steadfast and often humorous ministrations, the grip of fantasy/memory gradually slipped away until, for the first time ever, I had a Big O that erupted only from my body and not from my mind and its dreadful phantoms.

But it took several years. And it took a good man. And it took enough self-love to finally desire to heal.

Not only had I discovered the will to live, renewed health and affectionate companionship, the car accident also triggered an intense interest in spiritual matters. Religion had never been my cup of tea. Mom had dragged me to church, whining and complaining once a month "for my own good." And the nuns had had their crack at me. But none of it stuck. The priests could never answer any of my questions in a satisfying way, and I thought the Bible was just plain silly. I mean, if Adam and Eve were the founders of the human race and they had Cain and Abel, where did all the rest of the people come from?

By age nine, I knew you didn't breed the offspring of a mated pair back with the parent. And incest as the foundation for *homo sapiens*, although it answered a lot of questions about my species' general lack of intelligence and stability, just didn't seem to jive with what the Church was trying to get across. Being told I was "unworthy to gather up the crumbs from beneath Thy table Lord" didn't hack it with a Leo sun sign only-child either.

Doing life and religion the way my parents and most of society did, operating from a strictly materialistic mindset while paying lip service to words like spirit, soul and God in church on Sunday, had brought me almost literally to a dead end. Surely there was more to existence than working, paying bills, improving my credit score and talking about love, but never actually practicing it out in the world?

A chance conversation with a friend about angels and auras triggered an astonishing hunger in me. I started investigating alternative spiritual views, regularly visiting the local metaphysical bookstore. Soon I was tossing books like *Autobiography of a Yogi, The Nag Hammadi Library, The Dead Sea Scrolls, The Tao of Physics* and the *Gospel of Thomas and Mary Magdalene* into my suitcase before heading to the airport. It was a huge shift in gears, and my friends and co-workers didn't know what to make of it. Instead of drinking beer and watching more sports on TV with the guys after a game was over, I retired to my room to read. My mind was hungry, and I found the information astounding.

After a lifetime being taught that God was a guy in the sky with a beard and an attitude, I was now presented with a vision of the divine as an Unseen Intelligence; a Living Creative Force that had not only set Creation in motion, but that *was* me and every other thing, animate and inanimate in the multi-verse. Quantum physics was proving that all 'things' were actually one thing united! Mass was really energy. Sure, I'd studied Einstein's famous equation in school. But no textbooks taught what it really implied, which is that waves of energy unite everything and that physical reality is an illusion! And what teacher had ever told me the universe itself meets all the scientific criteria for being alive?

Seek and ye shall find. Knock and it shall be opened unto you.

I was seeking, and I was astounded at some of the information I was finding, especially the research about the role of women in world religions. Mary Magdalene hadn't been a prostitute like the Catholic Church said at all! Apparently, she'd been a highborn spiritual adept of the Essene sect of Judaea, which was why she'd been Jesus's most beloved companion and closest disciple. And Quan Yin of China was recorded as another woman who had attained spiritual mastery on a par with Buddha.

Hot on the trail of spiritual discovery, I threw all my time and efforts into this new pursuit. I dabbled with vegetarianism, got massages, bought a crystal, had my astrology chart done and purchased a pack of Tarot cards. I definitely wasn't so much 'fun' anymore. But I didn't care. Keeping my aura clear and studying Zen Buddhism beat the hell out of hanging out in sports bars, rehashing video replays and arguing about which player had the most runs batted in during the 1978 World Series.

The more I learned, the more obvious it became that I needed to go beyond mere intellectual study. Transformation was the name of the game, and I was far behind the eight ball. Apparently, I had spent my entire life under the spell of material illusions and my ego, and thus needed tools to discover my True Self. I needed to expand my mind beyond its limitations and vault beyond mere intellect. I needed to expand my psychic horizons. I needed to meditate.

The rewards of meditation seemed clear. If I could master my mind with its limited perceptions and tap into a larger universal consciousness, presto! No more misery, no more confusion, no more pain and suffering, no more stupidity. No more having to come back to live on this beautiful, suffering, sorrowful planet ever again. Electrified by the possibilities, I decided to take a shot at meditation on my own. I mean, how hard could it be? You just sit down, close your eyes and look within. Right?

Yeah, right.

After a dismaying month spent observing my incoherent mind dashing from thoughts of work, sex, bills, sex, the latest movie I'd seen, sex, and whether or not I needed to get an oil change for my car (all in under a minute), I grasped that I needed help. Several Atlanta meditation groups posted contact information at the metaphysical bookstore, and soon I was a regular member of a Dunwoody group that met every Wednesday night.

For the next two years, my life settled into a predictable rhythm of television gigs, books, kayaking, hiking, visits with Nick and meditation. A craving for BLTs and southern pork barbeque nipped the vegetarian diet in the bud, but most of the other New Age accouterments stuck. And all the while a desire for more definitive answers about the human mind and consciousness grew. There was only so much I could learn through random reading and conversation with members of my meditation group. In the spring of 1984, I applied to the Master's degree program in humanistic psychology at what was then West Georgia College in Carrollton, Georgia. Within a week of applying I also met my second husband-to-be.

Simon joined our meditation group in April. A handsome man with black hair and blue eyes, he had a quirky sense of humor and an out-of-the-box way of thinking that immediately intrigued me. "Take TV," he said the first evening we met at a group potluck party.

Please. Take it!

"Personally, I think it's better than a time machine for getting you into different experiences. I mean, I can watch a show and go to all sorts of places in my mind, seeing and doing things I'd never have the opportunity to do as myself."

My jaundiced attitude shifted marginally. *Hmmm.* "That's certainly a different slant," I responded cheerfully, munching chicken salad. Most 'spiritual students' classed television as a mindless tool of mediocrity, and I'd stopped watching the 'boob tube' years beforehand. Simon's view on TV and other things came as a refreshing surprise, and we spent the evening locked in each other's company. But when he asked for a date, I regretfully refused. "Sorry," I said. "I leave for San Francisco in a couple of days to work the Democratic National Convention and then the Republican convention in Dallas for CNN. And I'm driving up into Canada to go camping in between the two. I'll be gone for over four months."

Not a man to be dissuaded once he saw a woman he wanted, Simon decided on the spot to visit family in California and set a date to see me in San Francisco before the convention started. I drove home, interest piqued. What woman (at least, what straight woman) doesn't enjoy being pursued cross-country by a handsome eligible bachelor?

Arriving at my San Francisco hotel two days later, an enormous bouquet of red roses was waiting for me at the reception desk. Blushing, infinitely pleased, I endured the teasing of several crewmates as I rode the elevator up to my room, flowers bunched under one arm. True to his word, Simon flew out, and, despite my hectic schedule, we managed to have dinner before he had to return to his busy chiropractic practice. When I came back to Georgia in late August to start school, we started seeing each other. Soon we became lovers.

"Excuse me?" I asked.

"I said we should get married. We've dated long enough, and you know I'm the marrying kind." Simon grinned engagingly up at me.

I drummed my bare heels gently against the cabinet doors. Sitting on the open counter separating the dining room and kitchen in Simon's house gave me enough height to see the bald spot that was slowly expanding to meet his receding hairline. Despite the dancing eyes, at the moment that high, intelligent forehead was furrowed in sincerity. Yes, Simon was the marrying kind. I reached out and caressed his shoulders. "I've noticed," I said, forcing a laugh out of both of us. I would be what? Wife number three? Four?

"You're done with school the end of this quarter," he reasoned eagerly. "It could be a Christmas wedding."

"That's so soon." I locked my hands gently behind his neck. "Why don't we wait awhile?"

"I don't want to wait," he murmured, brushing his fingertips lightly over my breasts. "I know what I want. Waiting won't change that."

"Unh-huh," I flirted back, pulling his face to follow where his hand had just been. Using his preoccupation to gain a little time, I stared over his bent head out the kitchen windows as he nuzzled. Why not float a trial balloon?

"And what if I were to saaaay . . . no?" I made it come out teasingly, as if it were a question of no consequence. Simon pulled his head back and moved a little away, reaching for his wine glass at my left hip. He finished the contents and stared down into the dregs of his empty glass, avoiding my eyes.

"That isn't what I'd imagined you'd say," he said looking up, blue eyes flat with a slightly opaque look of emotional distance. "But if that's your answer, then I'd have to say it's over." Abruptly he turned away and walked across the kitchen to refill his glass.

Surprise and anger shot through me as his words sank in. He was giving me an ultimatum! Marry him or he'd end it? How dare he put me in that position?

I'm not ready to be done with this relationship yet!

We'd spent every weekend together that I wasn't working a gig. Yet after almost a year and a half I knew I wasn't in love with him. Not like I had been with Duncan, not even close. *Will I ever fall in love like that again?* Did I even want to? I pulled my mind back to the present, considering the situation. Simon and I had fun together. The sex and the conversations were great. He was kind and affectionate. He was into spirituality. He was a healer.

Why didn't I want to marry him? Why didn't I love him the way I should? *What's wrong with me?* Sure, I was working my way through my master's degree, struggling to maintain a 4.0 average. Maybe I was just preoccupied? Maybe I just needed more time? But time, it seemed, had run out. It was all going to end because I couldn't get my emotional act together and he needed the possessiveness of marriage to feel secure. It was all so stupid and unfair! Disgruntled, I tried another tack. "Sweetheart, you know what a hard move this is for me, getting out of TV?"

"Can't be soon enough for me," he groused. "Every time I see you, I have to put the pieces back together." But his eyes thawed marginally as the doctor in him rose to the surface.

"You do." I reached out for him. Slowly he moved back within touching range. "And I appreciate it. And I appreciate the offer to start my practice out of your offices when I graduate. But I still don't even know if I want to be a psychologist." He started to interrupt, but I rushed ahead. "I know it's a great opportunity and all. But I started this whole school thing because I was interested in the mind, not a career. Everything's moving so fast. Can't the decisions about a practice and getting married just wait?"

"You don't have to start a practice. I just thought . . . you know, that you'd be great at it." He looked up at me, one question in his eyes. "I love you and want to marry you. That isn't something I have to wait to be sure of. Do you?"

Crap! There it was. The 64,000-dollar question I didn't want to be asked.

Under the gun, unsure about anything except that I liked the status quo, my mind raced through potential answers, all of them the wrong one. Just when I thought I had no option but to drop a horrible flat "yes" to his last question and leave, the light dawned. If he could be selfish and demand marriage, I could be selfish and hold on to the relationship. So what if I didn't want to get married? What did marriage mean anyway? It was just a piece of paper you tore up when everything went south. Simon, of all men, should know that by now. I mulled over the shocking idea. *Just because he thinks marriage is important and significant doesn't mean I have to think so, too.*

Excitement shot through me. It was a brilliant solution. We would get married. Simon would be happy because things were going on his terms. And I would be happy knowing I'd done the deed on mine.

"Okay," I said, thrilled with what I saw as a mutual compromise, unconcerned that Simon had no notion of the deal. "Let's get married."

His face brightened. "You mean it?"

I lifted my wine glass in a salute. "Absolutely."

Ten days after our marriage conversation I found out I was pregnant. Aghast, I stared at the home pregnancy test stick, dreams of freedom imploding as I willed the positive pink to morph into negative blue. My life was over just as it was beginning! Simon, however, was thrilled. He loved making babies and having babies. Of course, he hadn't been around to actually raise and support the four he already had, so perhaps his excitement was justified. Sick with indecision and anger, I didn't know what to do. Then, before the situation had even fully registered, the gestation hormones kicked in.

From that point on there simply was no choice.

Hormones are powerful little buggers, affecting men and women's bodies, minds and decisions from puberty onwards, often running the show. Women vary greatly in how they're affected by their hormones, and, up until that point, I had always been one of the lucky ones. Normally I was completely undisturbed by such things as cramps and PMS. Which is perhaps why the pregnancy hormones knocked me for such a loop. Almost overnight I transformed from distraught, "Oh shit, I'm pregnant!" mode into an excited and willing mom-to-be. I kid you not. Within two weeks of finding out the bad news I was shopping for cribs, baby carriages and wedding dresses, calling my mother to give her the good news. Simon was walking on air.

Estrogen and progesterone vaporized a lifetime's dreams of independence as if they'd never existed. The fact that Simon loved the husband/father role and was high on testosterone all the time anyway just added fuel to the "Oh boy, we're a family in the making" fire. I finished my master's degree, said my goodbyes to TV and production crews, packed up my furniture and moved in with him. Before I knew it, I was married for the second time, helping Simon in his office, eagerly redecorating the spare bedroom into a nursery.

Being pregnant was amazing. Blessed with zero morning sickness, I felt wonderful and had enough energy for two. Sex with Simon took on a new and tender luster, and life suddenly had deeper meaning and clarity. Simple acts, like cutting up strawberries for dessert or walking down the street, were tinged with profundity. I was at the very hub of creation and marveled at how alive I felt. It was as if I'd been living in a black-and-white world that had suddenly been snapped into Technicolor focus.

With no thoughts or worries about the future beyond delivery of a healthy baby, the stress of TV and school behind me, I was utterly, inexplicably happy.

We spent the winter of 1985 blissfully nesting. Simon was attentive and thoughtful, constantly bringing me unexpected little gifts. I worked in his office, helping with administrative tasks during the afternoons. In the evening we cuddled in front of the fire, planning the home birth and trying on baby names. Spring was hinting at an early arrival, and I was early in my fourth month when, as I was getting dressed to go to a Sunday afternoon party, a sharp cramp doubled me over. Another cramp hit and I went to the bathroom. Seeing a small bloodstain on my underpants, I immediately went to bed. Simon was worried, but the cramps quickly eased and the spotting ceased. I reassured him.

"I'm fine. Go. Give my love to everyone."

He fussed and fiddled, delaying departure. We both knew these kinds of things sometimes happened during the early months, and after another hour had passed with no recurrence of symptoms, he left to make a brief appearance. "I'm not staying for dinner," he assured me, dropping a light kiss onto my hair. "I'll pick us up some Chinese food and a movie. Okay?"

His car had barely pulled out of the driveway when another wave of cramps hit. They were worse this time and I felt an icy wash of fear. Maybe if I just lay still for a bit, the terrible thing that I now knew was happening would go away.

It didn't.

A week later, I sat in a warm bath in the dark, the occasional drip from the faucet echoing in my tiled cave. *No baby.* Pulling my knees towards my chest, hugging them, I rocked back and forth, the water forming ever-higher waves in the tub, waves I couldn't see, just feel. Tears leaked from my eyes. My womb reverberated with an emptiness that filled me body and brain. *No baby.*

The words started as a whisper. "No baby." More tears scalded my face and plopped in the hot water of the bath. "No baaaby . . ." I sobbed and rocked, rocked and sobbed, my chanting becoming a moaning wail. Sorrow as battering as the physical agony of the miscarriage had been beat time like a drum. The bathroom door opened and Simon swiftly entered. Kneeling beside the tub he pulled my wet body to him and rocked with me in the dark, murmuring words I couldn't hear. *No baby no baby no baby . . .*

Who was I?

Idly I sat near the window, watching dust motes float in the weak rays of the sun. Maybe the better question was *what* was I? Was the behaviourist B F Skinner right? Was I just an automaton responding to external and internal stimuli? A puppet controlled by my society, telling me what to think and how to act? A female hormonal robot incapable of independent choice? Or had pregnancy actually opened a window, giving me a glimpse of the real me at last?

Well, maybe not the *real* me, but it certainly had revealed a more alive me. How shocking to realize that somehow I'd been living completely dead to the fact of being alive. *And I thought the car accident woke me up!* How many years had I been asleep to life? And now that I had been nudged awake, what was I supposed to do? After those precious vital weeks, what lifestyle or career could I ever work my way towards that could provide that level of sheer alive *presence* again?

A friend of mine who was a mom three times over nodded sagely when I explained my experience, saying, "Yep, that's pregnancy for you," as if pregnancy itself were the answer. But it wasn't the answer. For me, pregnancy had been the *means* to experiencing something else—a different way of being. It served as a neon sign pointing the way towards a better way to live life.

I haven't felt like that since I was a kid.

Blowing gently, I watched the little dust motes jig frantically in the sunbeam, amused by their antics. Just so, I had been briefly conscious of the living spirit that breathed all life into the dance of form. Just so I had awakened on that breath to the spiritual force that gave me everything I needed to play in the world as horsewoman, television engineer, student, lover, wife. So many roles the dance supported! Cinderella, Artemis, Hera, maiden, warrior, victim, athlete, Siren, bookworm—I'd played them all. Certainly a cold pragmatist had married Simon. So many masks disguising the living flame that fueled them!

Then came the short gravid months that rocked my world, betraying all the roles for the smoke-and-mirrors dance they really were. Then the window closed and I sat lifeless in the sun, eyes darkened once more.

Depression clung to me like a foul-smelling perfume. Aimlessly I pottered around the house, gaining back my physical health, wondering at the cause. Was it the hormones? Or was it a reaction to suddenly dropping back into ordinary human existence again? And what was so wrong with the rest of my adult life that it couldn't deliver the goods?

"Sweetie, we can try again when you're stronger." Simon was earnest, his blue eyes concerned. "You've got to put the past behind you and look ahead." He stroked my hand as we sat in the front yard, soaking up the spring sunshine.

I shook my head. "You know I never wanted children, Simon. And now that my pregnancy is over, I still feel the same way." I groped for words to express what I didn't yet understand. "I've been shown something. I've been hooked back up to . . . well, I'm not sure what. But I think what I experienced is what humans should be feeling all the time, but don't for some reason."

"I don't understand."

"That makes two of us."

The enormous oak tree overspreading the yard sported a full blush of pale green. Shy purple crocuses stuck up their heads through the clutter of bark and leaves around its base. We were quiet for a while as I sought the words that would make the next few minutes easier. But they eluded me. I pulled my hand away from his with slow finality. "I don't know how to say it except to just say it." The sharp pain of yet another parting filled me. *Does it have to be this way?* I knew that it did and forced the words out of my mouth. "I need to be alone for a while . . ."

Simon made a negative noise and started to speak. I reached over and placed gentle fingers against his lips, then turned the gesture into a caress. "I'm only sure of one thing right now, Simon. One thing in my whole life." I paused, knowing I was about to cast my fate to the winds. *Again.* "I need to be in nature. Out of the city. Out of the busy-ness of the world."

"We can move. I can go with you."

I shook my head. "Sweetheart, this is an alone thing." I took a deep breath. "The answers I'm looking for can't be found in anyone else, or with anyone else, or through anything outside me." I laughed shakily. "I guess that makes one other thing I'm sure of."

He heard the words and understood their meaning. But I could see in his face that he did not grasp the sense of it. How could he? He didn't share my need. His journey was not mine, and his spiritual quest was different. And besides, Simon never had been a solitary man.

PART VI

❖ ❖ ❖

THE QUEST
(1986–1989)

CHAPTER 11

Leap of faith

My search for answers and a renewed life took me to an abandoned farm—80 acres of pine forest with some overgrown pasture bordering a river up in the hills of north Georgia. After selling my car and most of my furniture, paying off bills and buying an old red Chevy pickup, I was left with $950 in the bank, my clothes, two dogs, a cat and a white Lipizzaner stallion a friend had given me. In March 1986 we all moved to the country together.

The rambling stone farmhouse built in 1899 had been destroyed in a fire and razed to the ground. All that remained was one large, oval-shaped room overlooking the river that I dubbed 'the cabin.'

The window frames had been burned out and the floor was bare rock, an uneven slab of pink granite that extended past the non-existent front door out to a waterfall on a bend in the river. The interior walls were the same soft golden sandstone as the exterior, most of which was smothered in English ivy. Ancient gardens lay buried in kudzu, an invasive vine native to Japan that flourished so well in the heat and humidity of Georgia that in the summer you could actually sit and watch it grow.

The ancient barn below the cabin was so decrepit even my horse turned up his nose at it. The cabin was incredibly isolated and access was rugged—a mile-long rutted dirt driveway that wound through the forest, forged a creek and skirted the top of the ravine above the river. The cabin had no electricity, no heat and no plumbing. The drinking-water source was a spring that bubbled up beneath the twining roots of an enormous oak tree in the woods behind the house.

My friends all thought I was crazy. But then, they were all city folk who thought Piedmont Park in downtown Atlanta was the wilderness, which I guess it was in a different sort of way. For me, the remote unkempt beauty of the place was a healing balm. And, at $25 a month, the rent was in alignment with my income, which was non-existent. Undismayed by the wreckage, all I saw was the property's potential. Would it have mattered if I'd known that Rich, the courtly southern gentleman who owned the place, had laid bets with his friends that I wouldn't last a month? Surely it would have made me even more determined to make a go of it.

All through April and May 1986, I worked on the place. Hailing back to the rough carpentry I'd learned as a kid, I built a shed for my horse. Sitting on the pile of lumber I'd ordered, I drank beer (which I kept cold in the river), puzzling out the steps of the building process, squaring the shape, digging the holes for the support posts, then adding the top plate, roof joists, sides and finally the corrugated metal roofing.

I hauled icy water from the river in buckets, hurled it against the cabin's filthy interior walls and scrubbed them down, forcing spiders and geckos to find new hidey-holes. I rebuilt the window frames, salvaged wooden casement windows from a demolition site and hung them. I found an old door in the barn, hung that; found a fat laughing Buddha doorknocker at a garage sale for an entry statement, then hauled in some pale green carpeting someone had thrown out and installed it over the stone floor.

I built kitchen shelves and a counter, placing a sink under one of the windows that looked up the hill to the woods above. For water, I bought a new 800-gallon concrete septic tank and placed it on an area I arduously leveled with a pick and a shovel next to the driveway at the top of the hill. I could get potable water delivered, and a gravity flow system piped down the hill from the tank into the kitchen worked fine. For a shower, I ran an offshoot line up a tree. It was outdoors and it was cold, but I was in a hidden valley well over a mile from the nearest neighbor and it worked. For heat and cooking, I bought and installed a used wood stove.

A single bed with a colorful counterpane against one wall served as sofa by day and bed at night. I brought in the few antiques I'd saved, a couple of walnut side tables and a carved mahogany chest that I filled with clothes and placed under the bay window facing the driveway. I put my old oak pub table in front of the three wide windows set in the curving wall overlooking the river and gardens. I placed matching lamps on the side tables beside the bed, which I hoped would one day shine with electricity if I could afford to bring it in.

With pictures hung against the rock walls, books in the shelves I constructed under the open casement windows, wildflowers on the table and the front door open to the river, it was colorfully charming and alive—the perfect hobbit house. Rich about dropped his drawers the first time he saw the place. Standing respectfully in the doorway, he ruefully rubbed his chin, admitted his bets and owned that maybe I'd stick it out after all.

Spring passed into the blazing heat of summer. I was nearing the end of my money and still didn't have a clue what I was doing, but for some strange reason I didn't worry about it. I locked the gate at the top of the drive, and woke with the sun and went to bed with the sun. I skinny-dipped in the shallow pool below the falls and sunbathed on the sand on the far side of the river where it caught the afternoon rays. I cowered on my bed as early summer storms raged overhead, lightning bolts striking trees on the hillside.

I rode my horse bareback through the woods, trailed by my dogs and bizarrely intrepid cat. I sweated and cursed clearing kudzu and brambles out of the gardens, worked the soil, ruined my hands and planted vegetables and flowers. I sat out under the stars, satisfied and exhausted, breathing in the deep, moist, quiet of the southern nights. And gradually peace seeped back into my weary bones.

When you follow your heart, even against all apparent common sense, life just seems to support you. I was out of money, bumming dinner off Simon at his house one evening, when I got an unexpected phone call.

"Cate? It's George at WIS-TV."

"George, wow, hi. How are you?"

"Um, Cate, I've got bad news. Andrew's dead. He drowned off Pawley's Island a couple days ago while he was on vacation."

I sagged against the kitchen door, stunned. My ex-boyfriend was dead? "Oh my god, what happened?"

"We don't know for sure. There'd been a big party, and he'd been up all night and went swimming the next morning. They think it was a heart attack."

God bless him, that sounded like Andrew. He probably had a Margarita in one hand and a joint in the other when it happened. I could see him grinning into the rising sun, tossing his ocean-soaked red hair out of his eyes, gloriously happy and stoned on his favorite beach in the whole world, taking a big hit before the plunge.

"Cate, there's something else you need to know."

The vision faded. I sighed. "What?"

"You're listed as co-beneficiary on his company insurance policy."

CHAPTER 12

Going within

I once read a book about the Australian Aboriginal tribes. The section on spirituality described the various initiation rites the men had to undergo. Starting in early childhood, the rituals were arduous, even brutal, taxing the boys to their utmost. It was not uncommon for some to die during initiations. But what seemed cruel to Western eyes was considered a necessity by the tribe.

The elders understood that boys needed much tempering and discipline before they could be fit members of society. Their selfish desires and unruly need to display physical prowess in constant competition had to be managed and refined. Their arrogance had to be broken. Guiding them to their spirit nature and making them conscious of the value of their feminine intuitive awareness was the essence of the boys' training. Like Native Americans, the Maori men's initiations extended into vision quests that were pursued throughout much of their lives.

At the end of the spirituality chapter there was a brief description of the only initiation rite for the girls. Predictably, their rite of passage was based in biology. When girls reached the onset of menses, they were ritually prepared to spend their moon cycle in solitude in an isolated hut. That was it.

The sequestering of young females at menses was a social pattern that repeated throughout most cultures. I was all too familiar with the ancient Judeo-Christian tradition in which women were considered untouchable during menstruation. They weren't isolated in huts, but they were kept separate from the men during this time of the month and were not allowed inside the temples. Seething, I finished the chapter, then hurled the offending book across the cabin. *Girls don't even get a fair shake in the bloody outback!*

It was years before I discovered the truth of why Maori girls traditionally had only one initiation rite. And it was a humbling experience to have not only my automatic Western assumptions of sexism exposed, but also the depth of my ignorance about my own feminine nature.

Sexism wasn't limited to Western nations, of course. Most tribal cultures had their own forms of discrimination against women. But the solitary initiation of the menses hut wasn't sexist. Turns out girls in the tribe didn't *need* multiple initiations to be tempered because they'd never been asleep to their essentially fluid spiritual nature in the first place. Calmer, more loving, in touch with their intuition, undistracted by testosterone, all the girls needed was a ceremonial recognition of their inherent unbound nature and the gift of time and solitude to develop it. This they did behind the menses hut door.

It was an inward journey that was renewed every month. Made conscious of the divine force that flowed through her and through all things, each woman then functioned powerfully as a conduit for life values that poured forth as a continual gift to her tribe through her social interactions, her guiding influence on her family and her daily tasks and decisions.

I spent three years alone in the cabin. It was, in essence, my introduction to the menses hut. A deeply feminine space, oval and womb-like, situated on bare rock in the midst of a forest, the cabin nurtured and protected me. With no television or radio, stereo system or telephone, I had no distractions. With no husband, no job and no children, I had time. Thanks to the consideration of a friend and ex-lover, at age 35 I had the financial means to drop out of the system for a while to take the long quest within.

Renewing the meditation practices that had been sporadic during the over-busy years of work, school and marriage, I sat by the waterfall each morning, trying to settle my mind and body into a peaceful space. And I utterly failed. I was one overwound chick. Thirteen years of being constantly on the go, over-stimulated by people, ever-changing places, jet lag, electronic equipment and the adrenaline rushes of live sports television, were not easily set aside. I sat for hours at night on my little bed, observing my mind—a confusing place with a zillion thoughts darting around with no apparent order or control. Often I fell asleep sitting bolt upright. Then I'd jerk awake and dive back into looking inwards. It was exhausting and disappointing work, but despite the lack of progress I persisted.

Somewhere in this mess called 'me' there must be something greater!

Then, after a couple of months of steady practice, one night I jerked myself back from the edge of sleep and . . . my mind stopped. Everything stilled. And in that timeless, unmoving moment, the borders of my awareness exploded outwards.

Or maybe they exploded inwards. Whichever, suddenly I was floating in an infinite universe of silence and peace, aware of pure existence. Within the context of that vast expanse, my infinitesimally small human life was utterly insignificant. And yet it was also precious. For the first time in my life, I wasn't looking at myself through the lens of personal agendas, emotion, nostalgia, worry about the future or regret about the past. And from this space of detached awareness my life made perfect sense. It just was. I just was. Everything was just as it should be, perfect and complete. How could I have ever thought it otherwise?

I have no idea how long it lasted. Five minutes? Hours? Time was meaningless in that exquisite state of mind. Eventually I lay down and gently drifted to sleep. Of course, I just about killed myself every night for months thereafter trying to get back to the same state of awareness. And because I was trying so hard, I failed. But it was an enormous moment. At last I had a personal talisman proving that the mystics and burgeoning scientists in the consciousness field had it right. There was more to me than eating and sleeping, working and worrying about money, watching my weight and looking for the next man in my life.

I was on the right track. I had tasted the 'peace that passes all understanding.' And I wanted more.

I got further brief moments of illumination like a blazing torch passing behind the slit windows of a darkened tower at night: quickly vanishing beacons of awake-ness. On my next trip home to Virginia I couldn't wait to share the insights and experiences that were rapidly turning into full-on visions with my mother. I stuffed spiritual books I thought she might like into my suitcase and eagerly flew home. At the first opportunity alone in the kitchen, I jumped into recounting the most profound experience I'd had to date, a vision which had occurred somewhere in the wee hours one night after I'd fallen asleep.

Dead to the world, I had been stirred back to consciousness by light. Not just light, but LIGHT—an internal blazing glory brighter than 10,000 suns that stretched into eternity: a Light that was a living presence of LOVE that filled every nook and cranny of my mind and body. Accompanying the Light was a high-pitched ringing harmonic tone, singing the endless promise of Heaven. Half conscious, I struggled to my knees to worship the Light, which to my stupefied mind could only be God Itself touching me. And yet oddly, at the same time as being infinite, the Light was also obviously an individual conscious Being. "Who are you?" I cried in ecstasy, hands outstretched and pleading.

The Light laughed, a rolling tide of playful bliss. It found my question enormously funny. And yet It loved and soothed me, giving me the answer: "You will know someday." It spoke, not in words, but in the simple gift of direct and total understanding. The Love ramped up, sending me into paroxysms of rapture. And then the Light faded. I lay awake, cradled in the arms of love and wonder until dawn.

Eyes closed, re-experiencing the most important moment of my life, I couldn't see my mother's face as I told the story. Opening them, I saw her face, ashen and gray, eyes narrowed, fingers gripping the edge of the kitchen table as her cigarette burned in the ashtray, ignored. A heavy silence filled the kitchen. The bliss recalling my story evaporated. "Mom, what's wrong?"

She stood up abruptly, tipping her chair over backwards. "You're nuts." Her voice grated, ugly as a nail pulled across concrete. "You're absolutely goddamn nuts. I don't want you to *ever* speak to me of these things again. Do you hear me?!" With that, she ran out of the kitchen and I heard her feet thudding up the stairs. Then her bedroom door slammed shut. If she'd pulled her pants down and peed on the floor, I couldn't have been more shocked. After a minute I got up and tried to talk to her. But she refused to even open her door.

Obviously, the spiritual terrain I was exploring terrified her. But why? I tried several times to get her to talk about it during my visit, but she refused. The books I'd brought she wouldn't even look at. By the end of my stay we were like strangers with nothing to talk about. After I flew back to Georgia, an awkward distance developed between us that just got bigger as the weeks rolled by.

Absorbed in my meditations, I soon forgot the pain of her fear and rejection. But, as time passed, I began to have reason to wonder if my mother hadn't been on to something with her crack about my being "nuts." For now every time I meditated, or simply lay down to sleep at night, waves of energy coursed through my body. Hissing, rolling waves that I could hear as well as feel, they grew in amplitude until they lifted 'me' right out of my body. A nightly experience both terrifying and exhilarating, I had no idea what was happening to me, or what it all meant.

Sometimes my spirit body floated gently up through the ceiling and out into the night. Sometimes I shot out of my body and hurtled through the cosmos at tremendous speeds. Sometimes part of my spirit body got stuck and I'd lie there, physical legs inert under the covers, while my spirit legs thrashed overhead like I was madly peddling some sort of invisible, upside-down bicycle.

But it wasn't the out-of-body-experiences (better known as OOBEs) that bothered me. It was the eerie phenomenon that often came with them. Sometimes as the waves of energy bathed me, I heard voices and strange laughter far away. Sometimes I could feel what were clearly hands on my body, pulling and tugging. Balls of white light would flash around the room. As I kept meditating, the phenomenon became more intense, and I started sleeping with the lights on. Thank God I'd got the money to bring in electrical service! But even with a lamp on, I could still see the lights whizzing about and hear the insane, echoing laughter.

"I felt the hands on my legs, pulling me out of my body. Then suddenly I was yanked out and hurled into this disgusting graveyard." Pausing for breath, I glanced across the small space between us the width of the expensive Persian rug. From my supine position on the sofa, Dr Erhardt towered above me. Legs negligently crossed, writing on a leather note pad, the best shrink my former graduate psychology advisor could recommend listened impassively to my story.

"Unh-huh," he said. "Then what happened?"

"Well, this terrible monster appeared from around a crypt, all fangs and claws and red eyes. I was so terrified I couldn't even move! But then this huge love suddenly swelled up inside me and I loved the beast and started to hug it. But it screamed and ran away. Then I found myself back in my body in bed, wide awake."

"Hmmm." He tapped his pad thoughtfully with his pen. "I think that's enough for a first session."

I sat up, nervously pushing a few strands of hair behind my ears. At the time it had been the most shockingly real experience. But telling the story to a psychiatrist made it sound much more like an encounter with an un-integrated part of my own psyche than an actual monster. "So," I ventured, not really wanting to know. "What do you think?"

He didn't answer, but I could imagine his thoughts: *I think you're a borderline personality disorder with integration issues.* The doctor got up and went to his big polished desk. There he jotted some notes and then pulled out his appointment book. Again the pen tapped gently. It was a gold Waterford. "I'd like to see you three times a week initially. Then, after six months or so, let's reevaluate and take it from there."

Three times a week? *Christ, he thinks I'm a schizophrenic.* I couldn't possibly afford it and told him so. But Dr Erhardt didn't bat an eye. "How much can you afford?" he asked.

Knowing his regular rate was $175 an hour, wishing I'd never walked into his office, I threw out a figure I knew he wouldn't accept. "Um, maybe $25 an hour?"

"Fine," he said, flipping pages. "How about 2pm next Monday?"

Frustrated, I paced the kitchen floor. "Just talking to this guy was enough to make me want to commit myself." I reached the cabinets between the kitchen and dining room and turned around. "For God's sake, I've got a Master's degree in psychology. I should know better than to let him intimidate me!" I reached the stove and turned back. "You should have seen his office—padded door a foot thick, bars on the windows behind satin curtains. Just being there was enough to make anybody feel crazy."

Simon shoved a glass of red wine into my hands. "Here, drink this."

Gratefully, I took a sip. "I'm sure he thinks I'm projecting all this crap from my subconscious."

He grinned at me. "Are you?"

"What? Projecting from my subconscious?"

"Crazy."

I stuck my tongue out at him. "Of course. One of the symptoms is sleeping with your ex-husband." The humor didn't stick for more than a few seconds and I fondled my wine glass pensively. "I'm not crazy, Simon. These experiences are as real as standing here, talking to you."

"Unh-huh."

"Don't *you* go giving me that noncommittal grunt, too." I took another sip of wine. "I can't believe he agreed to $25 an hour."

"He probably wants to do a paper on you."

"Great. Just what I always wanted to be, some shrink's Sybil."

Simon laughed. "That was a case of multiple personality disorder." He walked over to the telephone, picked up his address book and started turning pages. I watched over the rim of my glass. "You should have talked to me before you went haring off down the traditional path. I know a psychologist in Dunwoody who's into all sorts of alternative therapies. You should talk to her."

He jotted down a name and number and handed it to me. "Come on. Finish your wine and let's go to the movies. *Aliens* is finally out. What do you say?"

As if I didn't have enough to spook me. But at least my doctor ex didn't seem too worried. And it was a Friday night. "Sure, why not?"

The movie was predictably terrifying. Arriving at my farm gate near midnight, it was all I could do to force myself out of the truck to go unlock it. My hands fumbled with the padlock and I swung the gate hard, not wanting to have to push it and end up too far away from the driver's side door. *Chicken!* Around me, the August night pulsed with the sounds of cicadas. I got back in the cab, drove through and stopped, looking in my rear view mirror at the gate and the thick darkness beyond. *Hmmm.* I always kept the gate locked at night. Living in 'Deliverance' country, the last thing I needed were drunken rednecks showing up at my cabin. I stared at the gate, weighing my fears. The aliens won by a landslide. Laughing at myself, I drove down the rutted road towards the cabin.

An hour or so later, I was drifting into uneasy slumber when something startled me awake. I lay in bed, tense, breathing gently through my mouth the better to listen. It was music—loud country music. And it was getting closer. I got up, went to the open door and peeked out. Up the hill over the ravine, headlights were approaching through the trees.

I whirled, considering my options. The dogs looked at me sleepily, two big furry marshmallows. Being trapped in the cabin with one door seemed like a bad idea, and hoping whoever it was would drive up and then go away seemed naïve. People didn't poke around in the middle of a Friday night down long driveways in north Georgia with good intentions. A glance back out the door showed there were two vehicles coming. Not good. *Shit shit shit.*

Heart hammering, throat dry, I turned on the lights, yanked open the side table drawer and pulled out my .38 caliber revolver. I checked the chambers, making sure they were full. Grabbing the truck keys, I slipped on my shoes and ran for the vehicle parked close to the cabin, headlights pointed up the driveway in a good strategic position. Slamming the door shut, I locked them both, keyed the ignition, slipped off the safety lock, and put the gun on the seat beside me. Then I ducked down so I could just see over the dashboard and waited.

The first vehicle swooped around the curve coming down the hill, then the second, headlights raking the truck and cabin. Bass thumping, guitars twanging the night air, both trucks slowed. Then the first vehicle stopped. My hand crept towards the headlight knob. *Oh God, just keep going! Please!* Then they started forward, fast, sweeping around the circle in front of the lit-up cabin, back up the driveway and away. Dizzy with relief, I tracked their progress as they left. After a few minutes, I headed up to the gate.

No one was in sight. I drove to the next farm up the road, turned around and headed back. This time I got out and locked the gate. Aliens suddenly didn't seem so scary. As a lone woman on my planet, I had enough to worry about with the male of my own species.

"So . . . you're having out-of-body experiences. You see and hear things that aren't physical and you're having peak experiences." She finished jotting some notes and looked up. "You say this all started after you began meditating several hours a night?"

"Yes." That about summed it up. Coming from this woman, sitting un-fussed in her nice but modest office, it sounded almost normal. The tension inside me eased.

She smiled. "Well, I'd say you cracked your psychic centers wide open and activated kundalini energy, which is opening you up to the astral realms."

"Astral realms?" I asked, puzzled. I hadn't read about those.

"The closest unseen dimension beyond this physical reality," she responded. "I'm hardly an expert. Few people are. But it's believed that's where most out-of-body-experiences take place. Personally, I believe the astral regions were what Dante was writing about in *The Inferno*."

The upper reaches of hell? Oh, just wonderful. But it sure fitted with some of the things I'd seen and heard. "You mean I'm in contact with demons?" I stuttered, appalled.

"Oh, no, disincarnate humans. A lot of people aren't very pleasant alive, you know. Why would they be any different dead?"

I thought maybe we were splitting hairs here, but didn't say anything. She tapped her pen gently against her notes, so far the only similarity to the shrink I'd visited. "Don't worry about it," she said. "Paranormal phenomenon is unusual, but not abnormal. It's really kind of a blessing and a sign you're evolving. Things will probably settle down. Frankly, it's the issues around your stepfather I think we should address."

My relief must have been visible. But though her eyes twinkled a bit, she remained matter of fact. "I think if we meet once a week, we can work through everything in about six months."

My quest had me swimming in strange waters. My definitions of 'self' and reality were expanding exponentially. Inevitably, my inward journey brought me around to thoroughly examining everything I had been taught about God and religion.

Twenty years of sedate Episcopal sermons and three years of Catholic convent school had never once communicated to me that going within to 'embrace the spirit' could result in breathtaking moments of revelation and expanded mental clarity. Certainly no one ever mentioned it could bring me into contact with actual spirits. Priestly references to *those* had inevitably been riddled with warnings about demonic possession. Which was one of the main reasons I'd been so freaked out when my astral journeys had started. The only reason I'd ended up on the couch of a shrink instead of a chair in a local church office seeking counsel was because my life had given me no reason to have faith in either priests or religion.

Both had done little more than demand obedience, instill fear and consistently talk down to me. The Church's whole focus seemed to be following the rules in order to be good enough to obtain sufficient forgiveness to be granted access to a heavenly afterlife. I'd never heard of any religion espousing the possibility that bliss and peace were available here and now in the flesh. Or that it was possible to gain direct access to the Godhead without intercession, or that transcendent answers to human pain and suffering were within everyone's reach as a result.

Why didn't the priests encourage me to know God instead of fear God?

It was scary territory, asking these kinds of questions. Sometimes it even felt like blasphemy. But my spiritual and psychic experiences were giving me fresh context for my old religious understanding, granting me new meanings for what had previously been empty concepts and words. For example, in church I was taught that God is omnipresent in eerily Orwellian, 'Big Father is watching you,' overtones. Now that I was beginning to *experience* a hint of what the word really meant, that view evaporated. God was everything, everywhere, enfolding universes across all time and beyond. Nothing could be 'outside' of God, *including me*. And if God were all things including me, then being part of God meant I was potentially capable of being aware of everything else that was part of God, too.

My first oceanic meditation had demonstrated that this was a very real possibility. Granted, I had barely touched a fragment of the larger reality that might be called 'God' or 'Source Consciousness.' But even my small expansion hinted at great potentials. And if the mind of a regular woman like me could let down some of the personal identity barriers and beliefs that made me 'me' and expand in consciousness, it seemed the potential of what any human mind could contain was limitless.

Emboldened, I re-engaged scriptural clichés with fresh eyes. "My Father and I are One," said Jesus. "Follow me." What if we finally did? Not as sheep thinking he literally meant worship and follow him as slavish devotees, but follow his example and do as he did? What if millions of people learned to meditate and expand into a consciousness of oneness so they too could understand and say, "My Father and I are One?"

Everything would change! Who would do the worshipping if there was no one left standing outside the circle of divinity to worship? Who would care about going to war over a bunch of denominational beliefs *about* God if we could all experience being united in consciousness *with* God?

These were radical thoughts, and all the books, logic and direct experiences I was accumulating couldn't quite outweigh the old programming. The Big Guy in the Sky, the pissed-off Father in Heaven was not a dude I wanted to cross. Petty, jealous, vindictive, emotionally unstable, He could be angry one minute and loving the next, meting out punishment if I dared say, think or do the wrong thing. An unfathomable, unpredictable tyrant, this God's word was law no matter how stupid the law might be. And who wanted to be on the wrong side of that?

I laughed in rueful, shocked recognition. Jehovah or Allah, Yahweh or Zeus, it didn't much matter. Mankind's God sounded just like my stepfather.

"I'm beginning to think I had my stepfather all mixed up with God."

"What makes you say that?" asked Judy.

"Well, most kids think of their parents as some sort of God because they have absolute power over their lives. And I was taught in Sunday school that God is my Father, you know? And the Bible says God is angry all the time and that I should be afraid of Him. And, of course, Jack was angry all the time. So it was easy to confuse the two. Subconsciously, that is."

"How did that make you feel as a child?"

I leaned back on the sofa. "Frightened," I sighed. "And I didn't want to be around either one of them."

"Did you express your fear in any other way besides avoidance?"

Bless her, in eight weeks of counseling I'd learned I could always count on Judy to pull me out of the safety of what I *thought* about things into the realm of how I *felt* and how I expressed those feelings.

"Uh . . . no."

"Why not?"

"Who was I going to say anything to? My mother? She was scared, too."

Silence.

"Resistant. That's how it made me feel."

"And . . ?"

"Resentful. Nobody likes being made to feel afraid."

"And . . ?"

Damn. "What do you want me to say? That I was angry? Hell, yes, I was angry. But I couldn't say anything. I couldn't express it!"

"Why not?"

"It wasn't safe!" My body began to shake. "If I'd yelled back at Jack, I would've got my head knocked off. If I got mad at God, I'd go to hell!"

"Okay, so let's take a moment here." She clipped her pen to the ring binder of her notebook. "I want you to take a few deep breaths and close your eyes and imagine someone you can safely express all your anger and frustration to about male authority. I want you to talk to that person, right now, and just tell them everything that you as a little girl wanted to say, but couldn't."

Christ, I hate role-playing. "I can't," I muttered sullenly.

"Why not?"

I wanted to lash out, to scream and tell her if she asked me one more question I was going to . . . *what? Get angry? You're already angry. Let it OUT!*

"I can't!"

"Can't what?"

It felt like a tornado in my gut. "I CAN'T SAY ANYTHING!" I shouted. "I can't talk! I'm not *allowed* to talk! Jack, the priests, the nuns . . . none of them let me say anything! They know it all! They know everything!! Forget feelings. Forget questions! It's all just, 'Shut up, follow the rules and be a good little girl.' Well, FUCK that!"

"You're angry."

"Well, *of course* I'm angry!"

"How else do you feel?"

A sudden tiredness swept over me. I slumped on the sofa, emptied out.

"How did it make you feel as a little girl?"

I shook my head. "I don't know . . . ignored. Unimportant? Frustrated? After a while I just went along with the program and tried not to make waves because it was just too much goddamn effort and never got me anywhere. So I kept it all inside."

Silence.

Judy was pleased. I'd gotten angry—real progress there. Apparently, women didn't usually do too well in the anger department. Probably because we'd had so much directed at us with no possibility of dishing it back, unless, of course, we were willing to accept the consequences of speaking our minds. "Speak out," urged one of my favorite Crosby, Stills and Nash songs. "Speak out against the madness. Speak your mind, if you dare." As a kid I'd only dared if I had enough of a head start and room to run.

But that was a long time ago. I sat on the rocks above the waterfall with my fluffy cat curled up in my lap, watching gold and amber leaves drift down from the trees, dappling the water with color. Judy's urgings to the contrary, I really had no reason to speak out. What was there to speak out about? Simon was a thoughtful, gentle man. So were the rest of the men in my life, except Jack, of course. And him I kept at a safe distance in Virginia.

A sudden movement in the trees across the river caught my eye. Georgia Cat stiffened in my lap, sat up and then relaxed as we both watched a doe glide towards the pool below the falls. Hesitating at the edge of the trees, head up, soft eyes alert, she waited, then stepped onto the gravel bar. Two fawns, dapples almost faded from their brown rumps, bounded after her. Enchanted, I watched them move to the water and drink. The enormous ears of the doe twitched back and forth as she sipped. Every few seconds, she lifted her head to check her surroundings. Wariness born of living in a predatory world marked her every move.

How could life be so beautiful and at the same time so terrible that such a gentle creature had to live in constant fear, ready to bolt at the first signs of danger? My mind flashed back to the night the trucks showed up at my cabin, and ruefully I realized the doe's life was not really so different from my own. My sheltered valley and meditative existence fooled me into forgetting the world was still dominated by violence and anger, filled with armies and mobs, dictators and terrorists, redneck bullies and sex predators—all of them male. *Hmmm.* Maybe I had something to speak out about after all?

God help me, I'm beginning to think like a feminist.

But what was so wrong with that? It was true. Men could be brutal and dominating. Not all, certainly, but many, maybe even most. Aside from how to avoid their control, the question I most wanted answered was, why were men like that? What were they so afraid of? What did they have to prove? Why did they have to defend their beliefs and opinions to the point of coercion? And why, aside from fear of bodily harm, did women put up with it?

My mother always said, "If you want peace with any man, just agree with him." But at what price? What about the corrupt men in corporate and government positions of power, doing harm? Was it right to go along with their insane agendas just to keep the peace? And what peace was that? I was born after World War II, the war that was supposed to end all wars, which had been followed swiftly by the Korean War, the Vietnam War, and then wars in Columbia, Nicaragua, Cambodia, Venezuela, Afghanistan, Serbia, Iran, Israel, Egypt and Africa. War was everywhere. *And not one started by a woman.*

I groped around for something to throw into the river, my fingers closing on a blackberry branch. I jerked my hand to my mouth, sucking angrily at the blood. *Dammit.* How long could the world take it? How long could women take being the endless sport of soldiers and mercenaries, routinely raped to death as part of the fighting process, and over what? Men's territorial boundaries, men's opinions, men's money, men's lust for power, men's religious beliefs . . . the list of what men were determined to fight over went on and on.

Not liking my angry energy, Georgia Cat jumped off my lap to find a more pleasant patch of warm rock and sun. The doe and fawns moved downstream. But my thoughts were on a roll. *Even man's God is afraid.* Why else couldn't I question Him? Couldn't debate? Couldn't speak a differing opinion or hold a different truth? Wasn't there room enough in eternity for everything? Wasn't variety what made the world so beautiful? Surely this fragile, explosive God, so like men I had known—surely He was just a fabrication? A psychological extension of the ancient fathers who worshipped Him; a projected fantasy of an all-powerful, all-seeing MAN who had to be propitiated, worshipped and agreed with without question. Wasn't this volatile God of the Christians, Jews and Muslims just an out-picturing of man's fondest wishes for himself?

I was a spiritual infant. But even I was beginning to realize there was nothing personal about God. What could be personal about a Creator Source consciousness of infinite energy, love and peace? And if God really was this infinite, unseen *intelligence,* how the hell did we end up with a God sporting irrational human emotions, male genitalia and a He pronoun?

I lay in bed late that night, wondering. The autumn air whispered through the open windows with a coolness bordering on cold. On a whim I got up, lit a candle and stood in front of the large mirror hanging on the wall next to my clothes chest. In the light of such thoughts and the candle's fluttering glow, I studied my reflection. Then I stared in wonder. My face shone with an ethereal beauty far more arresting than any sensual attractiveness could lay claim to. What was it that scattered the light in such an exquisite way that I found myself suddenly beautiful? It was something more than the light and the physical arrangement of my features. Surely it must be the Spirit shining from within?

Stepping backwards, I tried to include as much of myself in the image as possible. My hands traveled downwards, molding cloth, briefly revealing my woman's body, round and full beneath the folds of the nightgown. The sight of my spirit shining through this feminine form was glorious. I inhaled the moment, intoxicated, reeling. Why hadn't I seen this before? Had I been so obsessed with my body as merely a body—keeping it fit and slender and sexually attractive—that I missed the life flame igniting it? Had I been so preoccupied with the roles this body played that I only saw the shadows and not the light that cast them? Was that why I hadn't witnessed this glory before?

My eyes were darkly enormous, absorbing the testimony of deeper dimensions. I pivoted slightly, first one way, then the other. If *I* couldn't normally see my own radiance, so obviously divine, shining around and within me, how could others? No wonder this beauty wasn't acknowledged by the world! On impulse I pulled up my nightgown and slipped it over my head, my nipples hardening with the passage of cloth and the touch of cool night air. Thirstily I drank the light, absorbing this new transcendent view of myself.

I have forgotten what I am.

How astonishing! How was it possible? And then the ache began, a dull constriction in my chest that blossomed as I realized I was not alone in my amnesia. *My sisters have forgotten, too. All of us have.* Unbelievable. Who could deny such a glory as woman? Had this vision been deliberately obscured? Was the light of God too much to bear shining from a woman's body? Was this why women had been torn from the altars of the Goddess and turned into whores? Declared unclean and unworthy of entering the inner sanctums of men's temples? Was this why I was stuck with the pale, bloodless Mary kneeling at the feet of her dead son? What image of the feminine was that to behold?

The eternal face of the sorrowful victim.

The candle guttered and I turned slowly, watching my wavering reflection. Was this unearthly grace and enchanting beauty somehow dangerous, even empowered as it was by divine love? My hair brushed the curve of my shoulders and swept along the shadowed cleft of my spine. I turned full circle, taking in my breasts and belly. Were men so weakened by this image, mistaking spirit for flesh, that the full vision of the divine feminine had to be buried and destroyed completely?

He who has the eyes to see, let him see.

Obviously, man's spirit was as weak as his eyes. Why else had women of power, wisdom and grace—women who recognized what I was seeing, who had the temerity to stand up and flaunt the embodied beauty of the Holy Spirit openly—been systematically slaughtered and maligned for over 2,000 years? I gazed long and lingeringly in the mirror, etching the vision of my Godliness onto my aching heart. *This is what I've been looking for!*

Recognition.

It was what I and all my women friends yearned for most: to be seen for what we really were. Not just faces attached to female body parts, breasts and vaginas to be suckled and probed; not just the objects of dirty jokes and objectification, but God itself radiating forth. I wove my arms across my breasts, embracing my body. I wept, absorbing the lush sweetness, acknowledging the truth banished by my society and so long withheld by my own mind: *In this body I am divine.*

I breathed in that thought with the night air and let it uplift and restore my soul.

PART VII

* * *

THE FEMININE
FACE OF GOD
(1989–1998)

CHAPTER 13

Images of power

Glimpsing the potent grace of the divine feminine that night in the cabin changed everything. And it changed nothing. One glimpse, no matter how powerful, didn't erase generations of programming whose sole purpose was my *not* seeing it. And yet, even as its impact faded, the vision guided me, showing me ever more clearly how absent the feminine was in my world. Even New Age literature and practices proclaiming the return of the Goddess seemed shallow and bloodless.

Wise woman tarot decks, velvet Renaissance gowns and bonfires on full moon nights did not make a goddess. What did make a goddess? I didn't know. But the few rituals I did investigate felt like a mocking whisper of something much greater: a modern game of spiritual charades. Surely if the Goddess was just linked hands, crystals and soft voices chanting in the moonlight invoking love and oneness, She wouldn't have been so deliberately and thoroughly scourged from people's minds?

Eager to find some modern Western acknowledgment of what I had experienced, I read books and attended lectures by amazing and evolutionary women such as Barbara Marx Hubbard and Jean Houston. But even these iconic feminine voices didn't give me a taste of what I was looking for. Then several channeled teachings dropped into this void.

Channeling, a process whereby a spirit allegedly takes over a person's body in order to give a message to the corporeal world, was still a relatively new phenomenon. Jane Roberts had channeled the Seth material and Helen Schucman had channeled Jesus's *A Course in Miracles*. That was about it until the late 1970s when a rash of channels emerged: Lazarus, Abraham, Mafu, Bashar and dozens of others. All my TV friends thought channeling was a load of crap—yet one more New Age gimmick designed to separate me from my money. How was it possible to know whether the channel was really channeling, they asked? Somebody could be a good actor or a functional schizophrenic and put on a good show.

But such was my hunger for a potent female image to find and follow, I paid no heed to their worries.

All of the channeled messages I ran across had masculine spirits at the helm—enlightened teachers, warriors, aliens from other dimensions, starship captains with reassurances for their Earthly cousins—and most of these male spirits were channeled through men.

For the most part these channeled teachings were nothing new by New Age standards. The overall message was, "You are God, spirits lost on the material plane of existence who have forgotten your true identity." But several channels spoke on the topic of the Goddess, baldly stating that women had had their divinity stripped from them by the male priesthoods in an age-old campaign to destroy all traces of feminine spiritual power. And a couple of these channels were women.

The sight of puissant spirits striding around in beautiful women's bodies (and all the female channels were beautiful) formed a one-two punch I couldn't resist. This was what I was looking for! Watching several videos at a presentation with Simon one Sunday afternoon, like most people in the room (and the room was mostly filled with women), I hung on each channel's every word. Some of the men, however, seemed restless. Simon was one of them. "Let's go," he said, touching my arm as I headed towards the buffet table during a break between tapes.

"What?"

"I said, let's go. I've seen enough."

I hadn't begun to see enough. "But . . . I don't want to leave."

His face took on a look of all too familiar stubbornness. "Then you're going to have to find a ride back home with someone else."

Home was over an hour north of Atlanta and hitching a ride was unlikely. I started to get pissed but then realized leaving early was a non-issue. I'd finally found the mirrors and the message I was looking for! I would get the contact information from our hostess, order the tapes from these people and go to their events.

"Why didn't you want to stay?" I ventured later as Simon angled the car up the ramp onto I-85.

"I'm not sure."

I waited a few beats. "Didn't you like what was said?"

"It wasn't what was said that bothered me."

"What then?"

He was silent for a while. Finally he sighed. "You didn't find it distressing?"

Of all the reactions I could have had distress was way down the list. "No. Did you?" His jaw tightened and he kept his gaze firmly on the road.

His reticence puzzled me. Usually our metaphysical interests tracked together, and I was in a fever pitch of enthusiasm and gratitude. Watching women deliver such powerfully enlightened talks had been an extraordinary experience. Each one provided an intoxicating image of potent male energy packaged in feminine form, and I wanted more. If female channels could have been synthesized into a potion like Alice's in Wonderland, contained in a bottle labeled "Drink me," I would have gladly downed the brew.

"It pissed me off."

Simon's voice jerked me back from my reverie. "What?" I asked.

He sighed. "It pissed me off that those women were chosen as channels." He glanced at me, obviously chagrined, and made the rest of his confession. "I wish it had been me. Or at least other guys, you know?"

Simon's ability for honest self-introspection was one of the things I loved most about him, but at that moment I wasn't impressed. "No, I don't know. Why would that matter?"

"It's just hard taking such spiritually advanced teachings from women."

"Excuse me?" My voice must have escalated two octaves in the tiny sports car. "Why should that make a difference?"

He looked at me, embarrassed. "Um . . . it's just so significant, it's hard for a guy to accept. Surely you can understand?"

Surely, I thought, folding my arms and shutting my mouth, *this is precisely the world's whole damn problem.*

CHAPTER 14

New Age agenda

Over the next couple years I attended many channeled events. Even Simon got over his initial judgments and started going. The cabin was a fabulous place to contemplate what I was learning and practice all the meditations and exercises I was given. I also started a new career as a newspaper reporter.

I'd wanted to be a writer ever since I published a poem in *The Chronicle of the Horse* magazine when I was twelve. The local paper, a Gannett-owned daily in Gainesville, Georgia called *The Times*, was a fine publication and I applied for a job. For weeks I politely badgered the city editor until he finally hired me as a part-time court records clerk—an unglamorous job recording births, deaths and divorces down at the county courthouse. My very first week, he also assigned me a feature story on an artist's gallery opening in town. I enjoyed writing the article, and apparently it wasn't too terrible, for after that I was assigned a couple stories a week. Six months later I was promoted to full-time reporter and released from the courthouse basement forever.

I often wondered what my apparently normal co-workers would think if they knew about channels and could see me starting my days meditating, chopping wood and taking cold outdoor showers under a cedar tree! Between working as a down-to-earth reporter and exploring out-of-this-world information, it was an exciting if eclectic lifestyle that kept me stimulated and fully occupied.

However, by January 1989 it became clear I needed to be closer to my spiritual teachers. Not surprisingly the majority were on the west coast. It was ridiculously costly flying cross-country for weekend workshops, and I'd always wanted to live in the Pacific Northwest. The summers were beautifully cool compared to the scorching humidity of Georgia. And where else could I ski in the mountains and two hours later be on coastal waters?

Yes, I loved my new work and it was emotionally wrenching thinking about leaving the cabin. I'd given it my blood, sweat and tears, and in return that little farm had literally given me back my soul. But after almost three years its peace and rustic beauty were part of me. I would take the place with me in spirit. Another reporting job I could always find.

I gave a month's notice at work and to my landlord, sold my horse, sold the rest of my furniture and traded in my truck for a used Chevy van. Finally, on a rainy February morning in 1989, I shoved the last of my clothes along with my dogs, Merlin and Savannah, plus Georgia Cat, into the spacious vehicle. Chugging out the driveway I waved goodbye to the oak tree and the spring, the high-walled ravine and the river far below. I locked the gate behind me, tucking the key in its hiding spot for Rich, swiping at the steady flow of tears. Then I drove away from the farm for the last time.

What can I say about Washington State? It was wet, cool, mossy and drowning in fir trees. After a brief flurry of residences and odd jobs I eventually rented yet another inexpensive rustic cabin on yet another river a short commute outside the state capital of Olympia. I also started freelancing newspaper articles for *The Olympian*, another Gannett paper. My new life was living testimony to the inside TV production crew joke about live sports telecasting: *same shit different location.*

For the next several years my main focus was the intense spiritual practices I was learning from a variety of sources. I was as intoxicated by the channeled power woman package as ever. But I was branching out, discovering teachings covering everything from ancient aliens to quantum mechanics, psychic development to consciousness studies. Informative and intriguing, some teachers coached people on how to transcend the body via astral projection and out-of-body experiences. Others taught psychic practices like remote view. Most focused upon developing the "power of manifestation," urging practitioners to use mental focus to attract the physical things they desired in life.

But fear was also part of the New Age agenda. At the same time as I was taught to manifest physical things I wanted, some teachers advised building underground shelters, storing food and buying guns to protect myself from the "end days" around the year 2012, when society would implode from the weight of its own insanity, aliens would drop from the skies, and starving terrified hordes would rampage the countryside looking for shelter and food.

Between the twin messages of inspiration and fear I whipped myself into a desperate desire to attain mastery of my body and mind so that I might escape the terrifying future and my own human shortcomings. I did the meditation and visualization practices I was taught as many hours a day as I could, and my psychic experiences and out-of-body journeys sharply increased, inspiring me to ever-greater efforts. Getting beyond this difficult and dreary world became my solitary goal; getting out of my body and "out there" to God my only dream and desire.

Looking back it's difficult to know what to fairly say about those years. Engaging in long solitary hours of spiritual practices at home, my consciousness vaulted far beyond where I would ordinarily have managed to get myself. But at the same time I also became rigid and fanatical in my thinking. New Age truth became my truth. Just like any other good religious follower in any other tradition, I thought my "church" was the right church. The only difference was, of course, mine was the real deal. I had the *truth* in my pocket and my smugness and spiritual arrogance knew no bounds.

The intense level of willful striving involved in psychic practices and "manifesting my reality" suited my all-or-nothing personality. I was no stranger to either merciless routines or driving myself physically and mentally. Whether it was training half-ton Thoroughbreds, working 24-hour editing sessions in network TV trucks, rebuilding a cabin, digging ditches by hand in the blistering Georgia heat or meditating all night long, it was all the same to me.

Between work and my spiritual pursuits I didn't have much of a social or family life. I dated a nice man, a computer programmer from London who was into a lot of the same spiritual practices I was. But a continent and an entirely different way of thinking stood between myself and Middleburg and my mom. I'd been with her through two open-heart surgeries in the 1980s, and had sent her reams of material about healthy alternatives to deal with her high blood pressure and angina. But she ignored all of it and her health continued to deteriorate.

Her resistance puzzled me. I'd honored her request and never spoken again about my ongoing psychic experiences and spiritual work. But what was so threatening about herbs and supplements?

I couldn't understand her blanket rejection of anything

remotely smacking of introspection and alternative medicine, all of which she labeled "woo-woo stuff." She'd even been uneasy about my going to graduate school to get my psychology degree. It wasn't until I was 40 years old on a trip home for Christmas in 1991 that her obstinacy finally made sense.

It was a beautiful snowy morning. A fire was crackling in the woodstove and Mom and I were sitting at the kitchen table staring at the unwatched, still shrink-wrapped natural healing tape I'd sent for her birthday in October. "The reason I send you stuff on alternative therapies is they'll give you options and help you discover the subconscious programs that are running your life, making you sick in the first place." I leaned forward earnestly. "This isn't woo-woo stuff, Mom. It's psychology. Once you get into it, life begins to make so much sense."

Restless, she stood up and walked to the French doors overlooking the patio. Her fingers plucked at the thin curtains, partially drawn back to reveal a dusting of powdery snow on the lawn. Finally she turned around and faced me. "Try to get this through your head once and for all. I don't *want* to know about myself."

I listened, uncomprehending. She saw I was about to object and something in her snapped. She advanced, fists clenched, shouting, "Listen to me, goddammit! I hate myself! I HATE MYSELF! I DON'T WANT TO KNOW MYSELF. IT TERRIFIES ME!" She burst into tears and then just as swiftly, stopped. Face blank and calm, she looked down at me. "So just drop it would you? All of it? Please? For me?"

It was the most nakedly honest moment my mother and I ever had. That she spent her entire life avoiding that moment or sharing any other moments like it was a tragedy. But I listened and I honored her request and never mentioned anything that I was learning to her ever again.

Two years later in February 1993 I got the sudden intuitive hit to fly back to Virginia to see her, but ignored it. With no extra money in the bank I didn't give the impulse a second thought. Then, a couple weeks afterwards, I came home to a message on my answering machine announcing, "Your mother died last night. I've made plane reservations for you on Delta Airlines for Thursday morning at 10 am."

That was all Jack said.

Devastated, I prepared for the flight, my thoughts roving painfully over my mother's life. An intelligent, sensitive, educated woman, she'd lived dominated by a paranoid, rage-filled alcoholic husband, trapped in a habitual respect for society's values. She believed that "familiarity breeds contempt," and had no intimate friends. She believed what the newspapers and the nightly news anchors said. She paid the bills on time and voted Republican. She made flower arrangements for her church and did volunteer work. She was neither selfish nor spendthrift and spent her life taking care of her parents, Jack and me. She lived her values from cradle to grave. And she found herself despicable.

She died of a final, massive heart attack—died of a broken heart.

CHAPTER 15

Saying goodbye

Jack picked me up at Dulles International Airport just as he had so many times in the 20 years I'd been away from home. But this time Mom wasn't waiting in the kitchen for me to walk in the door at the end of my hour's ride with him in the Jeep. She never would be again. And that was impossible to face or even understand.

The house was filled with the finality of death. There was some comfort knowing her spirit lived on and that, in theory, it was possible to connect with her. But that did nothing to change the irrevocable fact that I would never be able to sit down at the kitchen table, kick off my shoes and have a cup of coffee with her ever again. The one person in the world with whom I could be my most bitchy, selfish, loving, generous, strange self and be utterly confident of support was gone. As I wandered through her home, I realized with a sinking heart that I'd never really honored her. I'd been so fearful of repeating what I considered her mistake of living a simple life as a wife and mother that I'd never acknowledged her for it. Nor had I praised her for everything else she was.

And now it was too late.

I took what solace I could knowing I loved her and that I had often told her so. It may not have always come at times or in ways she could hear. Certainly I did things and made choices that made her doubt my love. But at least I said the words often and meant them. And though she was not an affectionate person and never once made the move to hug me, I always hugged her and knew she appreciated it. It would have to be enough.

The biggest spring blizzard in a decade swept through Virginia the night before her funeral. I spent the evening packing up her clothes, listening to the snow hiss against the windows as the wind lashed the eaves. Jack stayed in the kitchen with his bourbon and the dog, mourning in his own fashion, leaving me alone with her closet, her silver hairbrush, her pearls, the scent of her on her favorite Harris Tweed jacket and her well-worn, sensible loafers.

The next day the snow was so deep we had to cancel the funeral. Being snowed in with Jack without my mother's mediating presence was unbearable. As the snow-bound days passed, he dissolved deeper into gloom and alcohol. I didn't know what was hurting him more, my mother's absence or the passing of the monthly check from my grandfather's trust fund that had supported them. Not only had he just lost a wife, he'd lost his income.

"I'm gonna talk to my lawyer in the morning." His small, bloodshot eyes narrowed against the steady stream of cigarette smoke rising from his ashtray, a crystal and silver ashtray my mother had brought to the marriage along with so many other things tangible and intangible. At his slurred words, fear shot through me. I had little enough in the worldly goods department. Would he really try to take my small inheritance away from me?

"Can we keep our eyes on the ball here, please?" I snapped. "This is about Mom, not the trust fund."

"Easy for you to say. You're the one getting the money."

He drank, getting more and more belligerent. In the end I screamed all the terrible things at him I'd always wanted to say, shocking him into silence. Later in my room behind locked doors, shame overwhelmed me. I hadn't been able to practice my mother's forbearance for even three days. And a desperate fear arose in me as I lay awake, flinching at every creak the old house made, fervently praying Jack wouldn't come with a gun in the night and kill me for what I'd said.

By the time the roads were passable and I'd met with the executor of Mom's will, it was time to be on the plane back to Washington. In an attempt to keep a promise I'd made on my last trip home to "take care of Jack for me after I'm gone," I took only my mother's silver hairbrush and a favorite skirt I remembered. Her jewelry, her car and all the family heirlooms I left with Jack, along with as big a check as I could afford to write, hoping against hope to buy him out of my life forever.

He never did hold a funeral for my mother. He never even bothered picking up her ashes from the funeral home. I called and called, begging the funeral director to send them to me. But in Virginia a husband's legal rights to the remains superseded a daughter's and the request was denied. My mother's life passed, unnoticed and unsung, with no husband or daughter or friends saying goodbye. Her small caring ways, her impish nature, her love of fast cars, her sharpshooting abilities, her peaceful sweetness, it all died unremarked—as unappreciated as her remains gathering dust in a plastic bag on a back-room shelf in a mortuary on the east side of town.

PART VIII

***

THE SHAMAN

(1998–2001)

CHAPTER 16

Stopping

With the money from the estate I bought a small house on five acres of land at the end of a long country road. A sadly neglected structure, it had good bones, huge log beams, open spaces and polished cedar ceilings that cried out for nurturing. A sweet space for me, Georgia Cat, Savannah and the two wolf-hybrid pups I had recently adopted, I gratefully settled in, hammer and paint brushes in hand. After a few months of hard construction work, I fell back into the old routine of working from home and doing my spiritual practices. But as the years ticked past I gradually sensed my life coming to a standstill.

I got up at 5 am to practice the breath work and meditation I'd been taught for a couple hours before starting work. And I meditated a couple more hours at night. But despite all the work I could feel a huge block forming. It was like Spirit was standing in front of me with a raised hand saying, "You can come this far but no further." Encouraged by the world I lived in to be aggressive in my pursuits, encouraged by my teachers to be forceful, disciplined and focused, the only thing I knew to do was push harder and then harder yet, fiercely willing a breakthrough.

Peace and happiness eluded me. Meaning and purpose faded

into frustration and an overwhelming sense of distance—distance from God, distance from life, distance from myself and distance from others. My entire family, except for Jack, was gone. My boyfriend and I had broken up. My career was a bunch of disconnected freelance writing jobs done in isolation that offered no security or benefits and I scrambled every month to pay the bills. Surely there must be something more to life than an endless striving to keep a roof over one's head? Surely there must be more to spirituality than discipline and following all the rules to get to God?

Blearily I plodded down the stairs with my meditation pillow. As usual it was pitch black outside. I hit the light switch at the bottom of the stairs, dumped my stuff on the living room rug and started some music. Then I lit a couple candles, turned off the lights and headed to my cushion to start my morning routine. Music filled the room. An unutterable weariness swept over me as I stood staring down at my cushion.

Fuck it.

I plopped down on my seat. I didn't do the breathing. I didn't sit upright in the correct posture. I didn't do anything. I simply slouched there, closing my eyes, giving up. Within moments my conscious mind expanded effortlessly away from all human issues and concerns, opening me up like a flower until I was floating in an ocean of bliss, connected with the universe, linked with all life as One once more.

My morning's surrender changed everything. Between the space of one breath and the next I discovered I didn't have to push and force everything all the time. I didn't have to whip myself to accomplish something that was inherently un-accomplishable. For how can you accomplish being what you already are?

I ignored all the practices I had learned. Every morning I simply sat down, closed my eyes and allowed life energy to effortlessly rise up the column of my spine, sending my body into an almost sexual tide of bliss. The oceanic experience I'd had in the cabin in Georgia all those years ago returned daily—a pristine consciousness that knew no fear, worry, striving, or accomplishing. True, this amazing state of mind didn't last past the moment I opened my eyes, but it was enough just having a couple quiet dawn hours reawakened to something more than just "me." And the less I tried to do anything to experience this state the sweeter, easier and more expansive it became.

It felt like the weight of the world had fallen off my shoulders.

Spirit was in me, *was* me, always had been, always would be. What was there to strive for? I gave up reading spiritual "how to" books. I gave up going to teachers. Who cared about performing psychic tricks like remote view when bliss and Oneness were waiting? Who cared about a terrifying future? With joy in my heart for the first time in years I began to tend to the here and now. If I was joyous in the present what could possibly come into my life except more of the same?

1998 was a good year. Not only did I have a profound spiritual breakthrough, I also got out of the house and got a job as the NW Bureau Chief and editor for the national Native American newspaper *Indian Country Today*.

The first day, I arrived at the office to discover the former editor had already left and the secretary had been recalled to the paper's central offices in North Dakota. She handed me the keys, gave me a cursory tour, wrote down the computer passwords and walked out. I had five articles due by the end of the week, no contacts in Indian Country, no concept of proper protocols and no knowledge of Native culture and history. I also had an exploding international story in my backyard.

It was the height of the Makah Indian Tribe controversy over the resumption of their whaling activities after a 70-year ban. Death threats were deluging the tribe, and the reservation was in total lockdown against the flood of protestors and media besieging their tiny remote village on the westernmost tip of the continental US. So far, all the global papers had focused on were treaty guaranteed fishing rights, whaling bans, animal rights and Green Peace outcries. Nobody was digging into the Makah traditions and the reasons why ten young hunters trained all their lives to paddle a dugout canoe into dangerous ocean waters once a year to hunt one of the largest mammals on Earth, the gray whale. *That*, I thought, was where the real story lay, and at least spiritual traditions were something I could relate to.

The only other advantage I had was that I worked for a Native American paper. When absolutely no one, not even Forrest Sawyer, could get personal interviews with anyone at the Neah Bay tribal headquarters, working for *Indian Country Today* got me an interview with Keith Johnson, the Makah Whaling Commissioner himself. Sitting in his cluttered yet unadorned office, accepting a cup of black coffee, I got right to the point. "Keith, no one has asked you or anybody else here at the tribe what exactly the Makah spiritual traditions are and why they make this hunt so important. Could you tell me about that?"

He seemed a little surprised, but complied. "In our tribe, the whaling families go back generations. The canoe captain is always from the same family. Even though we had not hunted the whale in over 50 years, I was raised and trained by my father as a young boy to lead the hunt, just as he was trained by his father and his father before him."

"Trained for what exactly?"

He took a deep breath. "I was trained to connect with the spirit of the whale and then guide the canoe to him."

"Connect with the spirit of the whale?"

He hesitated as if he had already said too much. "Finding a whale is not a matter of paddling around in the ocean looking for one. When a whale is ready to give itself, it communicates its willingness to the one trained to hear his voice. The hunters and the whale find each other . . . are drawn to each other. After we find each other, the whale is blessed and the kill is made. And then . . ."

He stopped. "Our ceremonies and beliefs are not talked about to outsiders."

I didn't move or say a word.

He continued, almost angrily. "It's not about hunting and canoeing skills and prowess with the harpoon like everyone thinks. Although those things are important." He paused, tapping the fingers of one hand on the arm of his chair, looking at me. Finally he came to some kind of a decision. "I guess I can tell you this much. The main responsibility of the captain of the canoe is to connect with the spirit of the whale, which willingly gives its body up to the tribe to feed the people and make them strong. The sacrifice of its body is not only appreciated, it is rewarded. After the kill is made, it is the captain of the canoe who journeys with the whale in spirit to help guide it to its new life on a . . . on a new plane of existence."

He stopped dead. "I can say no more."

I sat back, closing my eyes, contemplating Keith's words. When I finally got what he'd just said, I was stunned. He was talking about reincarnation and the transmigration of the soul, a shared belief of Neoplatonism, Hermeticism, Christian Gnosticism and various Indian religions. In that one astonished moment I saw into the heart of the Makah whaling tradition: the 1,000-year-old connection that joined the tribe with the gray whale was an interspecies pact.

"So the captain is responsible for guiding the spirit of the whale that chooses to sacrifice itself, to the shores of its new life as a human being within the tribe," I said softly.

Keith jolted in his chair. "I didn't say that. I didn't tell you that."

"No, you didn't." I paused in wonder. "There's so much my culture doesn't understand or believe in. And we are the poorer for it. Thank you for speaking with me of your beautiful tradition."

Keith looked ready to weep, whether from the horror of being seen or from gratitude I couldn't tell. Either way the interview was over.

The white man talks about the Holy Spirit in his churches and says he believes in the soul or some sort of existence outside the body. But then he goes and lives as if he doesn't believe any of it. For the whites, everything is about the body, protecting the body and glorifying it. Even the Christian spiritual totem is a body on a cross. Sure, a token nod is given to the Holy Spirit, just as a token nod is given to natives and their 'spirit traditions.' But deep down, most white people think indigenous beliefs and talk about the spirit breathed into all life are nothing but a bunch of primitive superstitions.

The animal rights activists sending death threats to the Makah elders cared nothing for the tribe's traditions because they were unaware that the spirit really exists. For them, there was no difference between the Makah crew hunting one whale, risking their lives in a dugout canoe against heavy seas for a beautiful higher purpose and Japanese whaling crews slaughtering hundreds of whales from massive modern fishing boats for commercial profit. One body, many bodies—it was all the same thing.

I couldn't blame them for their ignorance. Native American ways are completely different to white ways, just as Native American history is completely different to white history, an astounding fact

I was made aware of almost every day. For if I dug deeply enough, there wasn't a single article I wrote that didn't have some ghastly backstory of greed by the whites at its heart; greed and theft of rights and resources and human dignity that had left scars and legal entanglements that hadn't been sorted out in 150 years.

It didn't matter if I was talking with a Native artist resurrecting bead-making traditions in California, a social worker in Idaho or a businessman in British Columbia; everyone had tales to tell. I heard about forced marches where women and children died on the road, their bodies left unburied to feed the vultures and crows. I learned about the internment camps, filled with starvation and disease; the little children ripped from their parents' arms to be sold into child prostitution and slavery, never to be seen again.

Some of the worst stories I heard, many of them eyewitness accounts, were about the residential boarding schools overseen by the Bureau of Indian Affairs. Well into the 20th century, little children were routinely beaten for speaking their native tongue, raped and sodomized by the priests who ran the schools, forced to sleep in the same beds with dying friends or their corpses, and even thrown to their deaths out four-story windows.

Nothing in my 46 years of living in white America prepared me for any of this. Sure, I'd heard "History is written by the victors." But that's just an empty cliché until you've sat with an aging grandfather or auntie in their dingy living room on the reservation, tears quietly running down their proud faces, telling you things that have broken their hearts and the spirits of their people; stories you don't want to hear, but can't refuse listening to because they need to be told by the ones who need to be heard, and heard by the ones who are ignorant; heard by the ones who have it too easy to care that we've been lied to by our government, the corporations, our church and our media for over a century about the true founding of this nation and the price that was paid for it.

A price we are continuing to pay.

CHAPTER 17

Ipupiara's questions

Wrapped in a cape against the cold, I sat watching the crackling bonfire, thinking about the strangeness of those things which resonate strongly—the people, words and moments that rise up out of life to grab you, shake you and change your life forever.

I had recently interviewed John Perkins for *Indian Country Today*, and his amazing story about the Amazonian shaman who came to America refused to escape my mind. I continued to think about it weeks after the article ran. In fact, I'd recounted John's jungle adventure story about the Shuar shaman saving his life at dinner that very evening. My best friends Tess and Francesca had been spellbound by the end as I recited the two questions the shaman, Ipupiara, had asked; the questions that wouldn't stop pounding in my brain:

"Where are your women, John? Why are they not telling the men to stop?"

My friends sat across the fire, chatting. Absently, I prodded the logs with a stick, obsessed with the train of thought John's tale had roused in me. What did give the Shuar women enough power to make the men stop cutting trees, killing the animals and using up resources unnecessarily? And what was woman's power anyway?

I was 47 years old and a professional journalist with a couple of college degrees. As a spiritual seeker I had faced encounter groups, floated amongst the astral stars, transcended my body, held hands in goddess circles and faced inner demons. But nowhere along the way had I gleaned any gritty insights into my power as a flesh-and-blood woman, certainly not in the way or to the degree the Shuar women expressed it.

It made me ashamed to admit it, but I didn't view women as powerful—not unless they had some sort of important job that made them so. And what women in what jobs were going to stop my culture's corporate-based, consumer-driven market economy? What a joke! Capitalism was a firmly entrenched and profitable cancer few people were interested in finding a cure for. How could anybody, let alone a bunch of women, command 'Stop!' and have anything happen at all? Besides, I could hardly sit around pointing fingers at men as the sole perpetrators of consumerism run amuck. As a modern Western woman I didn't know the meaning of the word 'stop' any better than they did.

In the United States, women spend over $4 trillion annually (over $6 trillion in 2011), accounting for 83% of US consumer spending—two-thirds of the US gross national product. I was part of that picture and just as driven as any man to succeed at making money and having things. I glanced across the fire at my fellow consumers. Francesca owned a clothing store and was a profess-ional storyteller. Tess owned and ran a construction company. All three of us were spiritually oriented, but being spiritual in my culture didn't mean slowing down and stopping or having less. It just meant adding one more thing to the to-do list.

Like everything else in my world, spirituality was an industry. And with millions of individuals focused on personal development, spending money on seminars, books, tapes, yoga mats, organic food and health products, it was a damn lucrative one. Most of the spiritual seminars I had attended were for-profit spirituality ventures with typical hierarchical staff structures just like any other corporation.

I took a sip of wine. The girls laughed and Tess winked at me across the fire, acknowledging my presence yet leaving me to my private thoughts. I prodded the fire again and fat sparks shot skyward.

There was an undeniable emphasis in Western spirituality on manifesting more material stuff as a talisman of spiritual advancement. The trend was so prevalent a new term had been coined to describe it: spiritual materialism. And for almost a decade I had been right in there, aggressively pursuing God and Mammon with the same passion. But that one magic moment where I stopped pursuing anything and simply allowed myself to *be*, changed everything. After a certain point striving and force were apparently antithetical for attaining one's desires—whether money or higher consciousness. And now, with John's story, I was getting the same message, "STOP!" from a different source. But how was I supposed to apply that lesson to the rest of my life and continue to live and do well?

Okay, so I 'stopped' for two blissful hours every morning. So what? The rest of my life was a daily grind trying to make enough money to make ends meet. My mortgage and other bills felt like a never-ending gas tank I had to labor hard to fill up. The world with its busy-ness was exhausting. And though I liked my job, if I didn't keep cranking out the articles, the income would stop. Then where would I be?

The divide between spirit and the rest of my life seemed unbridgeable. And yet it didn't have to be that way. I knew of other viable cultures that honored spirit and the earth *and* productivity. In fact, the most peaceful, happy nations in the world were those in which people's physical lives were balanced by lived spiritual truths.

In Bhutan, instead of measuring value in terms of Gross

National Product (GNP), the government defined value as GNH: Gross National Happiness. Founded in Buddhist ideals, the GNH index assumed that healthy human society resulted when material and spiritual goals were pursued side by side. The four goals of GNH were: 1) promotion of sustainable development, 2) preservation and promotion of cultural values, 3) conservation of the natural environment and 4) establishment of good governance. Every law the government implemented was created with these goals in mind. If a law was determined to not add to the population's Gross National Happiness, it was modified or repealed.

How astounding was that? In the US, so many of our laws were designed to make the acquisition of wealth easier for a few at the expense of the well-being of many.

I got up to get more firewood. Now full-grown wolves, Cheyanne and Master lay just within the circle of light, eyes green-gold sparks against the darkness. Adding another log to the flames, I dropped the rest in a pile next to the stone circle and sat back down, picking up my wine glass. Smudged with sooty fingerprints, one side was chill to the touch, the other warm from the fire. I closed my eyes, sensitizing to my environment, feeling the cold ground beneath my thighs, inhaling the scents of cedar smoke and damp night air, trying to feel what the night contained beyond the fire's glow.

But my thoughts wouldn't leave me alone. Catching a lull in the flow of words across from me, I entered Tess and Francesca's conversation. "So," I ventured. "We're facing resource depletion, pollution of water resources, economic collapse, climate change, genetic mutations and the possibility of all life as we know it ending. Our governments and corporations keep right on doing the things that are destructive. And yet most people, myself included, do nothing. Every day we go to work and act as if it will all magically work out somehow without our changing course. How did we get so out of touch with reality?"

The fire crackled in the silent space that opened up with my question. "Well," said Tess, "that's the last time we leave *you* to your own thoughts."

I chuckled ruefully. Cheyanne got up, stretched and moved away, her white coat vanishing into blackness. Francesca put down her wine glass. "I've got an answer to that if you want to hear a story."

"Is it a funny one?" Tess asked hopefully.

"No."

Francesca waited, then, taking our silence as encouragement, launched into her tale.

"One day, Coyote and Eagle traveled to the underworld to find their wives who had somehow wandered there. But, in those days, the dead were only visible in the darkness that occurred when a strange traveling woman consumed the moon at certain times of the month. Impatient to find and reunite with his wife, Coyote killed the traveling woman and immediately swallowed the moon himself. Once they were visible, he and Eagle put all the souls of the dead in a box and headed back home. When Coyote opened the box to release his wife, he accidentally released all the dead, and death itself, into the world."

She stopped. Synchronistic to the moment, a coyote yipped in the distance.

"That's it?" asked Tess.

"Yep." Francesca sipped her wine.

I made a little bowing gesture towards her. "Oh, She-Who-Speaks-Obscurely, please tell us, what the hell does *that* mean?"

Francesca didn't laugh. "You told that story earlier about the shaman asking where our women have gone, so I thought the Chinook legend fit." She paused, gathering her thoughts. "Women have gone away from the world. They've become like invisible shades in the valley of death. And men are so lost and desperate they'll do anything, even consume the moon, to get woman back."

She sighed. "Most peoples have myths explaining how death arrives in the world, even Christianity. Trouble is, we keep death at arm's length, locked in the mythic realms. We do everything to avoid realizing that death is a very real and natural part of living."

"What's that got to do with letting the environment go to hell?" Tess interjected.

"Well, how many people actually believe they're ever going to die and spend time thinking about it?" Francesca asked, looking at her, then at me. "Do you?"

Her question took me by surprise. I glanced at Tess. She was staring at Francesca. "No, I don't," she admitted.

"Neither do I," I said.

"Exactly," said Francesca, triumphantly. "And if human beings are so out of touch with reality they can ignore their own individual deaths . . ."

The light dawned and I finished the statement for her. "They can ignore what's happening to the Earth and act like the ride is never going to end."

PART IX

❉ ❉ ❉

THE WISE WOMAN
(1998–2008)

CHAPTER 18

Gaia

Galvanized by the conversation and my thoughts about a new potential role for women in our world, I started writing a book about the missing feminine. After three chapters of ranting and blame, spouting off the latest psychological research into the differences between men and women's thought processes and brain states, I hit a roadblock. I kept writing, but something major was missing. Eventually I shelved the project in disgust.

In 2001, *Indian Country Today* and I parted company. After three years I just couldn't write one more article about intertribal squabbles and ongoing battles with the US government over resource restitution and casinos. With my varied background in communications, I started a small marketing company aimed towards promoting businesses that contributed to higher planetary consciousness. But as a writer it was a decision based more on economic need than joyous creation. Meaningful expression escaped me.

"No wonder you're miserable."

"I didn't say I was miserable. I said I feel a little lost. Jeez."

"Okay, no wonder you're lost if your whole life focus is on 'spiritually transcending this world so you can float around happily ever after in the ethers,'" Tess made finger quotes as she minced around the pre-Christmas sales table piled high with oddments of camping gear, trying to look angelic.

"I didn't say it like that," I shot back, mildly irritated.

"If you ask me, that's the whole problem with people who pursue spiritual enlightenment. They always seem to think the Earth is chopped liver and that enlightenment has to happen in some magical 32nd Universe or something."

"Tess, this whole place," I gestured around the store where we were shopping, "is an illusion. Maya. A dream. It's not what really matters."

"So, if it doesn't really matter, why did you bother coming with me on this trip? Why bother with anything?" She tossed back her heavy mane of black hair then pounced on a rain poncho in a stuff sack. "Hey, how 'bout this?"

I looked at it. "Maybe."

"What's wrong with being here on Earth and being happy *and* enlightened? This," she gestured around the store, mimicking me, "is spirit, too, you know."

"Yeah, I know."

"No, you don't. If you did, you wouldn't be talking about 'spirit,'" she did finger quotes again, "as if it were better than the physical world. Which has been the whole trouble for 2,000 years. All this focus on Heaven gives everybody the excuse to trash everything on Earth as meaningless and pat themselves on the back for being good spiritual people while doing it."

A rather strong bell was ringing in my brain. *Where had . . . Ah yes.* "It's like that speech Dan Rather recently gave at some university graduation. At least I think it was Dan Rather. Maybe it was Bill Moyers."

"Um?"

"Whoever. Anyway, he interviewed some muckity-muck in Bush's cabinet who admitted the administration was all about destroying the Earth and depleting its resources as fast as possible so the Book of Revelations would be proven right and Armageddon would come faster and all the righteous ones, meaning them, would get to Heaven sooner."

Tess stopped ransacking a pile of wool socks, shocked. "Please, tell me you're joking."

I shook my head. "It's insane. But then so are our government's energy and environmental policies. It does answer a lot of questions."

"That's unbelievable."

"Yep, almost as unbelievable as us finally taking this trip together."

I'd been banging on about the beauty of the southwest desert ever since Tess and I first met and became friends at a spiritual retreat in 1989. Being Spanish, she'd never traveled in the United States. And although she'd moved to Washington in 1990, she'd quickly fallen into a relationship with another woman. Then she'd started a construction business. Completely absorbed between the two, there'd been no time to go galloping off with me on a road trip, no matter how enticing it sounded. In fact, "the desert trip" as we'd come to call it, had become rather a joke between us. And then came her early December phone call.

"Still want to go to the Grand Canyon?" she'd asked. "December is lousy for building and The Bitch wants me out of the house for a couple weeks. God, I can't wait to get away!"

Deep in the gray Pacific Northwest winter doldrums and in between freelance jobs, I readily agreed to go. I lined up a house sitter to take care of the wolves, threw my camping gear in the back of her Toyota 4Runner and off we went. So far, we'd faced a raging blizzard and whiteout conditions in the Cascades, swept down into Utah, sunroof open to the winter sun, soaking up the breathtaking desert vistas. We'd slept overnight in the car in another snowstorm outside Bryce Canyon and toured the Grand Canyon. Now we were headed east towards Canyon de Chelly, hopefully a little bit warmer and better outfitted for snow after our quick shopping excursion than we had been so far.

Best known for the Anasazi pueblos built into natural caves in the cliffs situated high above the valley floor, Canyon de Chelly had been occupied continuously since 700 AD until the Anasazi people disappeared from the region in the 1300s. Reoccupied by the Navajo, it was again abandoned when Kit Carson led cavalry into the canyons in 1863, destroying homes and forcing the Natives on a relocation march.

We arrived at the south rim of the canyon around noon on a crisp, clear day, although clouds were building on the western horizon behind us. At this time of year, the park was practically deserted. After a few miles we came to Tsegi overlook, stopped and got out of the car. Carefully stepping across deep fissures in the rock, we got to the jagged sandstone lip of the canyon. A 1,000-foot vertiginous drop lay at our feet. Across the canyon, Blade Rock stuck its knife-edge profile out into the fertile valley floor. The Chinle River flowed around it, its cottonwood-dotted banks overflowing with winter rains and silvery snowmelt. For a long time I stood there, letting the canyon's vibe enter into me. Cold desert wind washed my face.

Canyon de Chelly was puny compared to the Grand Canyon. But it was astonishingly beautiful and contained a strange magic. It was as if the canyon was fooling you into thinking it was smaller than it was: that any moment your eyes might stop deceiving you and added dimensions and hidden worlds would appear. It was a disconcerting yet lively feeling. I turned to Tess, eyebrows raised in question. "Here?" She took a deep breath and nodded, eyes never leaving the canyon and the vast horizons beyond.

And so it was here, in the heart of lands where ancient cultures, still connected to the star nations, lived in reverence, that Tess and I performed a ceremony and partook of a substance well known to facilitate spiritual expansion and insight called MDMA. Ceremony had been a major part of Tess's plans for this trip from the get-go. "I'm at a crossroads, Cate. I can feel it." She shook her head. "My relationship is awful. Zoe and I do nothing but fight. My business feels like a boat anchor, and I haven't got a clue what to do about any of it." She smiled wistfully. "I'm hoping a couple of ceremonies out in the desert will give me insight and direction. You're welcome to join me if you want to."

I understood her need and the impulse. Hadn't I run to the wilderness in my time of confusion? Granted, I hadn't used mind-altering substances since last smoking pot in 1975. And that had hardly been for ceremonial purposes! But I too was experiencing the sense of something missing in my life. It was a major reason I agreed to take the trip. Why not open myself to new experiences and possibilities?

By the time we finished preparations, meditating, burning sage and purifying ourselves, it was early afternoon. Saying a blessing over the tiny off-white capsules, we invoked Spirit and asked that the highest insights be given us, toasted with our water bottles and drank. Then, wrapped in our capes, we found a comfortable spot a few hundred feet from the parking lot near the rim and settled into the sweeping silence of the canyon.

For an exquisite couple of hours I watched the canyon change with the sun. Mercurial as Salome doing the dance of the seven veils, Canyon de Chelly was harsh and forbidding one moment, laughing and available the next: barren as an old crone, then lush with fertile sighs. The scents of sage and sandstone filled my nostrils and my heart filled with delighted peace.

Then suddenly, in one of those isolating snap zooms where everything is out of focus in a blur except for a central picture, I saw the cliff dwelling across the canyon and my perceptions careened every which way. Bringing the human element into the canyon's picture changed everything. My initial impression of hidden dimensions had been correct. The canyon was way bigger than it looked, and the pueblo clinging to the ledge about halfway up the cliff across from us looked miniscule and impossibly dangerous to access. In our first communication of the ceremony, I silently pointed out the site to Tess and heard her sharp intake of breath as her perspective shifted and she got how small our presence in this place really was.

And then, as I lifted my gaze back to the panoramic desert with its horizons stained ochre and rose in the rays of the setting sun, Gaia appeared.

The primordial deity of the Greek pantheon, Gaia is the spirit of the Earth. The first Titan to appear after Chaos, she is the mother of the seas, oceans, mountains, soil and all the creatures of Earth. And yet to name her as a deity is to immediately reduce her. To call her a goddess is to invoke a ridiculous human image of some gigantically tall, feminine form in flowing Greek robes striding across the desert. Seeing Gaia was nothing like that, for she was nothing in human form at all.

It was the formless *spirit* of the Earth making Herself known to me. And the enormity and force of that living spirit of Earth, thundering into my perception like an invisible wall of information, literally took my breath away. Between one moment and the next my planet transformed from a bunch of isolated rocks and plants, sky and dark gathering clouds, trees and river, bursting into my mind as a coherent, intelligent, overwhelmingly alive presence.

The shift in perception was exactly like what happens when you gaze at one of those perceptual tests you find in magazines—like the line drawing of the old hag with a wart on her crooked nose which suddenly morphs into a picture of a beautiful lady with a scarf and a wide-brimmed hat with an ostrich feather. None of the lines of the drawing change. The picture is the exact same picture. But your perception changes, and instead of a witch you see an 1890s' damsel! Similarly, the world stretching around me now was the exact same world it had been moments before. And yet, as my perceptions expanded to embrace a living Earth, it was totally different.

I reeled, psychically blown away. *How could I have missed this? How could I have missed seeing the Earth is an alive being? A living Presence?*

"She's alive," I whispered. Tearing my gaze from the horizon, I glanced at Tess and could see from the equally riveted expression on her face, the quick nod and shallow gulping of saliva, that she was experiencing the same thing. We sat, still as statues, acknowledging Gaia's presence until darkness fell and the wind drove the storm from desert to canyon and curtains of cold rain lashed our faces. Within moments our capes were soaked and it was pitch black with no way to see where the rim of the canyon lay. Crawling on hands and knees in the direction of the car, carefully feeling for solid rock in front of us until we reached the safety of the parking lot, finally we stood up, laughing, and ran to the car.

The storm was fierce and alive, vibrating every cell in my body. It was impossible to shut ourselves away from the intoxication of it by crawling into some metal box on wheels, so we both sat back down on the soaking sand nearby. Spiraling into the winds, I soared in consciousness to the top of the storm and then out into the universe. Feeling my way along the currents of movement that were the spinning of the planets, the wheeling of stars and galaxies, recognizing movement as the beginning of Creation and time itself, I expanded, at once exalted and yet totally aware of being a wet human huddled in sodden cold clothes in the middle of the desert night. Finally, I surfed the currents back down to Earth, feeling the changes in the wind in my consciousness, feeling every eddy, knowing the moment the raging blow would gentle into a zephyr. I laughed with the spirit of the wind as we shifted together in a lover's waltz of pure awareness.

"I'm cold." Tess's teeth were chattering.

I thought about it. "So am I," I agreed.

Laughing, we located flashlights and groped for towels and clothes amidst the mess of wet capes, food and camping gear in the back of the Toyota. Once dry and changed, Tess was exhausted and wanted to sleep. I felt like the Queen of the Night and decided to watch the sunrise in Monument Valley in southern Utah. Tess got in the back of the car and crawled into her sleeping bag, instantly asleep. I hauled out the maps to see where I was going, then pulled out onto the highway. The night was blacker than a stack of cats in a closet and the roads empty. I followed Indian Highway 7, connecting to roads ever north and eastward. An hour before dawn I drove into the wide dirt road entrance of the park, pulled onto the sand by the side of the road and fell asleep sitting behind the wheel.

Dawn revealed another jeweled spot in Gaia's crown. The massive towers of Monument Valley squatted like huge black dogs against the brightening sky, slowly gaining color and definition. The air was clean and cold. We rubbed the sleep from our eyes, hauled out our sodden capes and draped them over the back of the 4Runner to catch the early sun to dry. Then we walked a little way into the desert.

The sun leapt into view, splintering light in all directions, illuminating the rainbow-hued massifs. I turned to look at Tess and caught my breath. Head tilted back, lips parted in exultation, black hair cascading in a wild tangle over her shoulders, she looked like a Dryad magically birthed anew in this brilliant, austere land. Turning, she smiled, tenderly caught my cold fingers and raised them to her lips. In an outpouring of response so dizzying I couldn't even capture it, everything I thought woman was, all that I thought woman should be, was projected onto that one face. All the unrecognized, unacknowledged sweetness and grace, power and beauty of my own feminine being rushed out to embrace its reflection in the other.

The feminine, or at least my ideal of it, was in my life at last.

CHAPTER 19

In the company of women

I'd imagined doing a lot of things in my life, but falling in love with a woman wasn't one of them. Over the remainder of the trip I succumbed to the intoxicating spell of the goddess alive in my life, sitting beside me in a four-wheel drive vehicle, holding my hand. It was me I was falling in love with as we drove those desert miles. But I thought it was Tess mesmerizing me, not my own feminine essence reflected back, sweeping me away.

It was a mutual intoxication. Shyly, Tess admitted she'd been in love with me for years. Who knew? But I was so far out of known territory that the confession didn't even make me blink. By the time we crossed the state line back into Washington, the idea of being apart for even a few days was unthinkable. But Tess had a partnership to go back to, a bad one maybe, but she needed to be responsible. And I had . . . well, I didn't know what I had.

"You're *what*??" exclaimed Francesca, boggling. A few heads turned at tables nearby.

"I'm in love with Tess," I said, ducking my head and blushing. For once in her life Francesca ignored a menu. She stared at me, mouth open in surprise, hands frozen on the slick cover. Several questions almost came out of her mouth and didn't. Finally the most pressing one erupted. "When did you become gay?" she strangled, eyes wide, trying hard to resist the impulse to slide just a *teensy* bit further away from me on the booth seat.

I looked at her blankly. *Gay?*

"I'm not gay, Fran. I like guys. I just happen to have fallen in love with a woman. That doesn't make me gay."

"It doesn't?"

Did it?

"I don't think so. Sex and love are not the same thing, you know." It was an uncertain statement at best.

Francesca looked like a deer in the headlights. If it happened to me, maybe she could catch it, too. "So, how did it happen?"

I didn't have a clue. "Jesus, Fran, how does anybody fall in love? You just wake up and realize a certain person is special and important and that you want to be around them all the time. I just love everything about her. Her mind, her spirit, her zest for life, her heart, her . . ."

"Body?"

"Um. I was going to say laughter. Her body? Well. That's the problem, isn't it? I mean, she's beautiful and all. But I'm not a . . ." The word came with difficulty. "A lesbian." Francesca looked unconvinced. "I mean I'm not attracted to her physically. Isn't that what it means to be homosexual? That you're attracted physically to the same sex?"

Francesca laughed nervously, fiddling with the edge of her menu. "You're asking me?"

"Yeah."

"I don't know. I never thought about it. Haven't you talked with Tess? She's the lesbian. What does she say?"

I sighed blissfully, remembering her words. "That when she looks into my eyes she sees the face of God."

I looked around the table at the circle of female faces. Three lesbian couples eating barbequed chicken. *Jesus Christ, how did this happen?* A year and a half into my relationship with Tess and I was still astonished there wasn't a single man left in my life. No male friends. No male co-workers. Even my mechanic was a lesbian.

Talk about a whole new culture.

Of the six of us around the table, four had known since childhood they were attracted to women. But making the difficult personal journey of discovering what to do about it was easier said than done. Of those four, only Alex had not tried going the 'date guys and see if things change' route. Teri and Melissa told high school and college dating horror stories, exposing their forced attempts at being with guys and the terrible self-judgment that came with not being interested in them.

Melissa even got married. Not until she'd suffered physical abuse from her husband did she eventually escape to the 'other side'. Teri limped along through college until she finally gave in to the inevitable. Tess had had several male lovers and almost got married before she finally mustered the courage to tell her conservative Spanish parents the bad news. Both Nicole and I had been perfectly happy being with guys until we tripped over other possibilities.

In some ways, being in the company of lesbian women was like working in Indian Country all over again. I heard the most unbelievable tales: modern American parents subjecting their daughters to electro-shock treatments to 'cure' them of the disease of lesbianism, locking them in insane asylums, abandoning them as teenagers, hiring deprogrammers. Most of my new friends had endured relentless rejection by family, friends and society their entire lives.

"She *what*?!" The table erupted in gasps of dismay and laughter. My attention jerked back to the conversation. As the new kid on the block, I provided endless entertainment over my gay naïveté.

"She did. She got up and asked me to slow dance, right there in front of God and all those redneck cowboys sitting around drinking their beers."

"Cate!" Nicole exclaimed, eyes round.

Melissa, her partner, paled. "You just don't do that!"

"It's a fast way to get yourself beat up and raped, girlfriend," said Alex, her usually smiling face serious. "I've seen it happen."

"Cate, you're not with a guy anymore," said Teri, butting in. "You just can't be yourself and do what you want. Alex's right. You could've got both of you killed."

"So what did you do?" Melissa breathlessly asked Tess.

"I pretended she'd asked me to go to the ladies room, grabbed her arm and dragged her in there."

"Where I got a fast, whispered lecture about appropriateness," I shivered. The idea of dying in a really ugly way just because I loved a fine human being who happened to be female like me was not an easy thing to adjust to. Alex often joked, "It's always the straight women that get you in trouble." And she had a point. Being 'normal' all my life made me blasé to protocols that had ensured my friends' lifelong safety. Waking up to the reality of sexual prejudice wasn't just practical, it was a matter of survival. But as far as being with a woman was concerned, how ludicrous the prejudice was!

Contrary to slick TV shows like *The L Word*, sex wasn't the core of my relationship with Tess any more than it was with the rest of our friends. Our relationships were about love, play, comfort, connection and affection—with side benefits like the marvelous fact that women *automatically* clean things, cook and keep the toilet seat down. But sex as the main attractor? Sure, it was great and went with the relationship package. But it was hardly what the relationship was about.

For many lesbians, being with another woman was a safety choice. Men just plain frightened them, and a lot of them had good reasons to be afraid. Many had suffered sexual abuse at the hands of their fathers, brothers and uncles. Others had been raped and abused by boyfriends, male co-workers and husbands. Unfortunately, the sex part was all the religious conservatives could see. The rabid right apparently didn't care about love or companionship or safety. It was like they couldn't get *their* minds out of the gutter long enough to realize there might be something else going on between two people. And as far as men beating and raping lesbians to 'cure' them of their inclinations, you'd think the guys would wonder *why* some women preferred women and take it as an object lesson.

I took a sip of wine and watched my friends. Each one had wounds around gender and sexuality, deep ones. It was difficult to imagine them being able to heal with any man, especially in a cultural atmosphere where the feminine expression in general was discounted. And why would they want to force themselves to 'heal by being with a man' even if they could? Why did people think not wanting to have a penis around was an illness? Hands down, most women (not all) were more refined than most heterosexual men (not all). Most were much more available and responsive mentally, emotionally and physically. And there were plenty of ways to replace the male sex organ, so often misused or poorly applied by men anyway. Looking at it honestly, was there a heterosexual woman alive who had not wished to Heaven at some point in her life for greater sensitivity, connection, nuance and grace in her sexual experiences?

Certainly, all men weren't to blame for the problems of our world and for the diminishment of women. But, at the same time, wasn't the world basically falling apart because so many politicians, CEOs and petty despots were fucking it over? Wasn't the whole world dying for lack of sensitivity, connection, nuance and grace? Dying for the lack of woman and her touch? Dying for lack of enough sensitive men empowered to stand for change?

My thoughts and new perspectives from living with Tess shocked me deeply. I liked men. Had loved several and made love with quite a few. My father, Cliff, and many men I knew were decent, loving, honorable beings. And I had won the love affair lottery with Nick, my TV crewmate and friend of so many years. I *had* healed sexually with a man. But then I wasn't a lesbian.

I had no natural physical attraction to females, including Tess. In fact, I was highly uncomfortable being with her physically. Not surprisingly, that created problems in our relationship. But when there is such a deep love and attraction to the spirit and the soul of another, there is the will to find a way to connect physically. Tess and I found it by not 'having sex.'

Instead of falling into a business-as-usual focus on body parts and 'doing it,' we expressed our love by kissing and caressing, looking into each other's eyes and sensitizing to each other's energies. It was a rewarding, even compelling, experience; an intensely intimate physical/emotional/energetic act of 'being present' together that seemed similar to what I'd heard about the Dagara tribe's practices in Burkina Faso.

What was initially a deeply frustrating lack in our relationship became an amazing portal to new dimensions.

Lying together, consciously exchanging breath, we joined energetically, soaring in our spirit bodies out into the universe together. Yes, I was still aware of my physical body while all this happened. And yes, my body was aroused. But bodies were not the main event. And because we weren't trying to limit the experience to our physical bodies, we didn't create any boundaries to the experience. The journeys were like one long etheric bliss ride, and were so much richer and more fulfilling than any purely physical activity and physical orgasm that it blew us both away.

Laughter brought me back to the table. I reached for my wine, trying to pick up the trail of Alex's story. She was so funny. All of them were great to be with. *Do I really miss men?* I wondered. *Or just the way I am when I'm around them?* It was a scary thought, but I couldn't help but probe the territory.

When I was around men, there was always an undeniable libido charge that gave every interchange a subtle edge that was thrilling. *That old black magic.* But it was a magic that was strictly chemical. It was *my body's* natural hormonal expression that got turned on, not 'me'. And yummy as hormones made everything, it was an unfortunate truth that most of my interactions with men over 20 and under age 70 brought with them a litany of barely subconscious concerns typical of the whole man/woman dynamic. Was I pretty enough (to fuck)? Was I pleasant enough (to fuck)? Was I sexy enough, witty enough, available enough, fun enough, demure enough, a good enough cook, secure enough to attract and hold onto this man?

And what was the end goal of being all of these superficial 'enoughs' I was concerned with? No matter how I sliced it, for me the answer always pointed back to sex and the eventual promise of a full-time committed relationship and security. Companionship was in there, sure. But frankly, if that was what I was looking for, it was easier and more satisfying being with a woman.

Just look at how many tribes and sects around the world were happily organized around gender segregation, with women and men living in separate parts of the village, only coming together for sexual union and certain social and religious events. And everybody got along fine!

My God. Is my whole hook with guys structured around hormones, social norms and a need for security?

"Um, ladies?" Everyone turned to look at me. "I have a question."

"Yes?" Alex arched an eyebrow.

"After all these years, how does it feel to be hanging out with women all the time?"

Gales of laughter burst forth. "Wonderful! Are you kidding? Great!"

"So. How do feel when you're around guys?"

"Wait a minute," Teri said, before anybody could answer. "Before we get to that, how do *you* feel hanging out with women all the time now?"

"Yeah, you're still pretty new to this," Nicole piped in. Five pairs of eyes turned on me quizzically.

"Um, I was thinking earlier that it's been kind of strange. But I love you guys."

"We know you love us. But how does the whole thing make you feel?" Teri prodded.

Bless these kinds of woman questions! I thought about it. "It makes me feel . . . seen. You know what I mean? There's nothing I have to do or be. I don't have to be sexy and look great all the time. I don't have to be a certain way or accomplish anything for you guys to love me."

Tess snorted. "Accomplishment's a guy thing."

I looked at her in astonishment. Tess was one of the most career-driven women I knew. I patted her knee. "You should listen to yourself more often, you know that?"

"So it's good." Teri was making a statement.

"Of course it's good. Can I get the answer to my question now?"

Alex got up to take her plate to the kitchen. "I work with guys all the time and get along great because I think I am a guy. Always have." She shrugged. "They think so to. I mean, look at me. I'm a dyke."

"I get along with guys because I act a certain way," said Nicole.

"Like how?"

"Well, I don't flirt or act like a girl. I just stay focused on the job and do it."

"Same here," said Tess. "That way, there's no confusion and no problems."

"Even so, sometimes there's still problems," Melissa said, nervously twirling her thick blonde hair with her fingers. "You don't have to do anything." Silence. There was truth to that and we all knew it. All of us, except Alex, had experienced just how easy it was to stir up men's sexual interest without meaning to and how unpleasant the ramifications could be. "I just try to avoid them," she finished, looking pale and uncomfortable.

Teri shrugged. "Unless you're moving something heavy or want to have a baby, who needs 'em?"

I struggled to keep my jaw from dropping at this bald statement. Nobody else at the table even noticed. True, my own thoughts of just moments before had been angling in that general direction . . . sort of. But to hear it put in such a flat, unemotional way was disturbing. How amazing that so many women were so willing to reject half the world's population without a second thought! They would, apparently, be quite happy to live in a world without men. And the way they said what they said made it clear that they believed this point of view was utterly logical and acceptable. Relations between the sexes, in some camps, had got that bad. And everybody I knew just shrugged and accepted it as normal.

In addition to the frequently uncomfortable gender reflections the relationship provided, Tess also mirrored many of my own personal fears and lacks. It stunned me how underneath the seeming confidence and capabilities of an intelligent, middle-aged, early 21st century businesswoman, there could still be a lost little girl trying to figure out the mechanics of the world and her place in it.

"I remember when Papa would come home from work in Madrid," she said, "Bernardo and I were supposed to be all quiet and respectful. And mother would make all this fuss over him. And Papa would stand there in the drawing room in his three-piece suit, drinking his Fino, talking about his day. It all sounded so grand. I remember wondering how he did it."

"Did what?" I asked.

"Did this grown-up thing of making money." She shook her head. "I'm almost 43 and still don't feel grown up. And I sure as hell don't seem to be making much money." Disconsolate, she smoothed her hand across the sheepskin rug we were sitting on in front of the woodstove, rubbing the fur one way, then the other.

"Well, you couldn't have picked a more difficult industry if you'd tried, you know."

"What?" she shrugged. "Trying to promote sustainable building to a bunch of good ol' boys who work in a business that on average lags 45 years behind current technologies?"

"Something like that."

Her face hardened. "The worst part is presenting facts and alternative product ideas over and over again and having other contractors ignore them until some guy tells them the same thing I did. Then it's all 'Wow. What a great idea!'"

"Come on, Tess, what do you expect? Construction is the manliest man world out there. And you're a woman dragging woo-woo ideas about healthy environments and saving planetary resources in the door."

"Right."

"Look on the bright side. You know what they say about failure being the prelude to success and all that."

Tess smiled ruefully. "If that's really the case, I guess I've got it made."

No man could have so completely reflected my own insecurities. And, as much as I hate to admit it, at that point in my life no man could have shown me frailty and worldly uncertainty with no defenses and won my respect. Poor men! Having to be strong all the time, or at least appear to be, was their weary cross to bear. And yet Tess could expose fear and doubt freely, like offerings on an altar, giving me the chance to examine my own weaknesses as I did hers, without judgment. At the same time she also showed me the beautiful parts of myself, the sweetness, the high-minded intentions, the gentility and grace, all of it my own, still unacknowledged, inner bounty.

When the deputy sheriff showed up at my gate asking for "Cate Malone" one day, the unexpected use of my maiden name, Jack's name, filled me with instant dread. I'd managed to shut my stepfather entirely out of my life, ignoring the raving midnight phone calls threatening lawsuits and personal mayhem, changing my number to an unlisted status and tearing up the hysterical demanding notes I received after Mom died. Over the years I'd gotten a few calls from the Virginia State Police saying Jack was in jail for drunk driving, or had been placed in the county mental ward for observation.

"What do you want to do about it, miss?" they would ask.

Feeling a bit like Judas, I always answered, "Nothing." But in truth, what could I do? Invite the viper back into the bosom of my home where it would continue to bite and savage me? Jack had destroyed my mother's life and was now destroying his own. As much as I pitied him, I wasn't going to let him do the same thing to me.

It was hard. He had been the father my mother had chosen for me, and my child's love, my social programming and all my early religious training screamed at me to take responsibility for him. But who would consciously choose pain and violence over peace and happiness? If I had learned anything in my spiritual quest, it was that love was enough unto itself. Distance could not lessen its all-powerful effect. I could send him love from afar and wish him well, and I did so, having utter faith that his soul would receive it and that on some level it would help. It would have to be enough for both of us.

His trail of havoc eventually lead to a Florida trailer park—at least that's the information the Thurston County Sheriff gave me that day, along with the telephone number of the Intensive Care

Unit at the hospital he was in. He had pneumonia, a systemic infection, cirrhosis of the liver, God knows what else and was on life support. "What do you want to do about it, miss?" came the all too familiar question from the attending doctor. "As his only family you have the authority to take him off life support. Please inform us of your wishes."

I'm not proud that my first concern talking to the doctor was not about Jack, but whether I would be responsible for paying his medical bills. I didn't have the monetary resources to take care of his situation, and I was very much afraid of what this would do to my life. *What else is new?* Fear had always been part of my relationship with this man—if not physical fear, then always the fear of what he would take from me: self-esteem, innocence, freedom, choice, money, emotional resources . . . hell, he'd taken my mother and turned her into a shell of a human being with no will of her own. True, she'd let him do it. But still . . .

And now I was being asked to take or spare his life.

It was all rather surreal, and after two days of constant phone calls trying to get a sense of the situation, I still remained unsure whether he could recover and what his quality of life would be if he did. The male doctors covered themselves with vague contradictory answers. It wasn't until I got in touch with the nurse on the midnight watch that second night that everything came clear.

"You want my honest opinion, honey?" came her soft, southern drawl. "Forget what the damn doctors tell you. I wouldn't let a dawg live in the condition he's in."

With clarity came relief. The next morning I gave the order for Jack to be taken off life support. He died within 24 hours, and I felt absolutely nothing except remorse for the misery he had caused himself and others. Then came the decision about what to do with the body. I didn't want his ashes, and I didn't want to have to pay the thousands of dollars it would cost to have him cremated. The alternative, I was told, was to let the State of Florida handle things.

His body would be cremated, and his remains would go to a pauper's grave. Florida being a coastal state, that meant the Atlantic Ocean.

And so Jack was cremated and his ashes placed in an anonymous plastic bag to be shipped out of a Miami terminal on the next commercial freighter leaving the US. Perhaps the captain said a prayer over the remains of all the ashes dumped overboard that morning, and perhaps not. I never knew. But I did find it rather ironically fitting that the waters he so feared, the one place where my mother found her greatest peace and solace every summer, was now his resting place as well.

CHAPTER 20

Yin and yang

In many Eastern traditions, everything from elementary particles to elephants is seen in terms of yin and yang, the feminine and masculine aspects of life, dynamic polar opposites that comprise and balance everything in the natural world.

Yin and yang have very different, very specific qualities. Yang is aligned with the positron force, or the positive. It is masculine in nature and is associated with the color white, Heaven, the sun, and the qualities of action, creation, intellect, stability, hardness and aggressiveness. The electron force, or the negative, is feminine in nature and is associated with the color black, Earth, the moon and the qualities of passivity, receptivity, intuition, fluidity, softness and yielding.

"If being feminine means being passive and yielding, then all I can say is forget it." I strode determinedly down the dirt road. "Like I'm supposed to just sit around eating bonbons while Weyerhaeuser plunders the entire Pacific Northwest?" I gestured at the mess of clearcut forest we were walking through. "This isn't timber harvesting. It's rape."

Tess stopped abruptly, hands shoved deep in her pockets, taking in the devastation, the gouged earth, the shattered tree limbs and swath of stumps extending through a wetland area and far up into the hills. "Hard to believe we're still using the same timber methods that stripped Europe 500 years ago."

"And the masculine is represented by the sun, the heavens and intelligence? Where's the evidence for that?" I raised my arms to the cold gray skies. "Beam me up, Scotty! Please!"

A crackling of underbrush behind me made me turn. Cheyanne bounded out of a mass of salmonberry bushes on the other side of the road, her thick white fur a mess of mud and burrs. She trotted past, pink tongue lolling happily, enormous paws leaving deep imprints in the dirt. "She's not coming in the house like that," Tess squeaked. Another distressed noise came out of her as Master came trotting into view, equally filthy in his smoke-gray elegance. "Neither is he."

We walked for a while, strides evenly matched although I was taller. A sudden puff of frigid air caught us, and Tess zipped up her jacket. "Maybe we don't know what the feminine stuff really has to offer."

"Huh? What do you mean?"

She shrugged. "Men have been at the top of the heap for a long time and society filters everything through a masculine lens. Maybe we just don't get what the Eastern philosophers were trying to say."

"Like what?"

"Like the word passive. Maybe what we think it means now in relation to the feminine is different from what the Taoists meant. Maybe instead of meaning weakness and the inability to act, passivity really means something like stillness."

"As in the opposite of action?" I replied. "As in the realm of pure *being* instead of the world of doing? That makes sense. I think," I added cautiously.

What a different view to my immediate knee-jerk interpretation! I walked along, rather shocked by how automatically I filtered ideas through modern goal-oriented thinking and masculinized definitions. Looked at through the modern lens, the thought of cultivating passivity as a quality was revolting. Looking at it the way Tess had just proposed turned it into something else altogether. *Hmmm.* Was I so indoctrinated into the masculine 'doing' order of things that I misunderstood what the feminine really was, right down to the words describing it? Was I so enchanted with masculine qualities that I had unknowingly become my own opposite, divorcing my feminine self completely right down to the words I could and could not use to describe myself?

No wonder Tess and I both had problems understanding the feminine. All my female friends did! We embodied it and yet none of us knew what it really meant. We'd confused being feminine with cuteness, softness, pink lace, PMS, feminism, right-brain thinking, emotionalism and extinct Earth Goddess religions—all associations that spelled weakness and ineffectiveness. The result? We diminished the feminine to nothing, banishing it from our lives.

The magnitude and subtle ramifications of society's exclusive embrace of masculine qualities and the resulting sexual marginalization of the feminine and the misunderstanding of feminine qualities boggled my mind. How many countless millions of women and men did the same thing I had just done, sidelining feminine descriptive attributes with a contemptuous mental head toss, not even understanding what the words really meant?

"So . . ."

"Brrrr. I'm ready for a fire and some tea."

We hastened our strides as I mulled things over. How could I answer my question about 'What is feminine power?' if I couldn't even properly define or understand the word 'feminine'? How could I grasp the subtleties if I didn't understand the words used to describe it and had a built-in prejudice against the words and the qualities of the feminine they described? And what about the word 'power'? Perhaps I was limiting my definition of that, too? What a thought!

My mind churned. Up until that very moment I'd never once doubted that I knew exactly what the word 'power' meant, which was fundamentally *power over* something, whether it was land or people or even oneself. It meant *control*: a force that was aggressive and overwhelming, an authority that dictated terms and brooked no opposition. Holy Moses! Wasn't that really just the masculine version? Wasn't that just how the men did it? And how could they help but approach power in those terms? They naturally depended on the might of their physical strength; leaned on it almost exclusively in some cultures and extended it into the world of ICBMs, nuclear warheads and hostile takeovers in others. But wielding power in this way was no longer a workable plan. Wasn't this exactly the kind of power that had lead Western culture to the brink of economic and ecological disaster? If we continued to wield power solely in this fashion, it would destroy us.

Yet now both men and women *are pursuing power in the same old way. We know no other.*

The insight and the dire consequences it pointed towards almost stopped me in my tracks. *Holy shit!* I'd spent my entire life defining and seeking power in masculine terms, cheering on the women making headway into the power bastions of Capital Hill and the corporate hierarchy. Suddenly, the fallacy of trying to be equal to men by being the *same as* men hit me with stunning force. *That's just buying into the current game and giving it more credibility!* Sure, getting more women into boardrooms and onto Senate committees was vitally important. But wasn't the insinuation of women in greater numbers throughout the current power structure an approach doomed to failure unless these women were conscious of the need for doing things a different way? Wasn't it just more of the same if they didn't understand what the feminine heart path of connection and sustainability was, value it and stand up for it?

Mind awhirl, I missed the trail off the logging road, and we had to backtrack a couple of hundred yards before entering private lands headed back towards the house. The wolves crashed past through the trees and waist-high ferns following some new scent. I held a wet tree branch aside for Tess to pass. "So, what does being powerful look like to you? In a woman," I added.

"My ex."

That was quick. "Zoe? You're joking."

"She may be a jerk in a lot of ways, but she's powerful. Whenever she wants something, she kicks ass until she gets it. When we wanted to create something together, it happened," Tess sidestepped another low branch. "I miss that."

A twinge of guilt shot through me. *Nothing like being unfavourably compared to an ex-lover to get the insecurity juices flowing.* "In other words, the two of you had a miserable fast ride to money, cool cars and vacation houses," I snapped. In comparison, our life together was a blissful, barely getting-by, slow ride to who knew where.

"I'd like a powerful female mirror in my life again, Cate. There's nothing wrong in that."

No, there wasn't. Hell, I was ready to stand in line for the same thing. But what was a powerful woman supposed to look like? Margaret Thatcher? Hillary Clinton? Was it the Supermom kissing skinned knees and making school costumes after closing the merger at the martini lunch, popping Prozac the whole way? Or was it the New Woman? A combination of money, worldly success and blatant sexuality, the New Woman was a female who stomped the competition in the boardroom by day and strapped her man (or woman) to the bedposts by night. Was this Tess's idea of feminine power? The ultimate female action hero depicted in cartoons and movie characters like Ripley, Evelyn Salt, Hannah and Trinity? Powerful, big-breasted, gun-totin' babes who didn't take shit from any man, who took what they wanted, shaped the world as they saw fit, made love until dawn and to hell with everything else?

Wasn't this just a guy with a vagina?

Walking through the chill afternoon, I felt uneasy. It might be satisfying sitting in the movie theater watching the gals kick ass for a change, but in light of my current thoughts something told me this was not our next best evolutionary step as a species. For the life of me, however, I just couldn't see what the alternative could be.

PART X

❀ ❀ ❀

THE VAGABOND
(2008– 2010)

CHAPTER 21

Partings

For the first time in years, I stared in a mirror, really taking in my reflection. Hair pulled back, dressed in typical Northwest attire, which meant dark Patagonia top and jeans, I looked about as attractive as a stump. *Just wider.* My heart sank further. Where was the wild, incandescent beauty I'd seen shining through this same face and body so many years of nights ago in a North Georgia cabin? *Where did that woman go?*

She was buried under the weight of years and wine and complacency; buried under the stress of mortgages, bills and trying to make money happen; exhausted from running a marketing and Internet publishing business; diminished by spiritual goals that left the body behind; lost, rotating her life around another woman's face.

Shattered by change.

"Sweetheart, I still love you. I'm just not in love with you anymore." Tess's eyes were filled with concern.

"Gee, that's a consolation," I snapped. "I still can't believe you fell for her. What on God's Earth is the attraction?"

Her face grew even more desolate. "I'm not sure I can explain it," she said, voice trailing off quietly.

"Try."

"I don't want to hurt you."

Could it possibly hurt worse than it already did? I didn't think so. "Tell me."

"She . . . she's womanly. She's all woman." She bit her lip. "And you're just . . . not that anymore."

What? The fact that I'd gained 50 pounds during the 11 years of our relationship and forgotten what a tube of mascara looked like made me less womanly? "I thought our relationship wasn't about that," I said flatly.

"It isn't . . . hasn't been. But . . ."

"But?"

"I think I want something more."

"Well. Thanks for the heads-up."

The plane banked over the ocean on its final approach to the Lima airport. Steep cliffs formed a wall of white where the modern city met the sea, stretching far to the south. Instructions in Spanish flowed from the cockpit, undecipherable. I leaned my forehead against the Plexiglas window, dazed from the blur of endings that had marked the month of February 2008.

Despite the declining real estate market, the property Tess and I owned sold in three days for a full price cash offer. Heart and hearth gone, I folded my publishing business and handed the Internet newsletter I'd started when I was doing marketing for the film-makers of the international hit indie movie *What the Bleep Do We Know!?* back to film creator Will Arntz to manage. It deserved passion and enthusiasm and I had none. With regret and relief I said goodbye to all the writers at my other online publication, *The Global Intelligencer,* and tucked it away into cyberspace dreamtime. By mid-February I had sold or given away pretty much everything

I owned.

I glanced down. Two hundred feet below the wing a mélange of tarp-and-tin-covered shacks ran together in a never-ending bird's eye view of poverty. Children scurried along the dusty slum streets, waving as the plane's shadow passed overhead. Flying into Peru, I felt such a mixed bag of emotions it was impossible to sort it all out. Part of me was hooked so deeply to my old life it seemed impossible this was happening. A wiser part of me than my emotions agreed with Tess that it was time to move on. But pain and anger over the abrupt ending of what I had thought was a life-long partnership still dominated my life.

I was also afraid to be alone again—a realization which pissed me off even more.

Starting life all over again was not an unusual hand to be dealt a woman in her 50s. Many men left their aging wives during that insecure time of life, moving backwards towards their youth, trying to recapture it through the embrace of a younger woman. But the fact that the cards had been delivered by my best friend looking astray rather than a man confused and disappointed me. Somehow I had expected more of a woman.

CHAPTER 22

Ceremony

I took the cup filled almost to the brim with viscous dark liquid from his steady brown hand. For a moment I stared at the impenetrable brew, then raised the cup to my lips, kissed it and drank. The gag reflex was immediate and violent. Clapping one hand over my mouth, eyes watering, I swallowed and handed the cup back to Cush. He nodded approvingly, his mane of long black hair swinging, and moved back to the altar to pour another cup from the plastic Coca Cola litre bottle for the next person. At least I hadn't spewed the liquid all over his kidskin ceremonial pants.

The high Andes night was cold, and I squirmed more deeply into my earth tone alpaca blankets. Fifteen of us sat in a silent circle around the central altar, a low wooden table littered with feathers and rattles, a drum, pouches of tobacco and various bottles of Ayahuasca. One large candle guttered in the center, casting shadows around the circular, mud-plastered room. Outside a goat bleated. The mountain winds prowled, seeking entry under the red clay tiles of the roof. Soon the medicine brew I had just drunk would begin a similar assault, seeking entry into the hidden corners of my mind and body. What would it reveal?

The last person was served, and Cush sat back down on his

sheepskin-covered seat. Then he leaned forward, raised a fan of condor feathers and waved away the candle's light. A timeless half hour or so passed and the electric visuals Ayahuasca was so famous for started—faint phosphorescent green and violet buzzing squiggles and geometric forms at the peripheries of my vision. They increased, and as they did, I felt an unpleasant heaviness growing in my body: a leaden torpor mixed with nausea that infiltrated every cell. I fought against it, pulling up my energy to push back the building weight. For a short time it lifted. But it wasn't long before the heaviness returned and with it a sense of mind-numbing hopelessness.

Humming filled the room, then an ancient breathy chanted song. Rattles crisped the air, their sound writhing away from predictable rhythm. The strange visuals increased. The psychic dead indifference inside me increased, so crushing I longed for the joy of mere depression. I fought against the plant medicine, but her grip was relentless. Soon even the longing for a reprieve was too much effort. The nausea increased. The weight increased, and I dissolved under their combined forces like a minnow squashed beneath a boulder.

I am never ever ever doing this shit ever again oh god just get me through this . . .

Nothing existed but this waking rigor mortis and finally I surrendered to it. Within moments, electrifying recognition shot through me. I was experiencing my mother's mother's life at the psychic level! This was the deadly depression that had filled Ruth, paralyzing her with Parkinson's disease, the genetic inheritance that squeezed the juice from her life and limbs; the dead weight she had passed on to my mother, squeezing the life from *her* heart.

This was the dead zone that had been passed on to me.

I dived into the blasted space, the heritage of my feminine ancestors, back through the chain of time. Here lay soullessness—the rotting devastation of women left in dungeons, rats gnawing their flesh, the psychic imprint of thousands of years of slavery and abuse without hope of release; the lost feminine stomped into a bloody heap with no way out.

With all my heart I reached out to the women who had come before me, reached back through time and shimmering double helix DNA spirals, gathering, gathering, gathering . . . until all their threads were woven together. And then I released them. Seen. Heard. Felt. Experienced. Loved. They disappeared. The weight lifted from my body. A drumbeat echoed somewhere in a vast distance. The geometric forms danced. My heart opened. I had carried this ancient cancer in my cells never knowing it was there, quietly eating away my light. Now it was gone.

For a long time I sat, bathed in sweetness. Then a vision coalesced—the first of my journey. I was two years old, kneeling in a narrow dark hallway. My mother and a man were yelling at each other, their words red lightning striking all around me, their anger acid rain upon my skin. Couldn't they see what they were doing?! My little hands reached out, pleading with them to stop. But they raged on. The walls of the vision dissolved around me and I was tossed into a sea of children's faces, all of them pleading to be released from the ocean of poison adults poured upon them like blood from the skies.

I reached out to protect the children. Yet even as I did, I was spun into a kaleidoscope of light, hurled through universes, back and back in time to the very Beginning before there was Light. I watched all of Creation being born, watched it die and again be reborn. And then all was darkness and quiet.

I had never really thought about going to Peru. Working with plant medicine had never been high on my list of things to do either. But my close friend, Elena, had worked with Ayahuasca and other psychotropic plants for decades. She had close relationships with several indigenous shamans in Peru and, just when Tess and I broke up, was organizing a two-week trip for women friends who wanted to travel there for spiritual insight and healing. After the sale of our property, both of us had the money to go. And after our emotionally wrenching yet amicable breakup, I definitely needed healing—and on more than one front.

Not only was I struggling with my emotions about Tess, I was also struggling with a very real spiritual dilemma. Twenty-five years of meditation had introduced me to more of my essential spiritual nature and a state of universal oneness that contained no personal identity. Sitting with my eyes closed in this non-egoic blissful and peaceful state was infinitely preferable to my 'ordinary' personality—a consciousness still very much subject to the unpleasant slings and arrows of worldly fortune.

It wasn't the bliss that was problematic. Hardly! It was the assumption that came with it that this different state of consciousness, which I couldn't help but call 'heavenly,' was *better* than the physical world I lived in. Which was an easy assessment to make considering how miserable humanity (including me) had made the world emotionally and physically. How tempting to go off and become a hermit meditating in a cave experiencing nothing but spiritual nirvana! No wonder most patriarchal religions placed so much emphasis on the Hereafter and earning a place in Heaven through living a 'good' life. Shucking this mortal coil and sailing off into the sky to enter the Kingdom of God for all Eternity was quite enticing!

Bottom line, I was deeply uncertain about the value of the world and my continued place in it. Never mind Tess had spent much of the 15 years of our friendship pointing out to me over and over again: "If you spent half as much time focused on *creating* a beautiful world as you spend focused on *transcending* this world, maybe you'd end up with both."

Intellectually, I agreed with her. I knew the Earth was spirit-made flesh. But somewhere deep down inside I just couldn't quite believe that the world, with all its pain and suffering, was as divine as the non-physical dimension from which it flowed. And most of my friends held the same unconscious bias. We all wanted to float in an endless sea of Universal Bliss, not struggle to be 'good' people, paying our bills and battling cellulite. There was even a sardonic term for those of us thus obsessed: 'whales in space' pretty much said it all.

Yes, spirit and flesh were one. But believing something intellectually doesn't mean you live it as a truth. There were many miles to go before I would even begin to make ready the temple where Earth and Heaven could finally consciously meet.

Seven women were making the journey, intrepid inner explorers guided by Rossa, a woman shaman from the heart of Peru's Amazon jungles. All but one of the explorers I knew already. The day after our first ceremony with her friend, the shaman Cush, at his compound outside of Cusco, we took a small charter bus over the Andes to our next stop, the plains of Nazca. It took 19 hours—a journey filled with bad roads and fleeting images of impoverished villages, garbage, grazing Alpacas and dizzying vistas off the sides of mountains. Dropping from 17,000 feet down to sea level, we spent a brief, exhausted night in a hotel in the city, then prepared for our next ceremony.

"How far out of Nazca do they live?" Elena struggled to keep her blonde hair in some semblance of order as hot air from the open taxi windows blasted us.

"Not far," said Rossa, uncommunicatively.

The wasteland of the Nazca plains fled past the windows. "How long have you been working with the witches?" Sara asked curiously.

"Oh, many, many years now. Since I was a little girl." Rossa turned and said something to the driver in Spanish, who nodded. "They have joined me in many ceremonies."

We turned onto a dirt road amidst an ocean of dust headed towards barren mountains. At the end of the road several open-sided thatched-roof shelters dotted the landscape. Elena looked around, puzzled. She had been anxious about meeting Rossa's witch mentors, taking special care dressing that afternoon, trying on several different outfits before settling on a colorful Mexican skirt with an off-the-shoulder top.

The second taxi with the rest of the group, including Rossa's German husband/apprentice, Guido, pulled up in a flurry of noise and more dust. As soon as we were all together, Rossa poured each of us a very small drink of diluted Huachuma, a psychotropic cactus used in ceremonies throughout the Andes region. The drivers talked and smoked, watching the gringo women make faces over what was a mild concoction compared to Ayahuasca. As soon as the last of us had drunk, we trooped single file towards the nearest shelter.

The first witch, seated in the middle of a pit, was very old, very desiccated and exceedingly dead. Muffled words of surprise and nervousness circulated through the group. Elena couldn't believe her eyes. "There are 11 witches buried here," said Rossa. "Each one has special gifts and medicine. I work with three only. I want you to find the one you feel pulled to be with and sit with her."

I burst out laughing. Elena eyed me disapprovingly, surprised by my rudeness. I gestured towards the mummified skeleton, skull exposed, one bony arm laid across what was once her lap. "She's funny," I burst out in explanation. "She makes me laugh."

Rossa smiled. "Very good. She is known for her sense of humor, that one."

The gang moved on, and, content to remain where I was, I settled down in the shade to keep the skeleton with the funny bone company. The group's voices quickly faded, and soon all I could hear was the overhead rustling of thatch being whipped by the wind. It sounded like the roof was filled with an army of marching mice. Amused by the image, I leaned against a sand-scoured post and opened up to my surroundings. Before long, I had fallen into a light trance.

It's odd using that word. We think of trances as spellbinding states that capture us, narrowing our vision. Yet in the hours that passed that afternoon, just the opposite occurred. I was awake to every nuance of the world around me—the wind, the grit beneath me, the wood against my back, the mountains and my strange companion. My life in the States with all its busy-ness and phones, deadlines, emails and self-important work seemed much more trance-inducing than this wide open space.

I imagined the witch cackling her approval and turned towards her bones. The semi-toothless jaws remained fixed in what might have been a grin. I gave the skeleton a happy wink, and as I turned back towards the mountains, something caught my eye. An enormous jumble of rocks on the face of one dry mountain subtly shifted and eddied, slowly morphing into an image of a woman in a fringed ceremonial dress. Arms outstretched like wings, in her hands she clutched condor feathers. Head bent in concentration, she appeared to be dancing upon the mountain and yet, somehow, moving *within* the mountain at the same time.

It was my witch companion.

I gazed, delighted by her strong, flowing movements. Black hair cascading around her head, skirts flying, she was ecstatic in her elements of sky and dusty earth. Alive *and* dead, she was part of these mountains, part of this world, and yet not of this world in either capacity. I glanced back at the pit. The skeleton was still there. What a short journey from visceral womanhood to a clutch of wind-scoured bones in a shallow grave!

You are missing most of your journey paying attention to

unimportant things.

It was a sharp, if not unkind, comment—a ghostly reminder that my own grave was waiting. I closed my eyes, letting my senses drift. Not to be denied, the Condor Woman of the Mountain (or so I had dubbed her) whirled into my mind's eye. Pointing a feather directly at me, she tossed her head, dark eyes piercing. *You will face your greatest fear here.* Having delivered her brief message, she vanished in a swirl of black hair and feathered regalia, her laughter the last echo in my mind.

The antiquated bus rattled and squeaked, jouncing through the interminable potholes. I gripped the rusty window ledge with one hand, the soiled back of the seat in front of me with the other. Window curtains limply brushed my knuckles at each jolt. We'd been crawling down the dark rutted dirt road for hours. At least it seemed like it. Impervious to distance and discomfort, Rossa and Guido chatted happily with Benito, our driver.

Finally, the dull beams of the bus's headlamps illuminated a wide spot in the road bounded by a high chain-link fence. The vehicle ground to a halt, and the doors noisily ratcheted open. Several men materialized from the darkness, greeting Rossa and Guido as they descended the stairs.

Cahauchi was one of the most sacred sites in Peru. The first pyramid ever discovered in the country, it had been designed and built by the Nasca peoples around 150 AD. Constructed in Mayan fashion, with stepped sides and multiple entrances, the pyramid and ceremonial compound were part of a government-sponsored archaeological dig and closed to the public. But in the desert plains, as in the Andes and the Amazon, locals respected and feared the shamans with their ancient magic far more than the government. Trained in plant medicine from childhood by her father, Don Augustine Rivas, the unrivalled don of Peru's Amazonian shamans, Rossa was well known to guards at sacred sites throughout the country. For her, there was no such thing as a locked gate.

The pyramid was a massive hulking black shadow in the moonless night. Subdued by our surroundings, we stumbled across the ancient paving of the outer courtyard carrying our ceremonial gear to the fire pit. Guido quickly started a fire with the wood that had been prepared for our arrival. The rest of us nervously laid our blankets in a circle around the blossoming flames, huddling close for warmth, the light doing little to illuminate the thick darkness around us.

"This place is most sacred to our people and the guardian spirits," Rossa intoned solemnly as Guido handed out small plastic bags. "If you need to shit or puke, do it in the bags. Do NOT do it in the temple grounds. Understand?"

We all nodded. Sara and Alice examined their bags, obviously wondering if it would be possible to deposit bodily fluids safely into their interiors while reeling from the Ayahuasca. *Better not to think about it.* I unfolded several bags and placed them under my blankets close at hand.

Rossa sang songs invoking the spirits as Guido kept time with drum and rattles. Then she hauled out the ubiquitous plastic Coke litre bottle filled with dark liquid. My body recoiled viewing the container, and I turned my eyes away as she poured for the first person. Instead, I placed my focus on the dark mystery of the pyramid, recalling the message of the Condor Woman. Participating in ancient medicine rites tapping into the spirit realms was a scary enough process. Did this place in some way contain my greatest fear? And did I even want to know what that was?

When my turn came, I got the contents down. Gagging, I wiped my lips on a tissue. *Anybody who thinks this stuff is recreational has obviously never done it.* Trying to ignore the taste in my mouth, I poked around making sure I knew where my puke bags were, then settled down and closed my eyes. It didn't take long. Cahauchi had been a place of ceremony for almost 2,000 years. The vibe was waiting, and the spirits were alive and well. I heard the Condor Woman's laughter in the distance and anticipated her presence. Surely she had done her magic here many times through the long years of her life? But instead of her dancing figure, the first being that tore into my visual field was male, dark-skinned and fierce. A wizened figure lunging at me out of the shadows, he gestured violently for me to *GO AWAY*!

Body shaking with nausea from the brew, going away was not an option. Another spirit arrived. Then another. Soon dozens of threatening figures gesturing with rattles and other implements filled my visual field. Several thrust shrunken heads at me— ghastly things dangling from corded rope, black hair still long and flowing, eyes sunken, lips pinned shut with thorns. Unexpectedly unafraid, I laughed, delighted by the show. I even encouraged the spirits to come closer and do their worst. For a time, the frenzy increased. Then the first spirit reappeared, his crazed grimace melting into a welcome smile. The ancient ancestors gathered around me, now peacefully nodding and gesturing. What did they want me to do?

Ordinarily, you do not move out of a ceremonial circle unless the latrine calls or until the shaman says the ceremony is over. Except for the shaman who is responsible for clearing any negative energies out of participants by using sacred chants, songs, drums and rattles, Ayahuasca ceremonies are also silent affairs. Sometimes tobacco, Ayahuasca's sacred ally plant, is used. Smoke is blown into the participant's face and around their body or blasted from the shaman's mouth on top of their heads when something is really stuck—that, along with doses of sweet Florida water sprayed out of the shaman's mouth on the person's body.

As the ghostly figures surrounded me, Rossa got up from the other side of the fire and came over. Crouching down, she set her lips close to my ear. "They are inviting you into the temple. You may go to one of the entrances and sit there with the spirits if you want to."

I nodded and, with her assistance, got unsteadily to my feet. Wrapped in my blanket, accompanied by my ghostly companions, I carefully made my way towards the high bottom step of the pyramid. A stygian entry loomed before me in the structure's side. I crawled up onto the step, sitting down with my back to the door, facing the fire and my more Earthly friends.

My physical response, such as it was, seemed enough to satisfy the temple occupants. They swarmed around me and more spirits hovered around the fire, blessing the white women's respectful ceremonial presence in their world. The joining of the Eagle of the North with the Condor of the South had been officially approved. Eventually the spirits re-entered the pyramid where I dared not follow. I was left with the silence of the night, broken only by the crackling of the flames and Rossa's low humming.

It was as if I'd always been seated there. Indeed, as I looked towards the fire with its huddle of blanket-wrapped women, I knew this moment had been alive since time began. This ancient ceremony done in modern times was simply rejoining us with the elements and the spirits, reawakening us to our participation in what was, and always had been, the living consciousness of the world. We were part of life's dance whether we knew it or not. Drinking from the root of the vine harvested from the navel of the planet, our modern make-believe superiority was stripped away. Here, we joined the ongoing efforts of the Awake Ones—shamans of all lineages and ages—who were holding the door open to vibrant life, while billions slept in a deadly inanimate dream of their own making.

Rossa quietly offered another cup to those who wanted it.

Although I was in a good space and the idea of moving, let alone drinking another cup, was repugnant, I started to rise. It was my nature to always do more, pushing the envelope.

Or was it?

As I started to get up, I felt a cool hand pressed firmly against my forehead. *No.* I sank back onto the hard stone, puzzled. The pressure of the hand remained palpable. *Just be with me, daughter.* It was Ayahuasca herself communing with me, teaching me in words for the very first time. *Just be yourself and know it is enough.* The tone of the message was gentle yet firm. *Let the beauty of who you are draw the things that are equal to you into your life. You need not chase anything, especially me.*

And so I simply sat, inhaling and exhaling, watching the stars. I was a human being and that was enough—always had been enough. I had simply forgotten. When the time came to leave, I walked easily back to the bus, helping Elena who was moving with difficulty. And then there was the long trip back to Nazca. I sat, eyes closed, rocking with the motion of the bus, listening to its deep-throated growls as Benito shifted gears. Soon the obvious truth about the bus became . . . obvious.

Held together with wire, paint, rust and love, like everything else in the universe the bus had its own living consciousness and purpose. How amazing I had not seen before that the bus was a living being! My thoughts flashed to the Shuar shaman, Ipupiara, and his delight about communing with a Manhattan skyscraper. His words, "Your people are in much worse trouble than I thought if they don't know they breathe life into their creations," rang clearly in my mind. My earlier frustration with the bus and the long drive made me laugh.

Everything is irritating when you're dead to the world.

It was so obvious that the bus loved Benito. It eagerly responded to him, doing everything it could with its aging body to accommodate his needs. My heart poured out its joy, knowing I was being tenderly carried within the body of a living being created by man.

So this is how creation extends itself into eternity.

Light was dawning on the desert horizon as we got to our hotel. At the bus door I turned to Benito. "He loves you very much, your growly bus." I patted the dashboard. His face lit up at my words, obviously delighted his metal child had been acknowledged. "Si, Señora, si!!" He stroked the steering column. "We work together much. Long time. He very good friend."

I floated up the stairs to my room, happily wrapped in the discovery that it was impossible to be alone in an alive and feeling world.

Our last night in the jungle at Don Augustine's camp on the banks of the Amazon River was supposed to be a dinner celebration. But at breakfast that morning, the Don invited us to do a second Ayahuasca ceremony with him. All of us were tired from the first one the night before, and none of us relished the idea of drinking the noxious brew two nights in a row. But when the Don wanted something, he got it.

"Papa says you are strong women." Rossa smiled. "He likes you and wants to honor you."

Elena shrugged. "Darlin', it's what we came for!"

Despite a general unease, we prepared for the night's session, slathering our bodies with boa grease, a vile-smelling unguent Guido had made from a boa constrictor he killed that was supposed to keep away evil spirits. Topping the grease with mosquito repellant, we slid into our reeking long-sleeved shirts, pants and socks—the only things keeping us from being eaten alive by the mosquitoes. Despite the intense heat, I buttoned my shirt to the neck. Tying a red kerchief around my hair to keep the insects out of it, I followed the rest of my friends into the large ceremonial room. Skirting Don Augustine's enormous drum, I took my place on one of the built-in benches that ran around the periphery of the room.

The slatted wooden walls opened onto the river and the bugs flew in and out. Thick wooden doors opened onto a ramp facing east to the river and another ramp going out the opposite side to the pit latrines set in the decking, eight feet above the ground. The other two sets of opposing doors opened into our sleeping quarters and the dining area and kitchen with its huge fire pit lined with adobe bricks. Outside there was mud, water, thick jungle and darkness. Rossa went through her safety spiel a second time.

"Do not leave the house. Do not fall off the ramps. Do not walk in the jungle. There are snakes, poisonous frogs, alligators and jaguars out there at night. And worse things."

We looked at each other nervously. What could be worse?

As per the Don's translated instructions, we were each to drink two cups that night. *Urk.* Downing a raw toad mixed in a blender would be easier. But none of us shamed ourselves as we stood before the Don's altar filled with his drums, flutes, pipes, rattles, feathers, tobacco, carved wood cups and plastic Coke bottle of brew.

From the start, the whole ceremony felt weird. An incessant throbbing of drums from the village downriver filled the night. My journey began with one repeating image of black-tipped arrows and spears raining down on the camp from the sky. At one point what sounded like a hail of pebbles hit the corrugated metal roof and something solid bounced off the back wall with a sharp crack. I could feel dark energies pouring towards us. I opened my eyes and looked around the darkened room. Don Augustine was humming one of his oddly inharmonious tunes. My friends were quietly slumped in various positions on their benches, attention folded inwards. With a groan, Elena staggered up to go to the latrines. Wordlessly, Tess joined her. Bent double, they helped each other out the back doors.

Everything *looked* okay. Uneasily, I closed my eyes. A few minutes later a walkie-talkie crackled shockingly to life. My eyes flew open. Don Augustine grabbed the walkie-talkie and replied rapidly in Spanish. Then he got up and left the room—an unheard-of action for the shaman conducting a ceremony. Marlene, his wife and ceremonial partner, ran out after him. Rossa was already headed out the back doors to get Tess and Elena out of the latrines. A minute later she was hauling them bodily through the entry, wrestling them, protesting, to their seats. Guido closed the second set of double doors behind them, slamming a heavy hewn log down across them as barricade.

The walkie-talkie spat urgent men's voices into the air somewhere close by. Rossa disappeared, returning almost instantly with two large plastic buckets. She banged them down in front of Tess and Elena, her meaning clear. Muffled gunfire exploded in the near distance. "The ceremony is over," said Rossa in a calm voice.

No shit.

"Those of you who can, help us take your things and put them in the private rooms in the sleeping area. Leave no trace of your things visible."

With a general confused muttering, the women staggered to their feet, shuffling slowly into the sleeping room. Rossa and Guido were already hurling backpacks, shoes and clothing into the two windowless plywood-framed rooms that passed for private accommodations. Completely sober, I joined them in the hurried move as the rest of the group stood around or sank on rubber legs to the floor.

"You all will sleep in these two rooms tonight," Rossa commanded.

I helped drag extra mattresses into the rooms, leaving them sheet-less on the floor beside the double bed in each stuffy cubicle.

"What's going on?" I whispered urgently into Rossa's ear. She looked around to make sure no one else was nearby and leaned in, her breath hot on my ear.

"A terrorist group has stirred up the men in the village downriver to come and kill all the American women in our camp to start an international incident."

"What?" Fear slammed through my body. I looked into Rossa's dark worried eyes. This was no joke.

"Papa's gone in the boat to see if he can talk to them. He's well respected here." She turned away as Guido rushed up. I helped Elena off the floor and along with her, Tess and Danielle, allowed myself to be herded into the little 12 by 12 plywood box. Danielle sank onto the mattress beside the bed. Elena careered to the back wall to puke in a bucket. I went to the door with Rossa. "Lock it!" she hissed.

"Get me a gun, Rossa. I know how to use it." Her eyes widened in surprise.

"I don't have one," she said flatly.

"How about a machete?"

She looked at me, assessing. "I'll try. Now lock the door." She shut it in my face. Tess joined Elena at the back wall.

"I've gotta go," she groaned.

"Just do it in one of the buckets," I whispered.

"But it's gross. I'll stink up the place."

"No one cares. *Trust me.*"

Terror sucked me into its eddy. The drums downriver beat louder, relentless and violent. The camp dogs started barking, and another shot rang out. *This can't be happening. Should I tell the others?* Danielle was flat out on the mattress. Elena and Tess were crouched against the wall, fixated on their buckets, unaware of externals. No sense scaring them as well. To keep my mind from going berserk, I looked around for potential escape routes. There was nothing but the bed and bare plywood stretching eight feet up to the rafters. Could I get up there somehow? *People rarely look up.*

I stood on the bed and reached past the mosquito netting. Yes, I could shinny up the bedposts on the outside of the netting and get to the top of the walls. From there, I could get into the shadowy rafters. Escape planned and nothing else to think about, my fertile Ayahuaska-soaked imagination kicked into gear.

I heard the shouting and gunfire, the sharp clang of machetes and the heavy-booted feet across the floor, the pounding on the flimsy door. I saw my helpless friends, faces shocked and confused. I saw the smashing of the door, saw the men on top of them, tearing their clothes off, ripping them with knives even as they plunged their exposed members into their terrified flesh. Screaming, blood and semen, terror, rage and lust filled the room. I watched Tess twisting in her death throes beneath a man's fetid body. *My love!* I closed my eyes.

My eyes were already closed. Somebody threw up. From the mattress came snores. *At least she can sleep.* Caught in a ridiculous C-grade movie plot of jungle drums and terrorist agendas, I was verging on quiet hysteria. But this wasn't a movie. There had been a similar incident only last year—something to do with nuns in Venezuela. *Shit.* Venezuela was closer to us than Iquitos at this point on the Amazon.

I wracked my brains for more information, cursing my stupidity for not reading up on the international situation before coming to a Third World country. I double-cursed allowing myself to be locked in a plywood coffin, weaponless, with a bunch of helpless women. Again. *This has happened before this has happened before this has happened before* my mind chanted insanely as a kaleidoscope of shattering images rushed past: huddled sobbing women hiding, awaiting their fate in huts, locked barns and caves, castles and moldy basements—and always the same violent ending.

A low whistle sounded in the pulsing dark outside. Another

answered from the other side of the building. Friend or foe? The dogs burst into another frenzy of barking. Could it get more tense? My mind spun through more unwanted images. An NPR story of an Afghan woman fed pieces of her own breasts and vagina as they were slowly carved off her body rose, unwanted, from memory. *Oh God, will this never end? Will men never get past savagery? I can't leave my friends to die like that!*

In that moment, I vowed to stay with them. *Fuck the rafters.* I would fight. And if we could not win, what then? If I could capture a knife, was I brave enough to give Tess the mercy of a slit throat? Finished at last with her bucket, she crawled up on the bed next to me. I longed to reach for her and hold her close. But that part of us was over.

And then the drums stopped.

This was never a good sign in the movies. Had Don Augustine's mission failed or succeeded? I strained to hear, listening for shouts and caught the sound of a boat motor far downstream, slowly approaching. Then another. And another. *Oh my God this is it. They are coming. Where's your spirituality now, Cate?* I lay still, heart hammering, as the boats chugged closer to our landing. The dogs went berserk. And then the sounds faded: the blessed Doppler effect assuring me of continued safety and life.

And so the night went. The drums started again. The drums stopped. Boats came and went. Frogs bellowed. The dogs barked.

When the first cock crowed, I about fainted with relief. As grayness crept through the cracks in the plywood sheeting, Danielle woke up, unlocked the door and stumbled unthinkingly off to her own bed. I hurried out and knocked on the door to the other tiny room. A few moments later, Guido sleepily opened the door.

"More orange juice please."

Dana passed the pitcher down the long trestle table. I plucked another squat banana from a nearby basket. Everyone's eyes were wide from listening to my story, Rossa's most of all. "But I didn't say it was a terrorist attack," she protested.

"What did you tell me then?" I asked, exasperated.

"I said the camp was under attack by bandits and that Papa had gone to help fight them off."

"Oh." I sat back, nonplussed—as if armed bandits weren't bad enough. "But I plainly heard . . ."

"You heard what Aya wanted you to hear," Elena interrupted.

Was that possible? "But I was completely sober," I protested, turning back to Rossa. "Is that possible?"

She shrugged, her long black hair sliding across her shoulders. "With Ayahuasca anything is possible. Maybe your ears weren't sober." The table erupted in laughter.

"I kept seeing black fire raining down on us from the sky," said Tess. I recalled the black spears and arrows coming down on the camp and mentioned my early vision.

"And the drums," Dana shivered. "They totally freaked me out."

Rossa reached for another thick slice of bread. "It was the last night of the festival driving out the demons."

"What??" A veritable chorus sounded around the table.

"Every year, there is a weeklong festival in the village downriver. The last night they drum all night, driving the demons and evil spirits out of the village into the jungle."

"Right to our camp," muttered Elena.

Rossa nodded, buttering her bread. "The light draws the dark." We all munched, thoughtful. I was still riding the high of just being alive.

"Cate!" I looked down the table at Danielle's excited face. "Didn't the Nazca witch tell you you'd be facing your greatest fear here in Peru?" I paused, half-eaten banana in hand, the hair rising on my arms despite the muggy heat of the jungle dawn. *Oh my.* Realization dawned.

The shaman's journey didn't scare me. I was a long way from the young woman in the north Georgia woods having her first out-of-body experiences. Nothing in the spirit realms bothered me anymore. My deepest fear was physical—the gut-level terror of being attacked with violence and hatred, helplessly raped and killed.

I looked at the rest of my orangey-ripe banana, skin half off the fruit, and set it down on my plate. Suddenly I wasn't hungry. Seeing my reaction, everybody left me to my thoughts as food and conversation flowed happily around me. A scarlet and lime-green Macaw flew into the branches of a tree outside. Everybody else stood up to get a closer look, exclaiming at its beauty. But I was captivated by the gift Ayahuasca had given me: awareness of the age-old terror that lived inside me as a silent spark just waiting for the right circumstances to ignite.

I could live in a nice house and marry a nice man and have a career in my nice clean world and pretend this fear and the reasons for it didn't exist. Aside from a few 'thank God that's not me' moments watching the evening news, I could believe everything was fine. But now I knew better. All the pretenses had been stripped away.

Living in modern America provided the *illusion* of safety and well-being. But now I'd glimpsed what those statistical women on the news all over the world had endured. I had felt the sickening immanence of certain violation and death. Whether it happened on a jogging trail in Kansas City, a bedroom in LA or a remote village in Iran made no difference. The experience was the same.

And in that moment I realized it was no longer okay that this horror existed. Even if the violence directed at women wasn't happening to me, it was no longer acceptable. The law of universal Oneness dictated that what happened to every woman happened to me. If I didn't embrace the existence of the violence and try to expose it I was simply hiding my head in the sand. If I didn't try to do something about it, I was condemning myself—I was condemning all women—to simply more of the same.

Mankind had to wake up. Womankind had to somehow show the way. If we did not, the nightmare on my world would never end.

CHAPTER 23

Paradise

When my friends left Iquitos to go back to the States, I remained in Peru. This was the true moment of parting, and as I watched Tess walk across the tarmac to board the little plane bound for Lima, I was filled with sorrow, excitement and loneliness, all mixed into one bag called 'Cate.'

I had no idea what I was doing, where I was going or what I was looking for. For several months I simply traveled, poking around South and Central America, learning Spanish and local customs as I went. Far from being the barbaric, terrorist-ridden countries that all the propaganda and fear mongering spread by the media back in the States would have them be, I found the people incredibly genteel, happy and polite wherever I went.

Eventually, I settled in a rustic little house overlooking the ocean a few miles south of the west coast beach town of Dominical in Costa Rica. A 1960s' hideout for drug smugglers, bandits, bigamists and hippies, by 2008 the tiny village was almost civilized with its restaurants, surf shops, yoga studio and numerous real estate offices. But the pace of Dominical was slow—slow as the sloth that hung upside down from the tree outside my bedroom window. And the jungle . . . could any words or pictures capture a tropical rainforest?

Flowers dripped from every branch, as vibrant and colorful as the hundreds of hand-dyed sarongs snapping on the vendor's clotheslines strung between the coconut palms down at the beach. Fruits hung heavy for the picking. The oxygen-rich air held the scent of wild orchids. Howler monkeys screamed the dawn awake. Scarlet macaws, green parrots, chattering packs of parakeets and Toucans, astonishing with their enormous mahogany, tangerine and lime beaks, filled the trees and skies with color and sound. Jungle life was the world on steroids. It stunned me on a daily basis to realize this paradise had been here my entire life waiting for me and that I had been oblivious to what it could offer. Peace, wildness and wonder were just the beginning of its many gifts.

Costa Rica's national culture was Nature's beauty and I immersed myself in it. I swam, walked on vast empty beaches, discovered fruit that actually tasted like fruit, reintroduced myself to aloneness and got used to slow time. I was 57, had no job, no career, no partner, no lover, no friends within 5,000 miles, no family, no pets, no mortgage, no furniture, no television, no radio, no iPod and no country. Even the language was not my own. I was as successfully stripped of personal trappings and distractions as a person with a duffle bag, a laptop in a backpack and a four-wheel drive vehicle could get. What I would gain from this journey was uncertain. But I fervently prayed it would be a renewed and open heart.

If there was ever a nation that could help a woman find her internal compass, it was this one. The first of 14 nations in the world to formally abolish its military, Costa Rica had the social heart to match its physical beauty. The government directed all the financial resources formerly spent on its armed forces to social programs. As a result, the country had some of the best healthcare services in the world, high educational standards and a 96% literacy rate. As a world peace leader it served as headquarters for the Inter-American Court of Human Rights and the United Nation's University of Peace.

Despite all this, poverty was still a fact of life for the majority of the population. The average wage was two dollars an hour. But this was a princely sum compared to other Central American countries. Thousands of Nicaraguans accustomed to wages of 50 cents an hour or less poured over the borders every year to work illegally for the American ex-pats as maids and gardeners, displacing an already displaced native work force that had been bumped out of independent farming into service roles for the gringos. Theft and burglary were epidemic. Roads were poorly maintained, traffic choked the pot-holed streets in the capital city of San Jose, and police and government workers were infinitely bribable.

But to me the most shocking thing about the country wasn't the low wages or the corruption or the discrepancy between native and foreign citizens. It wasn't the long hours everybody worked or the tiny concrete homes of the poor, the dirt floors and starving dogs, or the ubiquitous razor-wire topping of the fancy wrought-iron fences surrounding the homes of the rich. It was the obvious happiness of the people.

Costa Ricans walked down the middle of the narrow streets singing, day and night. Men, arm in arm, whistled respectfully at women passing by. Whether a grandmother or young woman, it made no difference—females were universally adored. Older men picked flowers for me and pressed them into my hand as I walked past. Police officers handed me speeding tickets, soulful eyes filled with regret, kissing my hand as I passed over the obligatory 10,000 colones ($20) bribe to make it go away. Handsome men, lithe in their bodies as young panthers, flashed devastating smiles and blew kisses.

Family, community and nature came before money and things. Friends visited each other's tiny houses, met in the streets and gathered in the open-air markets. If parents couldn't afford the cheap bus ride up into the mountains for a family picnic once a week, the children, parents, grandparents, aunties and neighbors would picnic under a tree on the grassy verge of the street in front of their house. Or they would gather at the end of the airport runway outside San Jose to watch the endless magic of a hundred tons of metal successfully hurling itself into the sky on its way to some exotic foreign destination.

Children were delighted with the simplest diversions—a partially deflated soccer ball to kick through the streets, a pool of green water under a waterfall to swim in, rope swings from which to swoop and dangle. And watching Latino adults with their children was a revelation. Endlessly tender and patient, if a child were fussing or misbehaving, s/he was always picked up by the nearest person, kin or not, and hugged and kissed until their sullen little faces brightened with smiles. In the year and a half I lived there, I never once saw a child scolded or snapped at in frustration by an adult.

It was a telling contrast to the ugly scenes I'd witnessed so often in American malls and grocery stores where whining children were routinely yelled at, manhandled and spanked by angry, maxed-out parents. Seeing the astonishing difference in the way children were treated in Third World nations, my heart was both gladdened and sad. Glad there were still places where children were unspoiled and had yet to become a burden in a toxic harried world. And sad that the culture I came from, despite its routinely spouted maxims about family values, seemed so devoid of tenderness and love by comparison.

Of course, it wasn't all perfection and charm. There were scars on the Costa Rican psyche, too. The Conquistadores had plundered the land in the 1600s, killing and enslaving the people. The priests came and forced their religion upon them. In the 20th century, developers bought property cheap, making fortunes turning the beaches and jungle into condo communities and golf courses. Fat retirees and ex-pats came from America looking for nubile flesh and found plenty of young women eager to 'better' their lives by latching on to older Westerners and their money. Traffic in drugs, prostitution and exotic wildlife boomed. And the nation's ecological laws were often ignored and bribed away into ineffectiveness.

But these were all ills my culture had introduced.

I stood in front of the mirror hardly believing my eyes. Who was this svelte, flaxen-haired gamine grinning back at me from the mirror? Sure, I'd lost 50 pounds, bleached my hair and gotten a hell of a tan. But it was more than that.

I'd made new friends and explored a whole new culture. I'd ridden horses in the backcountry jungles, swum in emerald pools, learned Spanish and hung out with the locals, absorbing their easy smiles and gentle laughter. I'd been baptized under a waterfall by Jewish/Pentecostal friends as a symbol of my new lease on life and written a screenplay—the first creative writing I'd done since I was a kid. But it was more than that. I was in love with life again.

By May 2009, when Betsy Chasse, one of the filmmakers of *What the Bleep* called about a script project, I was ready to come home. By June, I was back in the States. It was hard leaving Costa Rica. But I would return. And she would be there, waiting for me.

PART XI

❖ ❖ ❖

THE GODDESS
(2009–2010)

CHAPTER 24

Bhairavi

Mellowed by my year and a half in Latin America, restored by nature and the graciousness of a slow lifestyle filled with simple needs, the world was once again a good place to be. It always had been, of course. I'd just let career, grief and stress overshadow the truth of it—again.

There was a way of being in the world that worked. Coming back to the States, it was sadly clear that Americans didn't have a clue what that way was. Over and over—on the farm, during my pregnancy, in my meditations, in my medicine ceremonies, and then living in Costa Rica—I'd been shown that taking the time to be awake to life and humbly honor its processes was the most powerful healing modality possible. The present moment contained everything, whole universes of grace, information, peace and potential, if we could simply remember to stop and access it.

And I had learned something else.

If the bandit attack on Don Augustine's camp awakened a purpose, it also showed me just how much of a spiritual bubble I'd been living in. Meditation was wonderful and inner peace was great. But what good was it if I couldn't access inner peace when I needed it most? The terror I'd experienced that dark Amazon night woke me up to the unavoidable realization that I was thoroughly human. Despite considerable spiritual arrogance and beliefs to the contrary, I was in the world and subject *to* the world. And it was delusional thinking otherwise.

The old patriarchal paradigm elevating spirit far above the world, striving after some high-minded spiritual identification 'out there' in Heaven somewhere, was still strong in my mind. But it was a masculine religious ideal I had inherited that simply wasn't designed to work very well. Like a two-legged dog, it was unbalanced. On the one hand, it gave the world religious devotees striving to attain spiritual perfection, divorcing themselves from the flesh, hoarding their wisdom, separating themselves from the world, abandoning it to its fate. On the flip side, this separatist ideal gave us the secular masses.

Believing spirituality to be an 'all or nothing' affair demanding way too much sacrifice to embrace (with the priesthoods doing little to diminish this perception), most people ended up spooked by God, living as normal materialists, believing physical possessions and wealth could guarantee their well-being—never mind our suicide rates and devastated, resource-plundered planet were showing us how well *that* wasn't working.

Sure, religious asceticism apparently produced enlightened beings, a few of which had the perseverance and compassion to stick around to help the rest of us along. But as a wise and sustainable metholodogy for the vast majority? I was beginning to believe that neither the path of religious fanaticism nor the materialist approach was in harmony with life. Both sides had a lot to prove to sustain their agendas, and both sides manipulated people's perceptions accordingly. They also unnecessarily eliminated huge chunks of existence from their repertoire—the spiritualists denied the flesh and the materialists denied the spirit—and everything and everybody suffered because of it.

People on the New Age 'spiritual path' renounced lovers, possessions, meat, sugar, coffee and whatever else they believed they had to give up to know God. Long-sufferingly they endured the barbaric modern world, praying that enlightened aliens from the Pleiades would rescue them from the Republicans and corporate elitists. God knows, I'd been hot on that particular path for almost three decades before Tess gave the apple cart a shove. Fundamentalist Christians prayed for the End of the World and a cataclysm of mass destruction and Judgment. Jewish, Catholic, Hindu and Muslim mothers-to-be still prayed for sons who would enter the priesthood as testimony to their goodness and spiritual purity—precious genetic talismans to give their lives greater meaning. In comparison, the materialists had it easy. They didn't worry about God or the Pleiadians finding them worthy. And they didn't have to give up anything. They simply shot themselves in the head when the stock markets crashed.

Somehow, a balance desperately needed to be struck. It certainly needed to be struck in me.

"Something's missing."

Elena cocked her head at the laden table with its elaborate tablecloth and flounced overskirt, china and silverware, flowers and candles.

"I don't think anything more will fit," she replied.

I shook my head, laughing. "I wasn't talking about the table."

"I know." She headed back into the kitchen to stir the sauce that would glaze the artichoke hearts baking in the oven. "Get the capers out, would you?"

Rummaging in her overstuffed refrigerator took awhile. Everything about Elena was abundant: her house, her table, her art, her willingness to help those of like mind—even if they were a lot younger than her. *Ah!* There the capers were, hidden behind the twelve different kinds of hot sauce. I hauled out the jar and handed it to her. "It's like I've realized all this stuff about the feminine and I still can't grasp it well enough to write about it."

"Working on your book again?"

"Sort of," I admitted. After ten years and three false starts, I was in serious doubt I would ever be able to communicate the essence of what I was feeling.

She cracked open the new bottle with strong hands and added a sloppy spill of caper juice to the sauce cooking on the back burner. "You haven't embodied it yet, that's all." She stirred the concoction, then lifted a sample to her lips. "Hm. Habanera sauce. The smoky one."

It was a directive, not a comment. I turned to paw through the refrigerator again. An open can of coconut milk caught my eye, and I felt a swift pang of loss. Only three months back in the States and I could already feel the juicy sweetness of Costa Rica fading, just like my tan. I found the sauce and handed it over.

"Have you thought about going to California?" She opened the oven door, peered inside and, satisfied, turned off the oven.

Had I thought about California? I hadn't thought about anything *but* California ever since she'd steered me to Sadhguru's website and I'd read the blurb about the upcoming Inner Engineering class in Los Angeles. But a guru? *Gah!* I'd had more than enough of spiritual teachers for one lifetime. And wasn't I trying to get more balanced on the Earthy side of things? An Indian guru was the last thing I wanted. And yet . . .

I watched as Elena sped between kitchen and dining room and back again. There was a palpable energy and confidence to her that hadn't been there before, a feeling of integration and equilibrium. She'd changed more in the last three months than she had in all the years I'd known her. And wasn't balance what I was looking for? Perhaps some spiritual disciplines actually could foster it. The yogic tradition went back over 30,000 years. God knows there had to be something in that mighty spiritual arsenal that could give me the tools to integrate what I knew so I could live all the things I'd learned.

She paused in her dinner preparations, waiting for my answer.

"Yeah, I've thought about California."

"And?"

"I just can't wrap my head around following some guru. Giving my power away to one teacher was more than enough."

She laughed. "Who the hell said anything about following anybody? Is that what you think I'm doing?"

"Um."

"I'm too damn old for that. But I'm also too damn old not to be thinking about getting my karmic ducks in a row before I peg off this planet. It's the ancient yogic kriyas I'm after and where they can get me, darlin.'" Hands on hips, she eyed me sternly. "If I could have gotten this stuff out of a book or some New Age wannabee charging a small fortune, don't you think I would have by now?"

"Well . . ."

"I've shaken all those trees. By God I have! So if you think for one minute I'm *following* somebody . . ."

"Jesus, Elena, I'm sorry!"

"You took harp lessons. Did that mean you were 'following' your harp teacher?"

"I get the point already, okay? It's just once burned, twice shy, you know?"

"Darlin', you're lucky it's only been once. So?" She turned her back on me and started messing with something on the stove, giving me a chance to collect my thoughts.

Her outburst reassured me almost more than the obvious testimony of the yogic work she was doing. She didn't talk or act like Sadhguru's follower. And as long as I didn't have to worship him . . . *Oh hell, get on with it already, would you?*

"Yeah," I slowly answered. "I guess maybe I'm going."

I stepped out onto the balcony and surveyed the temple grounds. In front of me a waxing full moon was rising in the blackness over the dome of the Dhyanalinga. To my left came the splashing of water in the sacred bathing pool of the Theertukund. To my right the white marble columns of the Bhairavi temple, the temple of the new Goddess-to-be, shone in the work lamps left on to guide people past the mess of new construction.

The sound of 500 souls breathing and chanting through their early-morning sadhanas flowed out the door of the cavernous meditation hall I'd just exited. Damp air held the scent of India—jasmine and incense overlaid with a whiff of excrement and burned plastic. A nightjar sang somewhere in the trees across the compound and was answered by its mate.

India! After three weeks it still astonished me on a daily basis that I was there. I padded barefoot down the metal steps to ground level, turned right and followed the wide sweeping curve of the rough-cut stone path around the back of the Dhyanalinga temple towards the raised marble portico that was the entry to the temple grounds. On the way, I paused to examine the Bhairavi temple.

Three days to go before the consecration and birth of a goddess. *Not that I know what that really means.* I shivered. With the dawn, the frenzy of work would begin again, leveling the marble paving stones in the courtyard by hand, chiseling the friezes and erecting palm-frond awnings over the temple grounds to shade the 5,000 devotees expected to participate in the upcoming three-day ceremony. Whatever lay behind the marble columns with their massive pedestals of cobras and giants and the closed metal-studded doors set in the smooth white marble walls was a mystery—and a huge part of what had brought me here.

"Bhairavi," Sadhguru's voice had caressed the word lingeringly as he shook his turbaned head in rueful amazement. "It has been a long time since my mind has been so utterly captivated by a woman."

Sitting in the audience at the Fairmont hotel in Santa Monica, California, during my introductory Inner Engineering class with Sadhguru in September 2009, I hadn't understood his words then. Standing in front of the temple five months later, I still didn't understand the process I would soon join that would turn living stone into the 'goddess Bhairavi.' But during that first class when Sadhguru had talked about the creation of this feminine lingam and society's desperate need for the return of the goddess, I had been deeply touched. I didn't know what a Bhairavi was or where she was being created or even when or why. But sitting in the Fairmont ballroom that day, I knew I had to be part of her birth and had vowed I would go, no matter where or when the ceremony took place. Perhaps the consecration would mark a tipping point in the goddess's return to our planet?

I turned towards the empty portico where I would perform my morning practices, glancing backwards at the uncompleted temple. I was keeping the vow I had set into motion the previous fall. As I trod barefoot along the rough marble pavement, my mind spun backwards to the weeks following my introductory Inner Engineering class in California and the path that had brought me to this place.

Until I met Sadhguru, I'd thought yoga meant standing on my head, twisting my body into all sorts of weird positions. It turned out that most of the physical yoga taught in the West and focused purely on the body (naturally) only represented about 10 percent of actual yogic science. In India, the remaining 90 percent of yoga was inner kriyas or meditative energy practices designed to accomplish different things, among them the integration of mental, emotional and physical processes with pranic energy—the life force itself. The yoga taught in the West was comprised of many of the exercises yogis had developed to strengthen the body so it could support the other 90 percent of the work.

Within days of starting the first kriya I had learned in California, I could tell it was shifting thought patterns and energies within me. Within a week, I had signed up for two more courses taught at the Isha Foundation ashram in central Tennessee.

Most of October and November 2009 I lived at the US ashram, reluctantly driving my 58-year-old body into physical yoga postures at 5am every morning, segueing into the seated energetic kriyas I'd learned. It was only two and a half hours practice, but both my mind and body complained bitterly. For eleven years I'd started my day with meditation, followed by a gentle morning contemplation accompanied by a couple of mugs of black tea with honey and cream followed by breakfast. Now I was grunting and breathing my way through a very different set of disciplines that had my mind in a whirl and my body begging for a break and some caffeine.

In the evenings, my body wanted wine or a Margarita and steak with horseradish sauce, followed by a movie and popcorn. Anything but the regulation quasi-Indian vegetarian cuisine it was getting twice a day. Adding insult to injury, the mandatory 10 pm lights-out foreclosed even bedtime reading. What was I doing even *thinking* about going to India? So what if I'd made a vow to go to the consecration of the Linga Bhairavi temple? I was struggling at the US ashram. Wouldn't I be jumping from the frying pan into the fire spending two months in India? The heat in the south provinces was legendary. So were the mosquitoes and snakes. Was learning new practices worth it? Was chasing the elusive feminine and cozying up to the Goddess worth it? And if I didn't like the food here, what would it be like there?

Christ, what a candy ass I'm becoming.

Comfort zones screaming, I called Elena. She listened to my whining, then got right to the point. "So, what else are you going to do with the rest of your life, eh?"

Hmmm. "Enjoy it?" I ventured.

"Yeah, right. More like age ungracefully and die young from some stupid avoidable disease." Silence thundered down the line. Damn, but she had a point.

My mother had been old in her 40s, broken down in her 50s, dead in her 60s. Both my genetic father and Jack had died in their mid-60s. In contrast, Indian yogis often lived well past 100 in active good health. Sadhguru routinely stated that old age was supposed to be the best, most productive years of one's life, not time spent doing the 'hospital asana' as he jokingly put it.

Who wouldn't want robust health and productivity right up to the end? Inspired, I said goodbye and walked over to the small dining hall for the evening meal. Filling my plate from the limited buffet, I sat down, closed my eyes and waited for the chant of blessing to begin. Aum, aum, aum, sahana vavatu, sahanou bhunaktu . . . I stumbled through the Sanskrit, opened my eyes and looked down at my food. A mess of white rice, bland dhal and raw carrot salad stared back at me.

Damn. Barbeque pork sure would go well with that.

Despite my concerns, I signed up to attend an advanced meditation retreat and the Linga Bhairavi consecration being held in late January 2010 at the ashram outside Coimbatore in the province of Tamil Nadu. Back home in Washington I did the special prostration I'd been taught for the ceremony every morning along with the rest of my practices. Every evening, I struggled to memorize the long incomprehensible Sanskrit chants that would be sung. As required for these particular events, I removed meat, coffee, alcohol and dairy products from my diet. And, as much as I liked to complain about it, I had to admit that I felt a lot better for the dietary change.

Tess, who lived nearby and whom I saw frequently, was as skeptical of the whole guru thing as I was. The creation of the Linga Bhairavi, however, piqued her interest. "So what's he going to do to create this . . . what do you call it?"

"Linga . . . or lingam. The words are interchangeable, I think." I shrugged as we hiked through the frost-covered pasture not far from her house. "Beats me what he's going to do. All I know is what he said in Santa Monica."

"Which was?"

"He said the feminine energies have been misunderstood and ignored for over 2,000 years, and that if we don't reawaken goddess consciousness in the West, this planet is basically toast."

"Well, that's true enough."

"He said the United States is the key because all the Second and Third World nations want what we've got. But the heart center of America is closed. We're greedy and only interested in material possessions. If people's hearts aren't opened here—if this country doesn't learn to support feminine values of community and sustainability—it will be a disaster. That's why he's working over here."

"Hmmm," Tess kicked at a clump of frozen grass.

"I saw it happening in Costa Rica and everywhere else I traveled. All the young people want stuff like we've got. They don't see how much better off they are than us. They only see the iPods and flat-screen TVs and swimming pools. Not the stress, debt and resource depletion that comes with it."

"So making this B-Byravi thing is all he's doing?"

"No. After the consecration of the temple in India he wants to build Devi temples here in the United States."

"Devi?"

"Sanskrit for goddess. I think it means Shakti, too."

"And they're supposed to do what?"

"Shift the energy somehow, I guess. And create awareness of the feminine." I snapped off a frozen stalk of grass as we walked. "I know it sounds farfetched. But at least it's better than nothing." We walked in silence for a while, deep in our own thoughts. "I've approached the Isha Foundation with a book proposal."

"Yeah? About what?"

"I want to interview Sadhguru and write a book about his views on the divine feminine from the Eastern perspective. God knows, so far I haven't been able to crank out a book on it—Eastern or otherwise." *Dammit.* "The world needs more information about what the feminine is all about. Besides, I've got to do *something.*"

"You could start a campaign to castrate half the world's population and make testosterone an illegal drug," Tess suggested hopefully.

I started to laugh, then caught myself. I'd heard similar statements made over the years, and it was tacitly understood they were just 'words to say' giving voice to the immense frustration many women felt towards the male in general. But the enmity in Tess's words was just as deadly as anything men had meted out to women over the centuries. Did Tess really feel that way? Did my other lesbian friends? And what good did saying such things do? Anger and bad blood certainly wouldn't heal the situation between the sexes, and something in me said I couldn't let her crack pass go unchallenged.

"Do you really think a male-bashing lesbian approach to the world's problems is a good idea?"

Tess shrugged. "Desperate times call for desperate measures."

"How can you even say that? It's just a continuation of the whole damn make-wrong cycle. We've already experienced the swing of the pendulum away from the Goddess religions to the patriarchal camp. Swinging radically back the other way again and making men the enemy is no better than making women the enemy. We need balance and love for one another, an understanding and appreciation of our differences. The masculine and feminine are part of all of us. Neither side is bad or wrong. It's just when we're lopsided that things get all vershukta."

"Gee, you don't have to get upset!"

"I'm not upset. I'm just done with the old knee-jerk reactions that lay blame on the *other* side of things. Haven't we had enough of that medicine forced down our throats to not inflict it on men? No matter how seemingly well-deserved?"

In somewhat less than good grace, Tess eventually owned that, yes, indeed she had.

The stairs of the temple portico materialized out of the darkness, steps constructed uncomfortably high as if to remind the spiritual aspirant that the journey within is not necessarily easy or what one is accustomed to. I reached the top, unfolded my mat on the smooth granite floor, faced back towards the Bhairavi temple and began my practices. To my left, over the edge of the portico down on the dirt road, two night guards smoked and talked quietly in their native Tamil tongue.

The morning air was cool with few mosquitoes. Birds sang and crows cawed. Something huge crashed through the underbrush in the forest—a wild elephant? The guards stopped talking. Somewhere in the compound another meditator breathed the chalabati breath. Soon, a bus rattled past bearing the first of the morning's guests to the temples, native worshippers and weary overseas travelers arriving at Isha for the upcoming consecration. I completed the exercises for the Bhairavi ceremony and opened my eyes. The hills behind the ashram were waking, dark green against the paling sky. To the east, children in the Sanscriti school chanted. From the sound of clashing staffs ricocheting across the grounds, some were already hard at work practicing martial arts.

Two more meditators joined me on the portico, and I began the shakti chalana kriya, a long series of different breaths and mudras. By the time I'd moved through the shambhavi kriya, the sun had risen and the temple was bustling with activity. The smell of cooking floated on the breeze, competing with the scents of incense, flowers and granite dust. The steady pounding *chink chink* of workers chiseling stone by hand sounded in the distance.

Temple days have been starting like this in India for over 30,000 years.

Humbled to be part of this ancient pattern, I folded my mat and strolled towards the public areas of the compound. A gigantic statue of a recumbent black Brahma bull faced the Dhyanalinga temple entrance, fully 15 feet tall, poised with one forefoot planted on the ground, ready to rise. This, I had been told, was the proper posture for the mind: instantly ready to go to work, left outside to wait, while the meditator entered the temple of the divine within.

I woke at four in the morning. The three inches of ancient foam beneath me compressed to nothing, I might as well have slept directly on the polished black granite floor. Lethargy and stiffness filled me. *Crappy bedding must be a guru trick from way back to get you up in the morning.* The six other women in my dorm room were sleeping peacefully. But my mattress screamed at me to move.

It didn't take much preparation for the day: put on the ubiquitous white corta, a long-sleeve cotton tunic top over the baggy sexless balloon pants, throw water on your face, brush your teeth, grab your mat and go.

I left the dorm, joining the silent figures already moving through the fog ahead of me on the dirt road. This early, the cavernous practice hall was almost empty, barely lit by a solitary ghee lamp left burning on the small altar. Slowly I made my way to the right-hand side of the vast room—the women's side—spread out my mat and started my exercises. The Bhairavi consecration was two days away. What few thoughts I had as I bent and stretched all flowed towards understanding the nature of the Goddess.

Apparently, She found my attention pleasing, because that particular morning She tossed me a few bones of insight. *The feminine expression is the fertility of all creation.* Moving into seated meditation after my kriyas, I contemplated what that really meant. The word 'fertility' utterly failed to capture the real essence of the idea. The impression I was getting was that the feminine was not only the unlimited *capacity* for the begetting of creation and the wellspring of life/nature, it was the active principle of continuous abundance: the unceasing outpouring of God/Source into expression.

There was absolutely no limit to this outpouring. Limitation was a human concept, and only the thought of limits could constrict the flow of life—or rather *appear* to restrict it. A human having thoughts of limitation was Source expressing, too: "I can't have this. I can't do that." Presto! A vast abundance of limitation pours forth as requested!

It was essentially the same message I had gotten from Ayahuasca, the feminine healing plant spirit of the Amazon. And the contrast between this effortless movement into creation of all potentials (the feminine) and approaching everything as a constant struggle requiring a lot of hard 'thinking and doing' in order to get what I wanted (the masculine) was extraordinary. All my life I'd been doing things the masculine way, figuring out things, planning, analyzing probabilities, then putting my shoulder to the wheel to make things happen. I'd even taken this approach with spirituality.

It was the exact opposite of the intuitive feminine path that simply *knows,* for no logical reason whatsoever, that whatever is desired/needed will flow forth. The feminine just lets it happen. The less thought and struggle, the better the flow.

My mind flashed to Elena. Right before I'd left for India, the septic system at her house had overflowed. With no plans filed with the county, it had been anybody's guess where the septic lines and tank were. All the same, my feminine hero instantly just *knew* where the tank was. Of course, her husband ignored what she said and spent two days out in the rain with a pick and shovel with an expensive septic engineer, only to discover that the tank was right where she'd said all along.

ARG! This is how I've been all my life! Out in the rain with a shovel trying to make my life work.

With the exception of my timeout in the north Georgia woods and Costa Rica, what had I ever done but taken the hard road? And all those New Age manifestation classes with their vision boards and lists and cards and endless focus trying to direct my mind in order to get what I wanted? Just more stressful, results-oriented *doing*.

Sure, I needed to have clear intent and desire. And I had to be willing to do what was necessary once life supplied the path to my goals. But easeful trust and grace were necessary for the path to have room to show up. I had to let the natural flow of things bring to me what I wanted, and had to have the unplanned spaciousness to recognize odd potentials and doorways when they arrived.

I finished my practices, folded my mat and headed out the practice hall door to greet the dawn. Would I ever embrace this wisdom in my bones enough to live it?

Around and around her small rotund body it went, eight yards of cloth worn over a cotton petticoat and sleeved top. Kalpita tossed her thick black braid over one shoulder as she tucked the last panel of cloth into the waistband of her slip.

"Don't you hate having to wear so much clothing in the heat?"

"No. I am used to it. Besides, it is not really even hot yet."

It wasn't? Just walking from one building to the next in the scalding 105-degree heat was enough to make me yearn for short shorts and a tank top. But India was a modest country as far as women's attire was concerned, and the ashram's dress code was even more restrictive. The men could walk around bare-chested with their dhotis (a long, rectangular cloth wrapped around the waist) tucked up around their knees without notice. But for women, skimpy attire was a social no-go. "Don't you think it's unfair that men can dress so lightly, while women have to cover up everything?" I asked.

She giggled as she set a large golden earring into one ear, a girlish sound coming from this full-grown woman and mother. "We must dress modestly," she stated with pride. "Indian men are very easily aroused."

"Well, of course they're easily aroused if women's bodies are hidden all the time," I groused later, sitting with some American friends in the ashram's public outdoor cafeteria. "A woman can hardly talk with a man here without being accused of coming on to him. And God forbid she should show a little leg."

"It's the old 'what you can't see invites interest' routine," Jessica stated, dipping a straw into her cold watermelon drink.

"It's more than just that." Kathy took a sip of her own juice. "It's a matter of respect and protection."

"Protection? Against what?" I asked.

"Oh, come on. Against the lower psychic energies of carnal thoughts."

"Huh?"

Kathy looked at me surprised. "Sadhguru talks about this."

"He does?"

"He says women are a more advanced and subtle form of

humanity than men and that we need . . ."

"He does?" I interrupted again, astounded.

"Yes, he does," she responded patiently. "I've heard him say it on several CDs. Basically, he considers women a genetic upgrade."

That would definitely take some thought. "But what's that got to do with clothing?" I persisted.

"Haven't you ever felt weird—like something creepy was happening and then turned around to find some guy undressing you with his eyes?"

"Sure," I said.

"Well, women need to be protected from lower thoughts and any sort of disrespectful treatment. We're sensitive and it psychically damages us. Covering up the goods is one way to avoid that kind of negative influence."

"Huh. Maybe that's where the tradition of the burka comes from," said Jessica.

Great, humanity's answer to everything—cover up what disturbs you. "How 'bout men doing an upgrade on themselves and getting a handle on their urges?" I quipped. "That way, everybody can just parade around in the altogether and not worry about it."

Kathy snorted. "Like you don't have urges? Isn't that why we're here? Aren't we all looking for an upgrade?"

I couldn't sleep. So much was becoming clear! I got up, dressed and grabbed my laptop out of my suitcase. Easing out the door with my yoga mat, I dropped it on the floor of the portico, sat down and started to write by the light of the single light bulb in the ceiling overhead.

January 27th, 2010 – Journal entry, Isha Center, Coimbatore, India

At this evening's talk Sadhguru said one of the main things the Linga Bhairavi is designed to do is facilitate people's desires and make things happen for them. I was hugely disappointed hearing him say that. My first thought was, "Is that all the Goddess is good for? Supplying people's crass physical desires?" But what's so wrong about having what you desire? Doesn't that just open the door for more creations in an ongoing evolution? Isn't that the whole point of life? And total unreserved giving . . . isn't that a feminine hallmark?

All my life I've subconsciously bought into the Christian ethic that the physical world is a bad thing, a lesser expression than Heaven. But in all of existence there is only the manifest and the unmanifest. That's it. Two sides of the same coin called God/ Source: spirit and flesh/feminine and masculine.

The 'feminine' (for lack of a better word) is spirit in form. It includes everything: guys, gals, cheesecake, rifles, Barbie Dolls, mountains, oceans and X-Men. Anything that has a face, in other words a tangible expression, is the feminine. Even intellectual thought is feminine because it's a limited manifested construct of the brain. Bottom line, you can **see** the feminine, **touch** it, **hear** it, **smell** it, **taste** it and **think** it. **The 'masculine' (for lack of a better word) is abstract formless spirit**. You can't see it, hear it, touch, smell, taste it or think about it.

But formed or formless, it's all God. Feminine and masculine are the same thing. We've gotten confused because of all the gender connotations we've ascribed to the words masculine and feminine. We think in terms of opposites—man versus woman and spirit versus the flesh. But there's a larger context: a larger unified dimension to all this that has nothing to do with gender or opposites!

The Hindus have it right. The Goddess is all of Creation . . . the outward form of pure disembodied Spirit.

Life is the feminine face of the unseen God. Even every human fetus is female for the first eight weeks after conception! A male is formed only when a 'y' chromosome is present and then it kicks in later during gestation. And the Bible has it that Eve came from Adam's rib? Ha! It's the other way around!

When are we going to get the metaphor? Eve only 'comes from' Adam in the sense that 'the feminine principle' (spirit in form) springs from 'the masculine principle' (formless spirit). But they're both spirit and absolutely equal: Eve = Adam; feminine = masculine; flesh = spirit.

Unity. Hello!?

Yet hundreds of millions of people actually believe that physical woman was created from physical man. Worse, they believe this situation makes woman a lesser expression of the divine than man. What a mixed-up mess! No wonder all the fundamentalist guy religions fear the mystical side of spirituality. Once you get past dogma to actually experience spirit, you can't help but eventually recognize 'the feminine' as the first and **only** born. Hell, it's the only 'thing' born at all.

All around me, women, segregated from the men during the ceremonies, were bawling and screaming. Just behind me a sari-draped figure writhed along the ground like a snake, shocking my Western sensibilities. *Jeez, get a grip, would you, lady??* A female brahmachari, one of Sadhguru's disciples, came over and instead of telling the woman to "knock it off" as I had expected her to, compassionately guarded her as she wiggled out onto the pathway. *Oh . . . if only I could put my stupid mind with all its judgments on ice maybe I might learn something here!* Why not scream and writhe around?! Maybe these women were more in tune with what was going on than I was.

Maybe if I really got what Sadhguru was doing, performing the rare mystical process of prana pratishtha, creating a doorway through which a beneficent Mother Goddess who did not frown and judge could shine; a munificent Feminine Deity who was accepting and understanding; a Presence who endlessly offered people whatever they needed for relief from all suffering, lack, pain and sorrow—if I fully grasped creating a portal to that was possible and that that was what I was witnessing, maybe I would bawl and writhe too.

The drums pounded and torchlight flickered. Sadhguru moved through the ceremony, weaving magic as old as time, his odd motions and acts completely foreign to me. How could solid alchemical mercury—an impossible compound that couldn't exist at room temperature according to Western science—plus Neem leaves, normal liquid mercury, Turmeric, vibhuti, the sacred ash, and all the other ingredients he had poured into the vessel of the linga, then prayed over, danced over and meditated over, produce a 'goddess?' For that matter, how did transubstantiation work, turning wine into blood and a wafer into Christ's flesh?

There are more things in Heaven and earth, Horatio, than are dreamt of in your philosophy . . .

Certainly, the Dhyanalinga temple with its massive granite lingam like an erect male phallus was testimony to the power of the alchemical yogic traditions Sadhguru was heir to. He had consecrated that lingam in a similar ceremony years ago, dedicating it to the unseen God—Source consciousness—the 'masculine' un-manifested Spirit. The lingam's purpose was to induce a meditative state in whoever walked through the temple doorway, making the Unity consciousness of Source available to them. And the proof of his successful consecration of that lingam was the energy that had literally dropped me to my knees the first time I entered the temple. Meditation? No problem.

Why would the Linga Bhairavi be any different? Sure, the lingams had different uses. The Dhyanalinga was created to induce unity consciousness, and the Linga Bhairavi was being created to provide a flow of abundance and the physical manifestation of people's desires. I cringed slightly at the mental comparison. *Still?* Even with all that I knew, the Dhyanalinga's abstract spiritual importance still seemed so much greater to me.

But if I do not honor physical life, I will never transcend it.

Wait! Stop! That was my old way of thinking, the old masculine ascetic 'I gotta get outta this place' way of looking at the world. I finally got the joke—again. *Wake up, Cate. There's nothing to transcend. Spirit and flesh are One. They're the same thing.* How many times would I have to come to this same point of understanding before I finally really got it?

The world was the outpouring of an idea just as divine as anything else more rarified. Certainly God did not judge that which flowed from its formless bosom? That would be like a mother hating her own milk as it flowed to nourish her child. *And modern society thinks breastfeeding is crass?! Oh, how stupid we are!*

And so my mind went throughout the long first day of the consecration.

I woke well before my alarm, dressing quickly and leaving the dormitory to enter the temple compound long before dawn. Roaming the grounds, I found a hidden spot behind some bushes at the base of the portico steps to do my practices. First prostration, face down in the grass, I was weeping.

Never before had I bowed down to physical creation! Never once had I truly, in full consciousness, paid reverential homage to Nature. Sure, I loved the Earth and had adored and reveled in

Nature on the farm during my youth. In the early bloom of middle age I had loved my body and seen its beauty. I had been ecstatic when I finally perceived Gaia during that amazing ceremony with Tess on the rim of Canyon de Chelly. Later, the plant spirit of Ayahuasca had spoken to me, dispelling ancient grief locked in my DNA, opening me up to the grace of the feminine. But honor these processes? Honor physical life itself? Hardly!

I had bowed innumerable times to Christ. Had bowed and genuflected to the cross; had bowed to the Holy Spirit; had bowed to things unseen beyond me; had crouched on my knees beseeching Heaven. All those things I had done a thousand times. But stop and humbly bow down to the Earth? Not once. The knowledge of my ignorance and spiritual poverty burned in me. My tears flowed faster, unrestrained. *Lip service to the Goddess only. No wonder the Earth is dying.*

I made the prostration a second time, three times, four. Shaking, open and raw, I felt the outpouring of energy from the still incompletely consecrated temple and understood how creation was utterly devoid of any semblance of control. Life— Shakti—the Goddess roared into existence. She *was* me, flowed through me, around me, beyond me, unstoppable, unrelenting and eternal, taking every physical form and every thought form possible, over and over again. Breathing in. Breathing out. Creation/destruction, creation/destruction, creation/destruction . . . an endless dance beyond the comprehension of my pitiful human mind.

Oh, how proud I have been!

How arrogant, thinking I could understand life, putting labels on everything, sticking my small experiences into nice little metaphysical boxes. I thought I knew so much, and yet now I could *feel* how little that was. I rose and started another prostration. The Goddess smashed me gently into the dirt. I could feel Her force above me, beneath me, inside me, all around me, dissolving my ignorance, dissolving all my fevered intellectualizations, leaving me with nothing and everything all at the same time.

And I thought I could ignore this? Trivialize the world as unimportant compared to the 'spiritual?' *Oh, what a fool I've been.* I started another prostration. I thought I could ignore the raw presence of everything that was going on around me? Quivering limbs, the quaking of the earth, the roar of the wind, the death of a child, of a star, of a spider . . . the long, slow, grinding down and building up of mountains and universes. All this was happening into eternity and in my 21st century modernity I'd thought I had a handle on it?

I laughed a despairing, exultant laugh face down in soil alive with billions of microorganisms I couldn't even see. All my writing, all the work I'd done interviewing scientists about consciousness and quantum physics, all the things I thought I knew in the blindness of my supreme intellect and spiritual pride fell into proper perspective.

How small I had made Creation. How small I had made myself.

The tall, brass-studded, paneled doors were open. The walls of white marble hung with a thousand tiny brass oil lamps, lit and glittering. I approached the temple empty-handed, bearing no offering, not realizing how purely this revealed the continued poverty of my awareness. On the marble floor before the raised doorsill, the bas relief of a young woman carved in stone showed the proper form the prostration to the Linga Bhairavi should take: face down, left arm reaching out, forehead cradled on the bent right arm, left leg outstretched, the right leg crossing at the knee.

Cautiously I stepped over the sill.

This late at night there were few worshippers and no tourists in the intimate triangular temple. A massive bronze trident—the symbol of the trinity of body, mind and spirit—was set at an angle into the floor, partially obscuring my view of the linga. More oil lamps sparkled inside. The white marble walls were carved with unknown symbols and decorated with paintings of flowing crimson and green saris starred with gold. Down a short flight of stairs at the apex of the triangle a few still figures sat in meditation facing the linga. I stopped and stared.

The goddess Bhairavi was utterly alien to me.

Two crimson-robed attendants flanked the ten-foot tall bas-relief of a yoni surrounded by flames, carved from a massive panel of what appeared to be black basalt. Ten stubby, bracelet-girded arms reached out, five on either side. Gold-rimmed eyes with black iridescent irises stared straight into and through me. The goddess's third eye, also rimmed in gold, was shaped as a yoni. A brass nose ring placed where it might be piercing the left nostril (if there had been a nose) stood out against the stone, oddly comforting in its ordinariness. At the base of the carving was a large copper trough where gifts of coconuts, flowers and other food and offerings were placed. Incense burned in a large brazier. Smoke and a low chanting filled the air.

I prostrated, but was distracted by my proximity to the goddess I had come so far to . . . what? Pay homage? To understand? What a joke. At least my ignorance had lessened to the degree that I understood that understanding was beyond me. Awkwardly, I rose and sat to one side of the temple.

Word had gotten out that Bhairavi was a fertile goddess whose ears were open and whose power flowed strongly. From seven in the morning to late evening, wives came with their round-eyed children, husbands in tow. Girls arrived, dressed in their finery. Young men entered hesitantly, leaving their confidence at the door. Old men hobbled across the threshold, lean and bent from years of manual labor. Old women came, fat from a lifetime of cooking, round and glowing in their colorful saris, tears streaming down their aged cheeks, gnarled hands filled with coconuts, flowers and pineapples, whatever small offerings they could afford to make.

Young and old, rich and poor, they came to pray for their loved ones, for long life, for healing, a new job, for milk-rich goats, a baby, for money, cars, a strong new bullock, rain, a wealthy husband for their daughters and well-dowered wives for their sons. They came and would never stop coming as long as the temple and human need survived.

Now it was my turn, and all I could do was sit and stare. Mosquitoes whined gently around me. Another meditator came in, prostrated and lay there like stone. The two attendants whispered, heads together, two young women trained in service and surrender who had been on their feet for hours accepting offerings, giving back blessings, flowers and sacred ash. One of them giggled quietly, hand over her mouth, crimson shoulders gently shaking.

After a very long time I finally closed my eyes to let Her in.

CHAPTER 25

Embodying the feminine

It was so simple. Both man and woman were spirit made flesh—utterly equal, divine beings, exquisitely different in their expressions of that divinity.

At the most basic level, woman and man represented two halves of a whole. Separate from each other, they stood as unbalanced opposites. Blended together, the complementary qualities of feminine and masculine balanced all of creation. Individually, humans expressed both masculine and feminine qualities to varying degrees—although it was far more socially acceptable for women to come across as assertive and logically intellectual than it was for men to be seen as passive, intuitive and emotional.

I walked down the long driveway of the guest cottage I was renting from my filmmaker friend, Betsy. It was cold for late March in Washington State, and I zipped my jacket up to the neck, wishing for a scarf but too lazy to walk back to the house to get one. The shift from the 115-degree dry heat of South India to the freezing damp of the Pacific Northwest was a refreshing shock, but hard to get used to again. *One more example of polarity,* I mused.

Hell, duality was the very fabric of physical existence. Within seconds after the Big Bang, electrons (the negative force/'feminine') and protons (the positive force/'masculine') were some of the very first 'things' to come into existence. No wonder everything on Earth was divided into opposites! How could they not be? *Man/ woman, up/down, good/bad, right/wrong, pain/pleasure, joy/ sorrow, hard/soft, hot/cold, wet/dry.* My idiot mind kept up a chanted list of Earthly opposites in rhythm to my footsteps on the gravel drive. *Long/short, black/white, ugly/beautiful* . . .

Polarity played out intensely and obviously between woman and man. For centuries, the physically stronger, aggressive, intellectual, abstract, linear male had been in ascendancy over the weaker, passive, intuitive, concrete, holistic female. We didn't call it the battle of the sexes for nothing! Maybe few people lived as total black-and-white examples of these opposing qualities. But it was indisputable that men and women's innate tendencies and ways of functioning were very different: thinking versus feeling; protective versus nurturing; goal-oriented versus process-oriented; self-oriented versus other-oriented—all dualistic expressions of humanity playing out as the laws of matter dictated.

I reached the end of the drive and stepped onto the country road heading down the hill towards the Deschutes River. Soon heavy forest gave way to pasture and a view opened eastwards toward snow-shrouded Mt Rainier, the largest volcano in the continental US. A herd of cows hung around a barn, ignoring the frozen grass, waiting for someone to come toss them their afternoon hay. Several calves cavorted near the fence, flirting with me as I passed.

Although spring was on the horizon, the world seemed bleak and gray. Perhaps it was a depressed perceptual aftershock from India? I longed for the vibrant colors of glowing saris and shawls studded with sequins, missed the ornate architecture that enchanted the eye, the masses of people, cars, bicycles, motorcycles, carts and wagons, cows, goats and children competing for room on the streets everywhere you went. Such an astounding place and people, warm and beautiful, sultry and dense with mystery!

Coming back to the States was quite a letdown . . . again.

It wasn't just the typical ennui of returning to routine after visiting an exotic locale. My immersion excursion into a much more feminine culture had given me new eyes, and I now found myself thoroughly dismayed at Western society. Here, it was almost as if the feminine had been banished from the face of the Earth, and with her all spontaneity, aliveness, color and warmth. No opposition to the masculine ideal was allowed to exist. My native monoculture celebrated one thing and one thing only: the 'P' values of Power, Possessions, Profits and Progress.

In alignment with these values, here, hard work was the ethic and material wealth the sole criteria for success. Endless corporate expansion was the dream, control the ultimate victory, and the economics of scarcity the whip employed to keep people busy, insecure and bid-able. My culture was the *precise opposite* of the feminine expression whereby ease and grace were the ethics, health and happiness the criteria for success, ongoing creation the dream, freedom of expression the ultimate victory and the economics of unlimited abundance the rule, keeping people harmonious and fulfilled.

What the hell? How had I not seen that I was living under a totalitarian regime where only one philosophy was allowed? Where only one side of the coin of life was traded and valued?

Struggling to gain entry into this realm, I hadn't thought twice about the price to be paid getting into the ring. I didn't know there was a price to be paid. Like all the women who had gone before me in the Suffragette Movement and then the Women's Liberation, our efforts had been focused on eliminating our marginalization, not questioning the value of the system we wanted access to. Generations of women had worked desperately hard to join the party and we had accomplished the goal. Now we were part of the problem.

We mortgaged our houses, trusted our politicians, obeyed our CEOs, invested our 401Ks, sold our souls and worked our asses off right next to the guys. We watched the same corporate controlled news and absorbed the same messages: BUY and BE AFRAID. We fought in the same wars, voted in the same elections, believed the same things and bought the spiel that unending consumption was the way to freedom and a better life. We were so enmeshed in the only value system that counted, so busy marching to its frantic steps we never once stopped to wonder: *Who is benefitting most from this agenda?*

Were Western women *or* men happier? Were we healthier as a population? Were we financially better off? No! Millions of people were sick and depressed. Families were losing their homes. Debt under the disguise of credit was driving people into bankruptcy, and unemployment was reaching new heights. I wasn't a genius, but it seemed obvious that everything in my culture was being strategized to sell an ideal that supported a very small segment of society: the 'illuminated' corporate elite who stood to gain the most under this kind of regime; the one percent of the one percent—a bunch of good ol' boys who had it all and who weren't about to let the reins of power slip from their grasp. *Wonderful. Now I'm thinking like a feminist and a conspiracy theorist!*

'Bemused, my footsteps slowed. To my left, Mt Rainier shone briefly through the clouds. Afternoon rays of the setting sun bounced orange, lilac and gold off the 14,000-foot volcano, setting the mountain on fire. The sight stopped me in my tracks. What a glorious world this was! If only humans would stop buying into a system of values that was destined to destroy it.

A shadow passed over the sun, dimming the mountain's glory, and I walked on.

Without women speaking up as *women,* Western society was

like a car running on only half its cylinders—operating very badly indeed. If only we could show up in the world as ourselves! If only our 'softer,' currently scorned, values could be openly taught, received and socially embraced. The corporate bastions of greed and corruption would be sure to quickly fall. The terrorist agendas based on fear would falter. The continuing slaughter of the innocents would cease. Starvation, poverty and despair would disappear. And women would no longer need to be afraid.

"Sadhguru agreed to your book? Oh, Catie, that's wonderful!" cried Elena. "When are you going to meet him?"

"I'm flying to Los Angeles on the 10th April. We're meeting at his hotel after the Inner Engineering leadership retreat is over Sunday afternoon."

"Are you excited?"

Excited? *Hmmm.* It wasn't exactly the operant word. "I think I'm more intimidated than anything else," I admitted.

"Oh, you'll be fine. I looked at your composite chart. You and Sadhguru will get along great."

Right. "Well, the book's about him and what he knows about the Goddess, not me. Speaking of which, do you have any questions you'd like me to ask him about the feminine and gender issues? I'm preparing a list of questions."

"Oh, darlin', you'd better believe it." The fervency in her voice came clearly through the telephone receiver.

"Great. Email them to me by the end of this week would you?"

We stared at the bike. Aside from dust, cobwebs and two flat tires, it looked in good shape. Tess moved a few more boxes out of the way, and I hauled it out by the handlebars.

"When did you last ride it?" I asked.

"I can't remember."

We walked it out of the garage between us, the chain making a light *tick tick tick* as the flaccid tires wobbled over the gravel.

"I still think women want to hear about the feminine from another woman, not a man," she groused. "Even an enlightened one."

We reached my truck. I lowered the dusty tailgate, and we hefted the bike into the back and set it down on its side. Tess stared at me across the truck bed. "We've had guys telling the story for long enough. It's time for women to speak."

I shook my head. "It'd take too long. This way, all I have to do is play journalist and write down the answers."

"So, what's your hurry?"

We got in the cab. "Tess, I've been trying to write my book on the feminine for 11 years. That's hardly being in a hurry. Besides, I've got three screenplays banging on the door, each one screaming to be written first." I backed the truck around and headed out the driveway. "I want to move on."

She scrunched down in her seat looking thoroughly unconvinced. "I still think you should write it."

Chitchat was not on Sadhguru's menu, at least not with me. *So much for how well we'll get on.* We'd talked for all of 15 minutes before he closed his eyes, releasing me from scrutiny. Apparently, he'd soaked up my vibe and what I had to offer in the first few moments of our conversation and was now mulling it over. Mulling me over. *Being barbequed alive would, quite possibly, be more fun than talking with this man.*

His eyes opened.

"We can go to the conference room and you can ask me your reporter questions. And I will give you reporter answers." He cocked his turbaned head and reflected for another moment. "It will be a very one-dimensional approach to the feminine." He stopped and stared at me. Whatever he was trying to say I wasn't getting it and he could see it in my eyes. "I don't want to do that," he said.

What? No interview? My heart sank even as it still pattered nervously in my chest. What the hell had I spent the money flying down to LA for?

"A question and answer format won't go well in the West either."

More devastation to my plans! But after some conversation, I reluctantly agreed. A book like that would work in India and be well received amongst the Isha Yoga practitioners around the globe. But preaching to the choir was not what either of us had in mind. After a few more moments of contemplative silence, he raised his brown eyes back to mine, measuring.

"You should write a story," he said.

I sat on the sofa, watching the rain pelt down from gloomy skies. In the surrounding trees nothing stirred. No birds sang. My entire world was a huddle of cold, wet grayness. I leaned back on the sofa cushions, hugging my knees to my chest. *A story, a story, dear God, my kingdom for a story.*

I'd been sitting there for days. Actually, I realized glumly, it had been a week since Elena picked me up at Seattle airport, delivering me to the door of my little gingerbread cottage-in-the-woods. In seven days' time I had done nothing but stoke the fire in the woodstove, feed my cat, eat, sleep, stare out the French doors and mentally sift through my shredded book plans for some spark of inspiration—anything to get me going in some sort of creative direction. But nothing was coming. *Nothing. Nada. Zip.*

It would feel good to sink into depression. It would be satisfying to feel abused and disappointed that my original plans had been shot out of the sky with such pre-emptive ease, anything to distract me from the lack of creativity. But I couldn't fool myself. Not only was Sadhguru a guru, which in Sanskrit means 'dispeller of illusion,' he was, apparently, *my* guru. As such, he had a responsibility not only to his overall plans but also to me, a duty to kick me in the right direction for my own general enlightenment no matter what. And if he thought I should write a story, then, by God, I should write a story.

Wasn't that what I'd always wanted to do anyway?

I sighed and got up to make myself yet another cup of tea. While the electric kettle heated, I leaned against the sink, staring out the window into the thin stand of wet fir trees. Sadhguru had played his part. If only I could get my act together and hold up my end of the bargain! The kettle shut off with an audible click. I poured a cup of Earl Grey, then wandered back to the sofa, cup in hand. *Dammit, it's not about holding up your end of the deal, you silly git. It's about surrendering. The feminine just lets go and trusts. It knows what's needed will be supplied. It doesn't worry or try to figure things out. It waits for what's needed to show up and then it goes to work.*

I sipped the steaming amber liquid cautiously as the next realization clicked into place. Sadhguru was forcing me into *being* what I wanted to write about! It was, I realized excitedly, the key element that had been missing all those years I'd been trying to write my book. I just plain hadn't *been* feminine enough to write about it! And my recent plans for doing a journalistic exposé on the Goddess? Talk about hanging out in an old comfort zone! Could I have picked a more intellectual, uninvolved path if I'd tried? Just bim-bam, on to the next project, mission accomplished with a big fat satisfying red checkmark next to 'book on the feminine'?

How very masculine of me!

I had to laugh—although the sound that came out was rueful in the extreme. Sadhguru had seen through my bullshit big time. Reporting on the Goddess would never touch my core. It wouldn't teach me how to *live* as I had never lived before: gracious, loving, focused, patient and absolutely fearless in the knowledge that what was needed in my life would be provided. A subtle thrill moved through my body. At last I was headed in the right direction! Not with just the book, but with my life. I could feel the truth of this new insight, feel the crying need in me to fully embody the feminine, expressing life with no sex-determined limits, no curtailments, nothing left out, no capacities set aside, becoming a whole human being at last.

If I had to sit here until hell froze over with no words on a page, it was okay. What had Ayahuasca told me that night as I sat communing with her on the steps of the temple at Cahuachi? Ah, yes: *Let the beauty of who you are draw the things that are equal to you into your life. You need not chase anything, especially me.* These days of pregnant waiting were my dress rehearsal, my trial run through the feminine domains of patience and trust.

I stopped sweating and started dabbling with literary forms. A sense of ease and playfulness replaced my previous desperate mental effort. Should it be a novel? A fantasy? An epic poem? I toyed with ideas and waited for plot lines and characters to come. Another seven days rolled by sitting with an empty notebook at my knee. No brilliant ideas and no characters showed up. Only one thought repeating over and over in my brain: *The world has had enough metaphor, Cate. Enough fiction.*

People liked stories about people—real people who tried to learn from life and become better human beings. Real people who figured out stuff and who had something valuable to say as a result. Real people . . . *like me*? I groaned inwardly, horrified, facing a journalist's nightmare. *Oh, man, not a memoir. Anything but that. Please?*

I lay in my little single bed, staring up through the darkened skylight. Fir trees creaked eerily in the night wind, weaving their needled boughs in graceful patterns overhead. It was still cold, and the fire I'd banked in the woodstove downstairs cast a ruddy glow across the ceiling. My kitty Grace pawed gently, asking to be let under the covers. *Please?* she purred. Together, we snuggled beneath the blankets.

Dinner that evening with Tess had been pleasant. But I'd been glad to get in my truck to drive the six miles home through the cold dark to my own little nest. *How my life brings change. What'll happen next?* The money from the sale of our property was running low. I had no idea how long I could stay where I was living, where to go next or how I would afford it. Although I'd finished the screenplay project I'd come back from Costa Rica to write with Betsy, we hadn't found financial support for it yet, and I hadn't gotten paid. I had no job and no income and no clue when it would come.

And . . . I wasn't worried. I lay there, startled, rechecking my internal sensors. By God, I genuinely wasn't concerned. I knew it would all work out somehow, knew there was nothing to fear, knew the universe would take care of me.

My mind jolted.

The *universe* would take care of me? What kind of habitual, airy-fairy, cliché-ridden thinking was that? The universe would take care of me? *Right. Like some separate God 'out there' will take care of me.* How long would I keep holding on to intangible concepts that no physical human could ever really relate to? How long would I keep bowing down to New Age verbiage that inspired no genuine confidence? What about knowing that LIFE takes care of me?

I trust life—I trust life in the body.

I tried on the strange thought, letting it soak in like rain on drought-struck soil. Life wasn't anything to be afraid of. Even when I died, I'd just be moving into life's next chapter, the mysterious, non-physical side of life called death. *Oh my.* Under the covers with the cat, my body hummed, warmly fluid and vital. My mind hummed along with it, quietly content.

There's nothing to be afraid of. What a concept! Why haven't I gotten this before?

Why? Because life was scary, unpredictable, violent and painful. It was skinned knees, bad report cards and napalm dropped on unsuspecting children's heads. It was floods and famines and paperboys with evil intent. It was gangs of men coming to get me in the night.

All this time I've been afraid of life and didn't know it. How odd.

Or was it? I was raised in a society that had no real knowledge about life. Oh sure, we'd peered at the edges of the universe through the Hubble Telescope and dissected Creation down to the level of quarks and muons. But what were we really? Why were we here? What were we doing? Where were we going? To what end and purpose? How did each of us fit into the scheme of things?

We had zero answers for all of it. Hell, most people weren't even asking the questions anymore. And although lots of people and lots of religions, new and old, liked to think they had the answers, no one really had a handle on the whole truth. Even Sadhguru, the most enlightened human being I'd ever met, admitted he understood probably a billionth of what was possible to know. And that was on a good day.

How could I not be afraid of life? I'd been weaned on dry words and concepts about it. Spirit had been presented to me as an *idea*, not a real thing. The soul was a hypothesis. The flesh had been reduced to clay. I was taught that the Earth was an inanimate resource, not a dynamically interconnected, living consciousness. My worth and every other human being's highest value were determined by our gross economic productivity quotient. My woman's body had been judged an evil seductive barrier between mankind and God, then commercially exploited. My woman's soul had been doubted and denied.

No wise woman had been around to teach me how to vault past these terrible barriers. My own mother had lived a frightened life, shunning all internal investigation, as her mother had before her. No wise father or shaman had been around to humbly tell me mankind's 'civilized' beliefs weren't necessarily true.

The wise ones—the men and women who explored life from the *inside* in consciousness—the shamans who could bear testimony to life's infinite grace and magic had been systematically labeled savages and pagans, sinners and witches. They'd been hunted down, tortured, indoctrinated into Western law and religion at the point of a gun, their lands taken, their living world and medicinal wisdom destroyed. And for what? Why?

Suddenly cold, I sat up and pulled the heavy woollen poncho I'd bought in Ecuador from the foot of the bed, spreading it over my blankets. Disturbed, Grace shot from under the covers and ran down the stairs. In the woodstove below, a log popped. A dancing glow of flames on the ceiling flared then diminished. Despite the extra layer and the warm amber light, I shivered.

There is a purposeful destruction of life occurring.

Destruction was the ultimate goal of every fundamentalist religion, including Christianity, Judaism and Islam: the End of the World, Armageddon, the Apocalypse—the getting rid of all of the 'things' that kept mankind from Heaven. I shuddered. Tears leaked from my eyes. *They don't know God is every green leaf, every grain of sand, every indrawn breath, every thought, every crawling creature on land and finned swimmer in the seas. They don't know we are already in Heaven, right here, right now, on Earth. They know neither love nor stewardship, only fear.*

Out of blind willfulness humanity had taken the glory and abundance of the world and turned it into Hell. For what else could you call a reality run by corporations enslaving people and destroying the planet, harvesting money as the only prize? What else could you call a world where life was reduced to reading, writing, arithmetic, a social security card, a driver's license, stuff to buy and the furtive rubbing of bodies together in the dark, igniting brief spasms of pleasure?

No wonder I've been afraid. No wonder everybody was afraid, desperately grabbing whatever they could get their hands on in order to feel more secure.

Somewhere to the north a lone coyote barked, its solitary voice quickly joined by the singsong yipping of the pack—a mother with her maturing cubs on the hunt in the vast clearcut out beyond my cottage. Amazing how six half-grown coyotes could sound like 60. I listened to the staccato symphony. Then, just as suddenly as it had begun, the yipping ceased. The kill had been made. The body of some small animal was in the process of becoming the body of the coyote. Life continued.

But we don't know that anymore.

Humanity was focused on death. And caught between fear of death and fear of life, where could joyous living occur? Where lay ecstasy? In a pill? How had we come to this? The contrast between the abundant sweetness of life and the weary gray pall that hung over most people's Western lives was confounding. I lay there musing over reasons why this should be. And then a shocking thought rocked me. *This is why the feminine has been so despised! This is why she's being eliminated from the world!*

Woman most personified what man did not trust—life.

Her very fluidity and lack of emotional control, her flaunting of the life force in all its raw, unrestrained, exultant, beautiful, passionate, mercurial, tender, violent, all-encompassing, all-consuming power were alarming. Her vagina was a dark, unknowable cave of mystery and life-giving potential. How terrifying! Of course she who represented life had to be destroyed! Of course the Goddess had to be diminished and shackled!

Humanity always attacks and destroys what it fears.

Mind on fire, my body shivered as knowledge cascaded through me, the last pieces of an eleven-year puzzle tumbling into place. Grace jumped back on the bed and started cleaning her whiskers. I stroked her soft orange fur contemplatively and was instantly rewarded with a deep purring rumble. The next thought came easily, the inevitable progression along the path my mind was taking:

The unrestrained power that resides in woman resides equally in man. He fears only himself.

Laughter bubbled up from my gut. What a cosmic joke! I'd been on a fool's errand for over a decade thinking there must be some gender-specific attribute or ability that would give women the power to tell the men to 'stop!' But there was no such thing as woman's power. There was no such thing as man's power either. *Power isn't even a human attribute!* Power belonged to life and life belonged to spirit. The only way woman or man could ever express true power was by integrating and humbly living in alignment with that knowledge.

I lay marveling at what I had missed in my fevered hunt for a feminine response to male social domination. *Domination only happens because of fear.* And mankind's fear lay in its lack of inner knowledge about life and how that dance played out through man and woman. My mind flicked to John Perkin's story from all those many years ago. The Shuar tribe down in the Amazon knew how it worked. The tribe functioned sustainably because they clearly understood human nature and used their knowledge of the sexes' strengths and weaknesses, not to enslave and battle each other, but rather to work in harmony and balance each other.

It wasn't philosophy or an enigmatic law that gave the Shuar women the power to tell the men when to 'stop!' It was a living common-sense covenant based on self-knowledge that was so obviously, undeniably true, everybody agreed about it and acted on it. The result? Everybody and everything benefitted, including the environment. But how could my culture grow to understand the vital importance of that wisdom?

Half the modern world had read or heard of *Men are from Mars, Women are from Venus*. We weren't ignorant of gender differences. Yet both men and women kept reducing their exquisitely matched qualities to bad-joke status, pointing fingers, trying to make the other wrong. Both sides were still trying to dominate the other. And what an ongoing disaster that was! I sighed in the cool dark.

The whole issue boils down to a stupid battle between head and heart.

Man-kind expresses through the head. And what wonders and technological advances we had made with the head in control! In the meantime, the heart and woman-kind had been relegated to the sidelines—wonderful things for knights to joust over and troubadours to idolize and sing about. But being uncontrollable, defying all logic, neither the heart nor woman-kind could be permitted a say, let alone the opportunity to rule. No one seemed to realize that a head without a heart was as unviable as a heart without a head. And the whole world was currently paying the price for that shortsightedness with the rapid degeneration of both the environment and society.

Whisker cleaning completed, Grace took another shot at wiggling under the covers. Absently, I lifted the sheet and she crawled underneath, snuggling against me as I tucked the blankets back under my chin. A feeling of intense peace filled me, and for an unmarked time I floated, thoughtless, in its embrace. Then, effortlessly, everything clicked into place. *Duh.* This was the story! This was *my* story! I'd made this journey. Like everyone else I'd been blind. I'd been self-absorbed and greedy. I'd lost all sense of the feminine, drowning her in crude sexuality and indifference. I had stilled my heart's voice over and over again and suffered the consequences—as we were all now suffering.

And despite all this I've learned better. Because of all this I've learned better.

I surrendered to the sense of the inevitable. Was this what Sadhguru had seen when he closed his eyes in the hotel lobby in Santa Monica that day? Was this moment and this realization why I had been born? Had I always been meant to encapsulate this everywoman tale in my flesh and bones, experiencing the tears and the torment, the heartbreaking confusion and hope? Had I been destined to go so far astray only to come out the other side renewed, restored, balanced and whole? Wasn't this everyone's eventual unavoidable journey?

Absolutely it was. But in the meantime, apparently, it was my task to take my clothes off in public and write about it.

CHAPTER 26

Full circle

The next morning found me staring at the cursor blinking on an empty white computer page. The first sunny morning in days poured cold spring light through the picture window where my writing table faced the lawn and driveway. The fire in the woodstove popped and glowed, belting out the BTUs. Grace sat in 'ready' position in my lap, my orange Muse of perpetual purring. A mug of English Breakfast tea steamed gently next to my keyboard.

I started to type, bemused yet content, knowing where the words would take me. *At least I know the storyline.*

CHAPTER 1

The question

"What do you know about woman?" he asked, brown eyes flat, boring into me, through me. It was as if the universe itself was asking me the question.